ROUTLEDGE LIBRARY EDITIONS: 18TH CENTURY PHILOSOPHY

Volume 15

ROUSSEAU: STOIC & ROMANTIC

ROUSSEAU: STOIC & ROMANTIC

KENNEDY F. ROCHE

LONDON AND NEW YORK

First published in 1974 by Methuen & Co Ltd

This edition first published in 2019
by Routledge
2 Park Square, Milton Park, Abingdon, Oxon OX14 4RN

and by Routledge
52 Vanderbilt Avenue, New York, NY 10017

Routledge is an imprint of the Taylor & Francis Group, an informa business

© 1974 Kennedy F. Roche

All rights reserved. No part of this book may be reprinted or reproduced or utilised in any form or by any electronic, mechanical, or other means, now known or hereafter invented, including photocopying and recording, or in any information storage or retrieval system, without permission in writing from the publishers.

Trademark notice: Product or corporate names may be trademarks or registered trademarks, and are used only for identification and explanation without intent to infringe.

British Library Cataloguing in Publication Data
A catalogue record for this book is available from the British Library

ISBN: 978-0-367-13518-8 (Set)
ISBN: 978-0-429-02691-1 (Set) (ebk)
ISBN: 978-0-367-13803-5 (Volume 15) (hbk)
ISBN: 978-0-367-13805-9 (Volume 15) (pbk)
ISBN: 978-0-429-02865-6 (Volume 15) (ebk)

Publisher's Note
The publisher has gone to great lengths to ensure the quality of this reprint but points out that some imperfections in the original copies may be apparent.

Disclaimer
The publisher has made every effort to trace copyright holders and would welcome correspondence from those they have been unable to trace.

Kennedy F. Roche

ROUSSEAU
Stoic & Romantic

Methuen & Co Ltd
London

*First published in 1974
by Methuen & Co Ltd
11 New Fetter Lane London EC4P 4EE
© 1974 Kennedy F. Roche
Printed in Great Britain by
W & J Mackay Limited, Chatham*

ISBN 0 416 78690 1

Distributed in the USA by
HARPER & ROW PUBLISHERS
BARNES & NOBLE IMPORT DIVISION

Contents

Preface page vii
Abbreviations viii
Introduction ix
1 The Stoic Origins *1*
2 The Nature of Man *22*
3 Natural Man & his Downfall *28*
4 Émile, or the Natural Man in Society *39*
5 The Return to Nature *52*
6 Jean-Jacques, the Man of Nature *55*
7 Rousseau, the Étatiste *59*
8 The General Will *69*
9 How the General Will is recognized *77*
10 The State & Individual Rights *85*
11 The 'Prince' or Government *99*
12 The Best Form of Government *104*
13 The Types of Government *111*
14 The Small State *124*
15 The Religion of Patriotism *135*
16 The Lawgiver *150*
17 The Person & the Collectivity *158*
References 163
Bibliography 170
Index 175

Preface

My grateful acknowledgment is extended to the Senate of the National University of Ireland for its grant-in-aid of £500 towards the publication of this book.

I recall, too, with gratitude the vast amount of assistance and encouragement given to me in the earlier years of my reading in the history of Political Theory by the late Professor James Hogan of University College, Cork, and I have pleasure in thanking Professor Oliver MacDonagh of the National University of Australia, Professor Howard Warrender of Sheffield University and Professor Richard Cobb of Balliol College, Oxford, who very kindly read my manuscript and made many valuable suggestions, and Mr Patrick Aherne of the Library staff at University College, Cork, for his very courteous and highly efficient assistance to me at all times during my preparation of this work.

University College, Kennedy F. Roche.
Cork,
January 19, 1974.

Abbreviations

Contrat	*Du Contrat social*
De leg.	*De Legibus*
De nat. deor.	*De Natura Deorum*
De re pub.	*De Re Publica*
Dial. (I, II, III, etc.)	*Dialogues*
Disc. Dijon	*Discours à l'Académie de Dijon*
Écon. Pol.	*Discours sur l'Économie Politique*
Ep.	*Epistles*
Gouv. Pol.	*Considérations sur le gouvernement de la Pologne*
Inégalité	*Discours sur l'origine de l'inégalité des conditions parmi les hommes*
La Corse	*Projet de constitution pour la Corse*
Lettre à Christophe	*Lettre à Christophe de Beaumont*
Narcisse	*Preface de Narcisse*
Nat. Quaes.	*Naturales Quaestiones*
Nouv. Hél.	*Nouvelle Héloïse*
Sur le luxe	*Sur le luxe, le commerce et les arts*

Introduction

In 1766, a learned cleric, Dom Cajot, published a work entitled *Les Plagiats de M. J.-J. Rousseau de Gèneve sur l'Éducation* (La Haye, 1766), in which he denounced Rousseau as 'only a shameless and unskilful plagiarist of Seneca and other ancient writers'. It was a hasty, harsh and superficial judgement and it related to only part of Rousseau's work. Yet it does raise the question, not only of the extent of Stoic inspiration in Rousseau's thought on personal morality and on historic society, but of his efforts to extend Stoic principles to projects of social and political reconstruction.

Seneca and Rousseau held closely-connected opinions in common: the universal nature of man is basically good, but has been perverted by the institutions of society (especially property); they conceived of the past in the same terms: a Golden Age of innocent happiness, followed by a descent into moral evil and misery; they believed in the privileged position of primitive societies; their ideas concerning education coincided in important respects, both maintaining that moral formation comes first and intellectual education is secondary and that the contact of youth with society should be delayed as long as possible. It is true that these ideas were not confined to Seneca, but they are quite recognizably Stoic. M. Georges Pire maintains that there are proofs that Rousseau had under his eyes the *De Providentia, De Ira, De Brevitate Vitae, De Beneficiis, De Tranquillitate Animi* of Seneca.[1] Mr Peter D. Jimack has reservations and thinks that the direct influence of Seneca on Rousseau 'was less strong than those of Montaigne and Plutarch';[2] but these two writers, Montaigne and

Rousseau: Stoic & Romantic

Plutarch, also show marked Stoic features. These are questions which I endeavour to discuss in Chapter 1 of this book.

One could, of course, by an almost random dipping into the Epistles to Lucilius, meet some of the salient features common to Seneca and Rousseau: in Epistle 88, the lines of the *Discourse to the Academy of Dijon*; on the Golden Age, Epistles 39, 41, 42, 43 and especially 90; on property, Epistles 88 and 90; on society and its pernicious influences, Epistles 7, 8, 14, 41; on the natural goodness of man, Epistle 94; on the intrinsic futility of purely intellectual and artistic pursuits, Epistle 88. On the other side, to go no further than the *Discourse to the Academy*, we find sentences that might have been written by any Stoic: 'Since the savants have begun to appear among us, honest people have been eclipsed'; 'Happy the peoples whose kings have made little noise in history'; 'If men ever become wise, their history will divert us no more'; *Paucis est opus litteris ad mentem bonam* – 'A good mind has little need of letters'.[3] Instances of similarity by way of direct quotation could be repeated indefinitely.

If I might try to summarize the contents of this book, I would describe it as an attempted study of the Stoic ancestry of Rousseau's basic ideas and conceptions: Nature and the *recta ratio*, the 'right' or 'perfect' reason (Eternal Reason) which informs the universe and ought to rule man; the *ratio quidem* or degenerate and selfish 'reason of a sort', which is the source of corruption; the myth of the Golden Age; the origin of evil in the misuse of reason, or rather the use of degenerate reason; the growth of evil due to the faulty structure of society, which promotes selfishness; the revolutionary implications of this condemnation.

The remedies Rousseau proposes are twofold. First, there is the familiar Stoic injunction: the cultivation of the 'inner self'. Rousseau, the Man of Nature, disregards prejudices and vanities and follows 'true' instinct. The education of Émile closes the entries to vice and enables him to develop himself in every respect as a virtuous and independent man and to emerge into society as essentially a Stoic, unassailable by surrounding vice (the Stoic is a man 'who has conquered the world'). The true purpose of philosophy is the cultivation of good morals, and not the enjoyment of intellectual adventure. Intellectual activity is justifiable only in so far as it conduces to virtue; vain learning and technology ('inventions') have been calamitous –

Introduction

the latter pandering to luxury, bodily ease and pleasure. Early man knew nothing of these things and was far happier without them.

What of the second remedy? The reader may be startled at my attempt to connect it with Stoicism.

Stoicism was a personal, and not a social, morality: the masses do not receive wisdom. Rousseau tried to socialize it with his doctrine of the General Will. The 'uncorrupted will' of man is always right; such a will underlies the evil accretion which centuries of selfishness have laid upon us; it occasionally emerges among groups of men, even now, in certain circumstances, as the General Will. The line of argument which Rousseau takes, I have endeavoured to trace in my chapter on 'The General Will' and elsewhere. The prevalence of the General Will would be brought about by the Social Contract, which would produce the ideal State in the small community of virtuous men. This General Will, being uncorrupted, would accord with the requirements of Eternal Reason, the *recta ratio*, which Nature intended to rule the world. It would be infallible and impeccable and there could therefore be no thought of placing any restriction on it. The Sovereignty of the People in this perfect State would be absolute. *Tuto enim quantum vult potest qui se nisi quod debet non putat posse*, wrote Seneca. ('He who would do nothing but what he ought may safely be allowed to do what he wills').[4]

The education of Émile produces the individual Stoic; the prevalence of the General Will would produce a collectivity essentially Stoic. The small community, so governed, would experience a new Golden Age, characterized this time by virtue rather than innocence.

The ancient Stoic placed the Golden Age in a long-lost past and regarded the increase of evil among the generality of men as inevitable: virtue is only for an élite. Hence, the concentration on the self-cultivation of the individual. Rousseau, too, concentrates on this, and his intense concentration on the uniqueness of each and every man is one of the salient characteristics that mark him out as a great Romantic. In his ideal State the uniqueness of the individual member (despite what he says of the need to 'denaturalize' man by means of good institutions in a passage in the *Émile*)[5] would be unimpaired because 'natural', and, as the General Will would also be 'natural', there could be no tension – the 'unique' would harmonize with the 'universal'. 'Each one, uniting himself to all, obeys, nevertheless, only himself and remains as free as before'.[6]

Rousseau: Stoic & Romantic

This metamorphosis of Stoic ideals into a religion of patriotism was work of a romantically optimistic order. Rousseau's ideal State would be pacific, because morally perfect. Machiavelli would have been amused at it: there is little place for *recta ratio* in *realpolitik*. Such optimism would also have been rejected by an ancient Stoic. Was it really accepted by Rousseau? Not habitually, one thinks. That he had much lasting faith in the prescriptions of the *Contrat Social* is open to serious doubt: even there, he recognized the inevitability of decay: 'The body politic, like the body of man, commences to die from the moment of its birth and carries within itself the causes of destruction'.[7] Throughout his life his prevalent mood was sad. He was basically pessimistic.

Perhaps one's understanding of the mental processes of pessimists, on the one hand, and of optimists or progressives, on the other, may be improved by a consideration of some theories concerning the personality. Are *reason* and *will* distinct faculties, or are they merely conjoint functions of the same thing: the personality? If they are distinct faculties, may not reason be trained to dominate will? This was the view of some thinkers of the Enlightenment; others of the same school, who subscribed to the theory of the unitary personality, considered that reason subsumes will. If they are not distinct, then the pessimistic view may be taken that the deterioration of humanity affects both reason and will: they are both enfeebled, and corrupted reason becomes the servant of corrupted will. There is, therefore, in our corrupted society, no hope. (Hence, perhaps, Rousseau's basic pessimism and hence his flight to the imaginary society of the *Contrat Social*, in which uncorrupted will, the General Will, rules). The Stoics, with the exception of Posidonius, seem to have subscribed to the doctrine of the unitary personality: hence their theory of general and irrevocable decay. Seneca, in Epistle 90, expressly takes Posidonius to task for having asserted that reason promotes technology ('inventions'); all these things ('inventions'), he maintains, merely pander to our taste for comfort and debase us. They are the products of the *ratio quidem* ('reason of a sort') and, as they proliferate, they bring increasing degeneration and increasing moral evil, which will culminate in the destruction of the world. If mankind were to follow the inspiration of Eternal Reason (the *recta ratio*), which the generality of mankind has never done except unconsciously and very briefly in the Golden Age, men would live 'the simple life', holding

Introduction

all things in common and without need of coercive institutions, in a state of happy harmony with all creation. This is what Seneca and Rousseau maintain, and this cult of simplicity has been a feature of modern Anarchism and of millenarism generally.

If one accepts the doctrine of the unitary personality (reason and will are the same phenomenon), the question may arise: which subsumes which? Rousseau would seem to make the nominalist assumption that will subsumes reason. He lays the emphasis heavily on will: the purity of the General Will, the selfishness of the individual will. Men exercise their will in promotion of their interests: that is to say, in promotion of what they desire at any particular time. Men who find that they have such desires in common (or who find themselves born or thrown into such a position) coalesce into bodies or associations, varying in size, force and permanence, for the purpose of such promotion. Society is honeycombed with such groups. In relation to the members of each such society, the will of that society is general: it tends to the promotion of the interest of each and all. But in relation to the will of the great society, which is the State, it is no more than a private or particular will and tends to promote the wellbeing of a part, at the expense of the whole. Thus, the general will of a lesser society may, in relation to that particular society, be good, but in relation to the body politic, harmful. 'Such a man can be a devout priest, or a brave soldier, or a zealous patrician, and a bad citizen'.[8] 'One sees with what facility can be explained, with the aid of these principles, the apparent contradictions which are noticeable in the conduct of so many men, full of scruple and honour in certain regards, liars and cheats in others: trampling under foot the most sacred duties, and faithful to death to engagements which are often illegitimate. It is thus that the most corrupt men always render some sort of homage to public faith; it is thus that the brigands themselves, who are the enemies of virtue in the great society, adore its simulacrum in their caverns.'[9] The smaller the society and the baser the objectives, the greater is the impulsion of the selfish private interest. From this, it seems incontrovertible, that the wider the society, the more just is the will. The widest society, Rousseau would say, is the whole community: its will is, consequently, the most general and the most just. Thus, he says, we have 'an unshakeable proof that the most general will is also the most just, and that the voice of the people is verily the voice of God'.[10] These assertions, needless to say, im-

Rousseau: Stoic & Romantic

mediately raise the question: what does Rousseau mean by the 'whole community' or 'body politic'? His ideal community is a very small one. What bounds would he give to the exercise of the 'most general' and the 'most just' will? The bounds are supplied by community of sentiment. 'It is apparent that the sentiment of society evaporates and becomes enfeebled in stretching itself over all the earth and that we are less capable of being touched by the calamities of Tartary or Japan than by those of a European people. It is necessary that interest and commiseration be in some manner bounded and compressed within limits in order to give them activity. Since, therefore, that *penchant* within us can be of use only in relation to those with whom we have to live, it is good that human feeling, concentrated among fellow-citizens, should take on a new force through their being continually in sight of one another and by the common interest which unites them'.[11] This is the *optimum* within which universal justice can express itself by means of will, since only in a society of this size can the laws of universal justice find a natural sanction. Rousseau does make his *obéissance* to the principle of universality: 'All justice comes from God: he alone is its source. . . . Without doubt, there is a universal justice, emanating from reason alone: but that justice, to be admitted among us, should be reciprocal.'[12] In a perfect world, universal justice, derived from universal reason, would rule. A perfect world would be one great city in which the law of Eternal Reason would be the General Will. But this is a corrupted world and our degenerate reason is incapable of discovering the universal principles to follow. Eternal Reason does not reach the generality of us. The best we can do is to seek the source of uncorrupted will, and that source lies in the sentiment of sociability and natural pity. This sentiment is to be found at its liveliest in a society of equals, so small that everyone knows everyone else. Our task ought therefore to be to purify the will, and the purified will, as the nobler part of the personality, can be trusted to withdraw our feeble reason from its errors and to keep it firmly in check. 'Man in the natural state scarcely thinks at all'.[13] 'All the rules of natural right are better engraved in the hearts of men than in all the confused medley of Justinian.'[14] Rules of life do exist, but they are indiscoverable by our reason; we are brought in touch with them only by uncorrupted instinct which alone can determine our relations with the Supreme Being. Religion proper, all that pertains to the spiritual side, is purely a matter

Introduction

between the individual and God; there is no place for human organization here, least of all for a body claiming to be a Universal Church. Morality, in so far as it is social, pertains to the Sovereign People and to none other for its regulation. A universalization of 'right' or 'perfect' reason is the *maximum desideratum*, but it can come (if ever it could) not by means of a series of principles imposed by abstract thought, but as the flower of a growth as natural as that of a plant. God speaks to us, not through our reason, but through our uncorrupted instinct which should operate our will. One might perhaps call this thought a modified nominalism.

Some thinkers of the Enlightenment made reason subsume will. ('The will', says Godwin, 'is merely the last act of the understanding.')[15] If this be so, the reason, being continually enlightened by experience, will lead on to perfection. And this reason is the reason of individuals, since society is made up of individuals, who alone have real existence. The future therefore lies with the development of the reason of the individual in all directions. To Rousseau, this was deadly poison. The two viewpoints – those of Rousseau and of the Enlightenment – were therefore fundamentally and directly opposed. Perhaps, then, the bitterness of the controversies in which he found himself engaged with former friends arose, not from temperaments merely, but from basically different conceptions of the personality? Are reason and will two distinct faculties and, if they are not, which subsumes which?

A great mystification lies in the transformation of initially nominalist thought into highly idealistic moralities. Stoicism has been described as a pantheistic materialism. 'In entire opposition to Plato, they (the Stoics) held that the individual object alone has a real existence: the universal, the general term, exists only in the mind as subjective thought'.[16] Yet the Stoics wove their entire morality around the ideas of 'right' or 'eternal' reason, providence, honour and duty. It is true that their materialism consisted in their insistence that nothing is immaterial (God, reason, the soul, are material). Between materialism in this sense and idealistic immaterialism, the difference may be largely one of nomenclature. The Epicureans maintained that the distinction between right and wrong rests entirely on utility and has nothing mysterious about it. ('But morality itself is nothing but a calculation of consequences', as Godwin was to say).[17] It is unrelated to any cosmic purpose, since the universe is blind and unpurposive. Yet, they constructed on the basis of the pleasure-pain polarity a highly idealistic morality. Similarly, Godwin, starting with the same nominalist premises as the Epicureans, went on to view man as part of a system of universal moral order and to maintain that immutable truths must be the criteria of all our actions. The Utilitarians (to which school of thought Godwin basically belonged) were self-declared enemies of dogma, believing that the only way to discover facts was by trial and error. They believed that, by sociological experiment, a science of morals as exact as physics could be invented and went on to persuade themselves that experiment made to date had elucidated practically the whole truth about politics and morals. From this, it was a short step for them to draft constitutions suited to all mankind and economic systems professing universal validity. And that most nominalist of all schools of thought, the Marxist, concerns itself with the immoralities of contemporary mankind and sets up as its goal the attainment of the classless and Stateless society in which perfect justice and perfect harmony shall reign forever. It would seem that, in practice, the belief that there are universal and eternal standards is so deeply rooted in the human mind that even the most materialistic of nominalists cannot rid themselves of it easily.

1

The Stoic Origins

> O, Man, from whatsoever land you are, whatever your opinions, listen! Here is your history as I read it, not in the books of your fellows, who are liars, but in nature, who never deceives. All that will be told you here is true: there will be no falsehood but what I may unwittingly have mixed with it. The times of which I would speak are far-away: how you have changed from what you once were! It is, so to speak, the life of your race I shall describe, according to the qualities you have received, which your education and your customs have depraved, but have not been able to destroy. There is, I feel, an age at which the individual man would long to remain: you will seek the age at which you would desire that your race had halted. Discontented with your present state for reasons which forebode even greater misery for your unhappy posterity, perhaps you would like to go back: and that sentiment ought to make you sigh for your early days, to loathe your present and to tremble for the unhappy men who will come after you.[1]

The secret of Rousseau's success was his appeal to our discontents. 'Things were not always thus' is a human reaction to the limitations of life. Whoever tells us this is certain of an audience. If he goes further and sketches a simple plan to restore the happiness of old, he is doubly assured.

The idea that all was once harmonious was far from new: in one form or another, it has been part of the mythology of many peoples; that all would yet become, or could be made, harmonious was familiar to Rousseau's contemporaries of the Enlightenment. What was new in Rousseau was the passionate language and what was relatively new was the romantic conception of the proposed political ideal. He has been called Janus-faced because he at once looked back to the

Rousseau: Stoic & Romantic

golden legend of a remote past and forward to a great *idée-force* of the future: romantic, extreme nationalism. That he was a nationalist in any form subsequently recognizable has been disputed: he was too unhistorical for this, it has been argued. Yet, the nominalist element in his doctrine of the General Will, the fervour with which he contemplates the Sovereignty of the People and the description of the function he allots the Lawgiver could not fail to give him a very prominent place in the tradition of nationalism. The French Revolution, which elevated the Sovereignty of the People, became increasingly nationalistic, and the French dynamic, partly by emulation and partly by reaction to French domination, aroused nationalism abroad. One of the main planks of nationalism – respect for the historical traditions of a society – was rejected by him because of his pessimistic attitude to history; yet, there are exceptional passages in the *Gouvernement de Pologne* and there is the deprecation of what he considered the watery cosmopolitanism of his time.

The ancestry of Rousseau's ideas on man and man's relation to his surroundings can be readily traced in large measure to the Stoics and, in an especial manner, to Seneca, while his ideal of political organization goes clearly back to the ancient conception of the *polis*.* The two

---

* The degree of the directness of influence exercised on Rousseau by Seneca has been discussed in considerable detail by M. Georges Pire ('De l'influence de Sénèque sur les théories pedagogiques de J.-J. Rousseau.' *Annales de la Société Jean-Jacques Rousseau* (Geneva, 1953–5) Vol. 33; and by Mr Peter D. Jimack ('La Genèse et la rédaction de l'Émile de J.-J. Rousseau.' *Studies in Voltaire and the Eighteenth Century* (Geneva, Institut et Musée Voltaire, 1960) Vol. 13. M. Pire, who seems convinced that Rousseau was directly indebted to Seneca in important respects, writes at pp. 86 and 87 of 'Conceptions common to Seneca and Rousseau, but not touched on by Montaigne: the negation of original perversion in man, the evil effect of society, the necessity to delay contact of youth with society as long as possible, the privileged situation of primitive societies, the origin of inequality, the causes of the end of the Golden Age.' He refers also to 'certain citations in Latin not found in Montaigne or other authors considered sources of Rousseau' and to proofs that Rousseau had under his eyes *De Providentia, De Ira, De Brevitate Vitae, De Beneficiis* and *De Tranquillitate Animae* of Seneca. On p. 62 he declares 'that Rousseau put into practice the method extolled by Seneca is undoubtable', claiming that the lines of the *Discours sur les Sciences et les Arts* are discernible in *Ep*. 88, 90, 95 (at pp. 59 and 63) and again at p. 63 and drawing attention to the contention common to Seneca and Rousseau that the liberal arts contribute nothing to virtue ('Scansion, correctness of terms, legends, laws of ryhthm. Which of these diminishes fear, lightens desire, checks passion? Geometry, music, astronomy, painting?' *Ep*. 88). At p. 67 he refers to Seneca on the Golden Age in *Ep*. 39, 41, 42, 43 and 95.

Jimack, however, disagrees with Pire that Montaigne and Rousseau 'both

The Stoic Origins

main-streams of Graeco-Roman speculation to exercise a lasting influence on European thought are the Aristotelian and the Stoic, and the great preoccupation of these schools lay with the conception of 'nature'. This preoccupation descended as a legacy to Christian Europe and marks all the political doctrine of the great theorists of the seventeenth and eighteenth centuries. In Rousseau, it may be termed an obsession.

In what senses has the word been used? In a primary sense, *nature* has been used to describe the entire ordered universe, the totality of the created beings and entities that compose it, the laws which govern them and the ends of their specific actions.

Metaphysically considered, *nature* is held to mean, in the first place, *birth* or *origin*, and, in the second, the *essence* of a being, communicated to that being by *generation*. Thus, St Thomas Aquinas says that: 'The word, *nature*, comes from the word, *nasci, to be born*', and quotes Aristotle's definition of it as 'The principle of movement which the being finds itself impelled *per se*, and not *per accidens*, to obey'.[2] *Nature*, according to Aristotle, means, in the first place, an innate potentiality of development, and, in the second, the actualization of this potentiality. In other words, every being has a certain function and a certain purpose allotted to it; the potentiality of fulfilment of this function and attainment of this purpose is inborn and inherent in the being. In fulfilling this function and moving towards the attainment of this object, the being acts according to its innate potentiality. Hence, the actualization of the potentiality is a process in accordance with *nature* and the epithet, *natural*, is to be applied to it. Applied to the living being, then, the term, *natural*, has both a static and a dynamic significance. And to the appointed immediate end towards which the being moves in the course of this actualization of its potentiality, the term, *natural*, is to be applied.

---

used the same source, to wit: Seneca' and considers that 'it seems to us impossible to separate with certainty the influence of Seneca from that of Montaigne' on Rousseau (op. cit., 350–3). He concedes that the moral philosophy of Rousseau is inspired in a great measure by that of the Stoics and that 'M. Pire establishes at least that Rousseau must have known directly the writings of Seneca and, showing that the theses of the two Discourses are already completely those of Seneca, he affirms that the two authors share "principles fundamentally identical"' (op. cit., 350–3 and Pire, op. cit., 73). Nonetheless, he declines to go as far as Pire and concludes with his own judgement that 'Despite the manifest parentage that unites Seneca and Rousseau, the precise influence of the Roman philosopher remains uncertain' (op. cit., 353).

Rousseau: Stoic & Romantic

There is a hierarchy of ends in the universe; the *immediate* end of every being is its own perfection as a member of its own order. The *natural*, therefore, signifies the inborn potentiality, the actualization of this potentiality and in the third place, that which inheres in the final development. All beings, then, possessed of the same potentiality and, consequently, of the same final purpose are said to belong to the same *kind* or *species* and all essentials that distinguish each being as a member of its kind are said to be of the specific nature of that being.[3] According to St Thomas Aquinas, the nature of the being is 'that which constitutes the thing from the point of view of its proper *genre* or kind, and that which we designate by a definition of that thing, in replying to the question: "Quid est?" '[4] A logical distinction to be observed in the employment of the terms, *nature* and *essence*, is, however, pointed out: the nature of a being is to be described as its essence 'as far as it is ordained to its proper operation', that is, in so far as it is designed to move *per se* towards its appointed end. To burn, for example, is the nature of fire. Thus, the being and the element, when considered from the dynamic point of view, are said to possess *natures*; the inanimate object may be spoken of as possessing an essence, a substance, rather than a nature; we do not, for instance, speak of the *nature* of a stone.[5] To sum up, it may be said that the conception of *nature* embraces the three-fold notion of a specific potentiality, a specific actuality and the process of becoming by which the specific potentiality becomes a specific actuality: it involves a specific essence, a specific potentiality and the process of becoming by which they are linked.

Again, we cannot touch on the consideration of the *specific* nature without going on to consider another conception of the nature of a being: the *particular* or *individual* nature. Every corporeal being is made up of *form* and *matter*: the term *natural* may therefore be used in a universal and in a particular sense of each. All that relates to the essential characteristics of the *kind* or *species*, to the *universal*, is to be described as of the *specific, formal* or *universal* nature of every member of that species. Thus, for example, it is of the *formal, specific* or *universal* nature of man to think, to plan, to laugh. Over against this *formal* nature, we find the *individual* or *particular* nature. The inborn peculiarities of the individual, those innate characteristics of such-and-such a person, which have no necessary appurtenance to the whole human race, pertain to the *individual* or *particular* nature of that

The Stoic Origins

person. Thus, for example, it is natural for such-and-such a man, on account of heredity, to suffer a certain infirmity.[6]

The eighteenth century, following the Stoic tradition, assigned the term *natural* to all those states or conditions the contrary of which the cosmic laws (as the thinker conceived them) do not enjoin. According to this usage, the products of human art are 'unnatural' – or at any rate, those products which are not necessary to our conservation. Thus, to be unclothed is natural, seeing that human art, and not the inner necessities of his being, has provided man with clothing. Unthinking instinct and spontaneous emotion are 'natural'. The word *natural*, when employed in this sense, signifies the primitive: that which exists anterior to civilization, that which stands in contrast to the works of human art. In the making of this distinction, the Cynics were perhaps more extreme than the leading Stoics. The practice of making this contrast, so dear to the Stoics and to Rousseau, is a legacy of the semi-cyclic theory of history, according to which mankind in its earliest days lived in happy simplicity, spontaneously obeying the laws of divine reason or providence which then permeated the entire universe. These laws, on the human plane, were moral laws and obedience to them supplied man with all the requirements of happiness. All else is vanity. 'Inventions', says Seneca, 'come from reason of a sort, but not right reason': *Omnia ista ratio quidem, sed non recta ratio commenta est.** [All those things were discovered by the exercise of reason of a sort, but not by perfect reason.] The true role of philosophy is the discernment of moral truth; this is the only thing 'right reason' is concerned with; all the rest is the work of 'reason of a sort', and its effects have led to the deterioration of the human race.

All Aristotelian and Stoic thought centres around the principle of order. The universe is thought of in terms of a rational, ordered whole. The totality is viewed as a regulated unity, governed by deeply-laid, unerring laws. The Stoics in particular see in it the work of a Supreme Reason which appointed to all things appropriate functions and purposes, supplying them, in accordance with their needs, with the means of fulfilling their roles and attaining their ends. All reality is an ordered hierarchy, culminating in a rational source, a source

---

* *Ep.* 90 (24). See also *Ep.* 16 (3). *Non est philosophia populare artificium nec ostentationi paratum. Non in verbis sed rebus est.* [Philosophy is not an occupation of a popular nature, nor is it pursued for the sake of self-advertisement. Its concern is not with words, but with facts.]

which operates, not arbitrarily, but in rigid accordance with fixed and unalterable law. Divine law, Divine reason, is of the nature of Deity itself and, being so, is at once eternal and immutable, since Deity cannot contradict its own nature.[7] The depth of the contrast between this comprehensive conception and the surrounding chaos of barbarism, with its fragmentary world, its warring, capricious gods, the figments of childish fancy, needs no emphasis.

Divine reason reflects itself in man. Deity permits man to know something of itself and its workings and equips man to live according to a design of its own making. And this equipment with which Deity endows man is the human reason. Human reason is thus a reflection of and a participation in the Divine Reason. It is that innate and inherent faculty wherewith man is enabled to distinguish between good and evil, between that which the law ordains and that which is opposed to Eternal Justice; it is the candle which Deity gives to man to light him through the labyrinth of life.[8]

Greek philosophy from the earliest times concerned itself with the specific or universal in man, and this element it found in the faculty of reason. In man, it found an innate intuition of what is morally right, a disposition to seek truth and practise justice. In this quality of rationality, all men partake.

The law of reason, coming as it does from the principle which regulates all things, is anterior to and takes precedence over all man-made or positive law, and, being common to all humanity, is independent of time and place, of compact and custom. Positive law ought to be designed to give effect to the demands of reason in particular cases. Submission to the wrong decision of an established government is an affair of composition, an imperfect duty that bids us suffer certain evils in order to avert greater.[9]

The elaboration of this theory of a pervading rationality gave the Stoics a lasting influence on European thought. Reality, according to the Stoics, is pervaded by the divine principle of reason which expressed itself progressively in successive stages or types of existence, namely: in the inanimate, the brute and the human. The first, the inanimate, is governed by physical and chemical laws; the second, the brute realm, by fixed laws of instinct which, although necessary, are not as directly and evidently so in their operation as the physical and chemical laws of matter. On the human plane, we come to the highest level of all, in which the divine reason that permeates the universe

The Stoic Origins

attains to self-consciousness. Man, then, is essentially rational: the tendency to categorize in moral terms is innate and inherent in all men; consequently, knowledge of the moral law, the law which the principles of innate and universal reason build up, is attainable by all men who use their reason. Stoicism will have none of the Aristotelian doctrine of inequality, based on difference in the degrees of rationality.* Mankind occupies the highest plane, the plane on which the divine reason attains to self-consciousness. Humanity, then, as occupant of that one plane, is one: all its individual members, occupying as they do the same plane, are essentially equal, no subdivision in respect of essentials being possible. There exists, therefore, no natural inequality of master and slave; all mankind is a society of equals.[10] By this term, *natural*, the Stoics mean *rational*: that is to say, in accordance with the laws of the universe. Deity, reason and nature are one.

Thus Stoicism issues in a panlogism, a rationalistic pantheism, the implications of which were to set Chrysippus on the search for a principle which would serve as a basis for the affirmation of human freedom. The affirmation of free will has presented difficulties of vast dimension to philosophers, both pantheist and transcendentalist. Most people would affirm that free will is a fact of experience, but to prove its existence or its extent from the resources of human reason has not been universally considered easy. The Stoics were materialists in the sense that they believed that all is matter (that is, corporeal substance): the soul itself, the *pneuma* – that which maintains and prompts the growth and the decay of everything, is a mysterious fluid or gaseous substance which gives coherence and dynamism – is matter; space itself is matter; nothing is non-material. The essential reason of everything is itself material, its relation to the thing being that of a gaseous to a solid body. As corporeal substance may decay, then so may the reason acting within it decay and become the *ratio quidem*, the 'reason of a sort' which panders to our baser desires. This is the general Stoic opinion and explains their view of history.

In some respects, Posidonius introduced some extraneous elements (to some extent platonic in origin) to Stoic thought: the implication of a dualism of God and matter, the rejection of the old Stoic doctrine

---

* *Politics*, 1254, Bk 1, ch. V: 'Those, therefore, who are as much inferior to others as is the body to the soul, and beasts to men, are by nature slaves and benefit, like all inferiors, from living under the rule of a master. He, therefore, is by nature a slave who can (and therefore does) belong to another, and who shares in reason to the extent of apprehending without possessing it' (Warrington, pp. 11-12).

Rousseau: Stoic & Romantic

of the unitary nature of the personality (reason and the proper states of emotion being inseparable) in favour of a tripartition among reason, spirit and passion as parts or distinct faculties of the soul.* He also seems to have taken a more optimistic and more extrovert view of the capacity of human reason than that of the old Stoa and that of Seneca, exhibiting as he did a lifelong interest in the sciences and in studies which Seneca considered as distractions from the true purpose of the mind, which is the pursuit of moral truth and the practice of virtue. We ought, Posidonius considered, to take an active share in the ordering of the physical world and follow Nature, not only by contemplating it, but by joining in its organization.† Hence his attribution of the invention of certain conveniences and comforts to the operation of reason for which Seneca rebukes him in *Epistle* 90. The world soul, Posidonius maintains, in common with all Stoics, has no evil tendencies in it, but Posidonius also believes that in man's soul there are innate tendencies to evil. Man can follow these tendencies and fall into disharmony with the universe, or he can resist them and, by exercising and strengthening his distinct faculty of reason, take a share in ordering the world. This belief clearly gives a role to

---

* J. M. Rist: *Stoic Philosophy*, 217–18. Godwin would appear to subscribe to the doctrine of the unitary personality in asserting that reason subsumes will: 'We need only to attend to the obvious meaning of the terms in order to perceive that the will is merely, as it has been happily termed, the last act of the understanding' (*Political Justice*, Vol I, 181). This is the very basis of his optimism and of his individualism: the higher faculty (although he would reject the use of the term) directing the personality, the ultimate result will be a human race of self-directed, perfect individuals.

† There should never have been a need to do this, Seneca maintains (*Ep.* 90). Nature provided the first men with everything necessary to them – water, food and adequate shelter. What we have done by plundering and dividing the earth is to give to some a superfluity injurious to their moral health and to leave the majority in a condition of physical and moral deprivation. What is needed is the cultivation of the true self, which is within, for what lies outside is largely dross. The wise man will keep his mind clear of the distractions of sense and of all worries about the past and the future. The true self cannot but be in accordance with the self of the universe, which is good. The social or existing self is corrupted by the divorce from Nature or the daimon of the universe which society has brought about. The function of wisdom is primarily introspective. *Recede in te ipse, quantum potes.* (*Ep.* 7, 8). [Withdraw into yourself as much as possible.] 'The most magnificent ideas of the divinity come to us solely by our reason. See the spectacle of nature, hear the inner voice. Has not God said everything to our eyes, to our conscience, to our judgment? What more can men tell us? Their revelations only degrade God in giving him human passions' (*Émile* in *Oeuvres*, VII, 68).

The Stoic Origins

free will, but the extent of the role one attributes to it will depend on the extent of one's confidence in the power or purity of reason. This conception of the duality of God and matter and of duality in the human soul seems to have removed the foundation of the old belief in the psychosomatic action of a unitary universe and a unitary person and to have brought Stoicism much nearer to Platonism. The Roman Stoics tended to abandon the consideration of the physics of the system and to convert it more and more into a pure morality, but their legacy of panlogism remained in sufficient strength to prevent them from reaching a satisfactory solution to the problem of free will.

The idea of Fate is never far from Stoic thought. Fate is the eternal will of nature, or God, or the universe. It sends disasters and tribulations to us, but these are not moral evils. Moral evil comes from ourselves. There is a law of Necessity, which they conceive of as something extrahuman in origin, over which the individual has no control and submission to which is freedom.[11] To struggle against it is the mark of the slave. *Ducunt volentem fata, nolentem trahunt.* [The fates lead the willing man and drag the unwilling along.] The great soul is the man who gives himself over to Fate; the weakling and degenerate struggles against it and maligns the order of the universe.[12] Everything that is not morally evil is sent by providence and is therefore in accordance with divine reason. It is intrinsically good, coming as it does from nature or God. This conception of Necessity, a divine or an impersonal force, figures prominently in Rousseau's *Émile*, in Godwin's *Political Justice* and, indeed, in the literature of anarchism generally.[13] It has an apparent clarity, until we recall that many occurrences that seem at first sight the product of non-human forces are contributed to (even if very indirectly) by human will. Complementary to the duty of accepting what providence sends is the duty of obeying the dictates of 'right reason', which is also of the nature of the universe or God, and therefore of man (since man is but part of the universe or God). The world is entirely perfect:[14] its laws lie in impersonal necessity and 'right reason'. He who obeys both is free. What is freedom? asks Seneca. And he answers that it is 'not fearing either men or gods', 'not craving wickedness or excess' and 'possessing supreme power over oneself'. *Non homines timere, non deos; nec turpia velle nec nimia; in se ipsum habere maximam potestatem.*[15] [Not to fear men, nor the gods; not to crave wickedness nor excess; to possess supreme power over oneself.] It is true that

Rousseau: Stoic & Romantic

in the *Naturales Quaestiones* Seneca says: 'When I shall treat of that question (destiny) I shall show how one can, without diminishing the power of destiny, accord something to the free will of man'.[16] It is equally true that he did not achieve his purpose.[17]

The world is entirely perfect; yet man's nature is not perfect, but can become so.[18] The actual is the ideal, then, only in so far as men are purely rational. Man is rational, but men misuse their reason or it becomes corrupted. Hence, the Stoic distinction between 'perfect reason' and 'reason of a sort'. The former is natural, the latter is debased and has been productive of evil. 'The voice of nature and that of reason', said Rousseau, 'never find themselves in contradiction, if man does not impose on himself needs which he is subsequently forced to prefer always to natural impulsion.'[19] 'Perfect reason', which is the law of all entities in the universe, governing and regulating the ends of the specific actions and processes of everything, is intended by providence to govern man. It is a law of strict duty, a law which prescribes action untainted by suspicion of unworthy motive. Yet, it is broken by the mass of men. Rousseau found himself in a difficulty akin to that of the Stoics. He, like them, found a benevolent providence whose laws are calculated to keep the world in harmony. He, like them, found the world was not in harmony. At one time, it must have been. There must have been a Golden Age. Why did we leave it? It must have been due to Fate or to some initial human mistake.

Faced as they were by this contradiction between the intention of a benevolent nature or immanent deity and the unhappy reality, it is not surprising that the Stoics resorted to the legend of the Golden Age. The world is in decline and has been so for ages past, ever since man disobeyed the law by seeking to make himself richer, more comfortable, more powerful.* To achieve this, he invented property, which gave rise to inequality, avarice, ambition; vice begot vice and

---

* The doctrine of palingenesis (periodic destruction and re-creation of the world) is fundamental to Stoic theory. The destiny of the world lies in the stars. Seneca quotes Berosos as holding that the world will be destroyed by flood or fire when all stars which now follow different orbits will reunite under the sign of Cancer and range themselves in line, so that a straight line could pass through the centres of all these spheres. The deluge will come when these same planets take up the same formation under the sign of Capricorn. Whatever the signs, they will be written in the heaven when God finds it good to put an end to the old world and to begin a new and better one. The progressive bestialization of morals is a symptom of the approaching end of the world. When the human race and the animals will have been destroyed, the cataclysms will cease and all will be created

The Stoic Origins

the disorder which ensued made coercive government necessary. Hence, the degeneration of the present which stands out in such sad contrast to the goodness and happiness of an age long left behind. The idea of the Golden Age – in which the ideal natural law prevailed in all its completeness, securing the spontaneous and joyful obedience of all, so that the ideal justice was the actual in human interrelationships and the ideal harmony was the actual in society – is one of the most important of the legacies that Stoicism has left the world. It would not be too much to say that this myth has provided the exemplar of all the humanitarian utopias of western history: there was no evil and therefore no need for constraint, no coercive government, no private property, no envy, no friction.

Precise ideas of the human condition in that age of happiness varied somewhat among the Stoic writers. To Seneca, it was an age of childlike innocence in which reason was not needed. In the early days of man, there was no philosophy: it was unnecessary, for men obeyed instinctively the promptings of nature or providence. Those happy people held all things in common; there was therefore no scope for avarice. The earth was more productive, since it was used in the interests of all. There were no rich and no poor: all was divided in friendly fashion. Such being the spirit, there were no wars. All was safe and tranquil. Men did not huddle in luxurious houses, but lived where they chose under the trees or the open sky. They knew nothing of wealth and inflicted no needless cares on themselves. They freely accepted the leadership of the best among them. *Sed primi mortalium quique ex his geniti naturam incorrupti sequebantur, eundem habebant et ducem et legem, commissi melioris arbitrio.*[20] [But the first men on this earth followed Nature unspoiled: they took one and the same person as leader and law, freely submitting to the decision of a man of

---

anew. The new race of men will know nothing of crime and will be born under the best auspices. But their innocence will last only so long as their souls are new. Wickedness will soon insinuate itself and will increase again with the centuries, until the world is again destroyed; and so on in an endless cycle (Seneca, *Nat. Quaes*, in *Oeuvres*, III, xxvii–xxx; *Ep.* 36, 11, etc.). Cicero maintained that the world would be destroyed by fire: the stars, being of a fiery substance, are nourished by the waters of the earth and shed them back again; some moisture is, however, continually being consumed and lost and the eventual result will be the drying-up of the earth and a tremendous conflagration which will destroy it; 'thus nothing will remain but fire, by which as a living being and a god, once again a new world may be created and the ordered universe be restored as before' (*De nat. deorum*, II, xvi).

superior merit.] For these leaders, 'ruling was a service, not an exercise of royalty'; they owed their power to the people and never tried to use it against them. *Nemo quantum posset, adversus eos experiebatur, per quos coeperat posse, nec erat cuiquam aut animus in iniuriam aut causa, cum bene imperanti bene paretur nihilque rex maius minari male parentibus posset, quam ut abiret e regno.*[21] [No one tried out the extent of his power over those to whom he owed that power in the first place. And no one had either reason or inclination to perpetrate injustice, since persons governing well were equally well obeyed, and a king could issue no greater threat to disobedient subjects than that of his own abdication.] Seneca disagrees with Posidonius that wisdom was used in those remote times to promote comfort or develop the arts: the cult of comfort, science and art belongs to a later age and originated, not in philosophy, but in ingenuity. These matters are the body's business. The business of philosophy is with the soul: that is to say, with right living, the pursuit of morality, which nature dictates to us and from which these things are a distraction. *Non desiderabis artifices; sequere naturam. Illa noluit esse districtos.*[22] [Follow Nature, and you will feel no need of craftsmen. She does not desire us to be so bound down.] The earliest men knew nothing of artifice, beyond the simplest. Their lives were excellent and guileless; they were *a dis recentes*[23] – 'fresh from the gods'. But although they followed the dictates of eternal reason in all things, they did so instinctively and without study. They were not virtuous, for virtue proceeds from the study and practice of morality, from the conscious and purposeful following of the precepts of 'perfect reason'. These happy people were merely innocent: they had never encountered evil.

Such was the life of the Golden Age, as Seneca conceived it. He does not indulge in any contemplation of that figment of Rousseau's imagination, the isolated man in the 'state of Nature'; but for Rousseau, too, the real Golden Age does appear to be the age of earliest society which immediately succeeded isolation. It is most remarkable that this ancient Stoic view should have been given by Rousseau with such memorable vehemence within two lifetimes of the theory of evolution, its very antithesis.

The ancient harmony came to an end when avarice broke in. *Inrupit in res optime positas avaritia et, dum seducere aliquid cupit atque in suum vertere, omnia fecit aliena et in angustum se ex immenso redigit.*[24] [Into this ideal state of things burst avarice, which, in seeking to put aside

The Stoic Origins

some coveted article for its own use, only succeeded in making everything someone else's property and reducing its possessions to a fraction of its previously unlimited wealth.] With avarice came private property; with property came inequality, poverty, luxury, vice and dissension. Vice and dissension created a need for laws and coercive government; government transformed itself into tyranny. So, having broken with Nature, mankind took its downward path.

Stoicism, because of its belief that mankind was on the decline, made of itself a socially conservative force: the immensity of present evil it regarded with a sense of impotence; the world being on a downward slope, a career whose progress human effort cannot stop, it is idle to think of general fundamental amelioration. The most that can be done in the conduct of public affairs is to check this downward rush in some measure by adapting positive enactment as far as possible to the demands of the ideal natural law (that is, the law of right reason). In order that the process of decline may be, as far as is humanly possible, arrested, coercive institutions are needed. To Cicero, the enlightened and virtuous mind 'is born to take part in the life of a State' (*cumque se ad civilem societatem natum senserit*) in order to promote what is honourable and check the wicked; to Seneca, 'the advantage of the State and that of the individual are yoked together' (*iuncta est privata et publica utilitas*) and the wise, who profit most by the security which the State gives them, 'must needs cherish as a father the author of this good' (*necesse est auctorem huius boni ut parentem colant*).[25] Yet, rational as the coercive State may be, it owes its degree of rationality to corruption: it bears a taint. When the natural law reigned in all its fulness, the coercive State did not exist. Neither did private property nor the other artificial restrictions of contemporary fallen society. There was material in Stoicism that could be made explosive.

If the Stoics had, by assuming that the world was on an upward curve, transposed the Golden Age to the future, how different a force would the doctrine have become, politically and socially? Then, one might think, in place of the sense of impotence there would reign the exaltation of mind that distinguishes the revolutionary; the sense of complete certainty that the millennium lies around the corner and the savage impatience with the human shortcomings that delay its advent. Old Rome might have had her Robespierres, St Justs and Bakunins, had her Stoics placed the Golden Age in the future. But the old pagan world was incapable of doing this. Its millennia all lay in the past: to die young was good, not to be born was best. Even to the deeply religious-minded Seneca, who clung tightly to the consolations of philosophy, the world was a darkening place.

> *In nos aetas ultima venit;*
> *O, nos dura sorte creatos.*[26]
>
> [The last age comes with us;
> O, we, created with so dreadful a fate!]

The infinite sadness that underlies so much of ancient thought, the daily experience of squalid evil, unrelieved by a supernatural religion of hope, made exaltation of mind impossible. It remained to the post-Christian world, with its distant recollections of the doctrine of the brotherhood of man and the idea of future blessedness, to transport the Golden Age to the future. The ancient world had its palace revolutions and, in places, its ideas of social justice which sometimes issued in class struggle, but it knew nothing of revolution in the modern sense of the word, based on political or social doctrine: progress in the sense of a continually ascending process of amelioration was foreign to it. 'Christianity grown wild' combined with ancient ideals to make the revolutionary creeds of the modern world, every one of which based itself ultimately on an optimistic naturalism, a theory of progress, of evolution either of rationalized matter or of materialized reason towards ever higher forms of life.

The pervading evil of the world drove the Stoic in upon himself. The law of reason, no longer generally accepted, still existed and could be discerned and followed by the individual who was prepared to seek it. This entailed constant self-denial and self-examination in the light of rational precepts. Philosophy, which is essentially a guide to right conduct, has to be learned laboriously in the decadent world in which we live; good conduct no longer comes to us through our instincts, which are now corrupted; it is no longer made easy by social pressures. But it is possible for the individual to find wisdom and to live by it. *Sanabilimus aegrotamus malis; ipsaque nos in rectum natura geniti, si emendari velimus, iuvat.*[27] [We are afflicted by ills that are curable; Nature herself aids us, since we were born to righteousness, if we wish to better ourselves.] A man can be stronger than the world.

The great mystification of all fatalistic systems has been the co-

The Stoic Origins

existence of fixed laws that determine the behaviour of the generality of mankind and of individuals who persist in defying these laws by exercising free choice. Mankind, according to the Stoics, is condemned by the historic process to deterioration. Yet the Stoics remained, continuing to maintain the primitive values and to show how nature intended all men to live. The development of the intelligence and of the vices takes place, according to Rousseau, 'in direct proportion, the one to the other, not in the individuals, but in the peoples'.[28] This is the assumption on which the entire *Émile* is based. Émile and Sophie were to be the exceptions from the lot of mankind and were to prove that the development of individual intelligence and sensibility is not necessarily accompanied by moral deterioration. The distinction between the individuals and the peoples is characteristically Stoic. The degeneration of mankind in general was explained in terms of the semi-cyclic theory of history, but the existence of exceptions cannot be explained, save on Manichaean premises. God, nature and reason are one; the trilogy attains to self-consciousness in man.[29] But man, the highest manifestation of Deity, is deteriorating and increasingly defying the laws of Deity. The laws are eternal, but between them and the historic process there is perpetual conflict, a conflict which the laws are losing on the human plane. The logic of the system would seem to be that Deity embraces two conflicting principles: good and evil. Yet, this is a logic the Stoics did not admit. Does society corrupt man, or does man corrupt society? This was to be the issue between Rousseau and de Beaumont. It would be difficult indeed to decide it in an immanentist context.

The Stoic response to the riddle which their beliefs set them was a mixed one: despair of the world and hope for the individual. In relation to the masses, the Stoic was the *Promeneur solitaire* ('more alone than Robinson on his island'), for the masses have nothing to teach one. *Immo vero crudelior et inhumanior, quia inter homines fui.** [Indeed, crueller and more inhumane have I become, because I have been among men.] Yet, every man is rational and can follow the path of wisdom if he determines to do so. Nature (that is to say, our rationality) gives each one of us the power to recognize true wisdom

---

* Seneca; *Ep.* 7 (3). Chrysippus and other Stoics maintained that 'there was no root of evil in human nature' and that moral evil in each individual is due 'to the bad influences of society' (Edwyn Bevan, *Stoics and Epicureans*, p. 104). Posidonius takes the view that in man's soul there are innate tendencies to evil (p. 8 above).

and to practise virtue, if only we would bend our wills that way. *Satis natura dedit roboris si illo utamur*.³⁰ [Nature gave us strength enough, if we would only use it.] Man is a social being and is consequently bound by his nature to help others. The duty of self-conservation, which is the first and holiest of all, entails continual effort at moral self-improvement and moral self-improvement entails active benevolence towards others. *Alteri vivas oportet, si vis tibi vivere.*³¹ [You should live for the other person if you wish to live for yourself.] It is true that the 'natural man' of Rousseau's *Discours sur l'Origine de l'Inégalité* can scarcely be described as social, for he lives in virtually complete isolation and in complete self-sufficiency. Yet, even in this extravaganza, Rousseau endows him with a 'natural pity which takes the place of laws' and goes on to transport him into the simple and innocent society described by Seneca in his picture of the Golden Age. Both Seneca and Rousseau moreover agree that the Age of Innocence can never be recalled and that the virtuous man is better off than the merely innocent. For both, the virtuous man is social. For both, the pursuit of virtue lies along the path of self-conquest, the eschewing of vanities such as speculation for its own sake, the shunning of luxuries (for luxury enslaves the mind to the body), the practice of simple living. The sage does not need much.

In their mistrust of speculation and their contempt for technological progress ('inventions'), Seneca and Rousseau are remarkably conservative.

> I have made him feel that all the ideas which are wholesome and truly useful to men are the first that were known, that they have ever constituted the true bonds of society, and that all that is left for transcendent minds to do is to distinguish themselves by ideas which are pernicious and dangerous to the human race.*

The notion, so fashionable in the days of the Enlightenment, that man can be trained to see what his 'true self-interest' requires and that knowledge of this requirement would necessarily ensure universal, indefinite progress in all spheres of life, moral, intellectual and tech-

---

* Rousseau; *Émile* in *Oeuvres*, VII, 151. To both Seneca and Cicero, the 'liberal arts' with which the savants occupy themselves are, at best, only mental sharpeners for the great work of pursuing true wisdom (the knowledge and practice of morality); they are a mere apprenticeship to the real work. In themselves, they are *istaeque quidem artes, pusilla et puerilia*. [Those arts of a sort, petty and puerile.] (*De re pub.*, I, viii, 30; *Ep.* 88 (2)).

The Stoic Origins

nological, was rejected by Rousseau. Not for him the visions of a Condorcet or a Godwin. The role of 'right reason', Rousseau would agree with Seneca in asserting, is to discern moral truths; it shuns the vanities of speculation for its own sake and the base pandering to comfort and ambition in which a *ratio quidem* ('reason of a sort') has been employed throughout the ages of decadence. Truly enlightened self-interest, Rousseau would agree, would dictate the same course as 'right reason', but mankind, having put itself under the dominion of the debased *ratio quidem*, cannot be relied on to discover the requirements of true self-interest. 'Human reason', he says, 'is in my eyes by this time so feeble and so miserable that I do not think it possible to demonstrate its proper feebleness.'[32] The dreams of the Enlightenment are delusory. If a future of happiness is to be sought for mankind, it must be one in which morality will reign throughout the whole of society, to the exclusion of all vanities. The wise man can achieve happiness for himself by following the promptings of right reason, but the generality of mankind is incapable of doing this unless it auto-limits itself: that is to say, unless it places itself in a position in which the demands of right reason are enforced upon it and in which it comes to love them and obey them freely in course of time. Men can auto-limit themselves to the practice of virtue (compliance with the demands of right reason) only by placing themselves under an infallible authority upon which no restriction is imposed, for infallibility should not be restricted. *Tuto enim quantum vult potest, qui se nisi quod debet non putat posse.*[33] [There is nothing dangerous in a man's having as much power as he likes, if he takes the view that he has power to do only what it is his duty to do.] The readiness to submit to such an authority can be brought about only by the sentiment of sociability, the only true guide to virtue left to the generality of man, and the submission is achieved by the Social Contract, which sets up the Sovereign People as the infallible lawmaker. The Contract can be made only where the social sense of men is strongest and where the associates can gather to make laws: that is to say, in the small region. In these circumstances, the lawmaker (the Sovereign People) needs no restriction, for in harming any one of its members it would harm itself, which is impossible. It would, of its nature, enforce only the demands of right reason, because, if it did anything else, it would harm its members; and in enforcing the demands of right reason, it would cause men to love these demands, through their experience of the happiness that follows compliance. Living under the rule of right reason would be truly living according to Nature, since right reason comes from Nature.

Both as to the goal of humanity and as to the means of reaching it, Rousseau is completely at variance with the Enlightenment. The goal is not mastery of the universe, but mastery of the self. The future of humanity is not to be a race of gods, but one of virtuous, undemanding men. And the means of reaching it is to shun the allurements of debased reason and follow the sentiment of sociability, that instinct which has come down to us with the least corruption from the early days of man.

In discussing Rousseau's debt to the Stoics, one is concerned with his ideas as distinct from his life, which was not remarkably stoical. He was a man of acute tension. His mind was partly formed by the calvinistic atmosphere of the city of Geneva to which he and his forbears belonged and by his absorption of stoical ideas in various modifications, which would have been congenial to the puritanically-formed; his nature was weak, his imagination lively, and the result was a heavy sentimentality. Everything had to be excused: every situation had to have its ingredients of modesty, purity and innocence; every misfortune to the hero had to be due to external circumstances. It is not surprising, then, that his moral ideals should have been pitched very high and that the professors of these ideals in their severest form, the Stoics, should have had a special attraction for Rousseau. Their austerity, their integrity and their personal independence were the things he envied most. The attainment of perfect morality without effort, as in the state of innocence or as part of the collectivity, was a dream which was certain to attract him. The Stoic would have abhorred the notion of absorption in the mass as an abdication of personal responsibility and might well have argued, as Godwin did, that there is no easy, automatic coincidence of absolute moral excellence with the decisions of any collectivity, however well-intentioned and homogeneous. For the Stoic, the romantic dream of the Golden Age was over and life was a stern test. Rousseau agreed, and could speak as eloquently as any Stoic of the beauty of virtue. The *Émile* is a prescription for the education of a Stoic of the Senecan stamp, combining absolute rectitude with a high degree of sensibility; the picture of the Man of Nature, withdrawn from and independent of externals, might well have been drawn in large part from Seneca; the

The Stoic Origins

despair of reforming a corrupt world, the very definition of *Nature* (short of identifying God with the universe, although the overtones are sometimes pantheistic) and the dichotomy of its benevolent laws, and the course of criminal folly which mankind has pursued: these outstanding features of Stoic thought formed the inspiration of Rousseau's themes. 'If we dare to prefer the manner of the philosopher to that of the orator', says Diderot, 'this is less the fault of the author of the *Essais* (Diderot): it is that of Jean-Jacques, who recalls Seneca to us at a hundred points, and who does not owe Cicero a line.'[34]

To trace briefly the ancestry of Rousseau's outstanding ideas from external evidence, one might cite, first, the same Diderot:

> I shall cite only one of them [The French authors]: it is M. Rousseau, of Geneva. It would be easy to prove that he owes to Seneca, to Plutarch, to Montaigne, to Locke and to Sidney, the greatest part of the philosophical ideas and the principles of morality and politics which have been most praised in his writings: he even owes to Seneca some of his sophisms and of his strangest paradoxes; that is a source from which, if I may use the expression of Montaigne, he was drawn like the Danaids, filling and pouring without cease.[35]

Next, one might cite Montaigne:

> As for my other reading, in which the pleasure is more tinged with profit and whereby I learn to order my opinions and behaviour, the books which serve me best are Plutarch – now that he is translated into French – and Seneca. I never seriously settled myself to any works of solid learning except these. Like the Danaids, I am for ever filling and pouring from them. . . . Plutarch and Seneca agree in most of their soundest opinions. . . . Their teachings are the cream of philosophy – at once simple and pertinent.[36]

It is true that Plutarch did not belong to the Stoic school; indeed, he rejected the elements of determinism in the system and reacted against the excessive severity of its ideas of virtue. Nevertheless, he accepted the Stoic belief in a particular Providence and always emphasized personal responsibility, which the Stoics (despite their fundamental determinism) never ceased to do, and he shared with them their cult of fortitude and nobility of character. In practical matters, his attitude might be described as modifiedly Stoic; his insight on human nature is as remarkable as Seneca's.[37] It is not surprising, then, that the success of Plutarch should have been linked with that of Seneca and that the term 'plutarchian stoicism' should have been used.[38] Even after his reaction against the severities ('the arrogance') of Stoicism, which developed in the 1560s, Montaigne continued to hold Seneca in affection and to think of him, less as a master of Stoicism than as a *médicin des ames*.[39] The charm of Seneca seems to stem from his kindliness and his sureness of touch in penetrating the heart: so it seemed to the eighteenth century, when his vogue, a little diminished in the late seventeenth century, revived and assumed great proportions in philosophic circles. Montaigne's 'retreat from Stoicism' brought with it a decline of faith in reason, a pessimistic view of the sciences and philosophy (even moral philosophy), an envy of the happiness of the ignorant and the tranquil patience of the poor. *Nature* is all that which has not been contaminated by human art, but right reason is natural, since it comes from Nature.[40] The happy man follows Nature and has no pretensions to science or philosophy. The noble savage is free from the diseases of our civilization.* This is a deviation from Stoicism; yet the points from which the deviation was made are clearly recognizable. Rousseau's indebtedness is equally clear: 'Rousseau', says Faguet, 'is an unbalanced Montaigne.'[41]

It is true that Rousseau is more explicit in acknowledging his debt to Plutarch than to Seneca. One can attribute this partly to the influence of Montaigne (who turned more to Plutarch from 1560 on),[42] but chiefly, it seems, to the similarity of the political antecedents of Plutarch and Rousseau: they were both the products of small com-

---

* 'They live in a pleasant country and so temperate, as I am informed, that one rarely hears of a sick person. Moreover, my witnesses tell me, they never saw a native palsied, blear-eyed, toothless, or bent with age. It is a nation with no kind of commerce; no knowledge of letters or numbers; no name of magistrate or political superiority; no wealth, poverty, or need of servants; no contracts, inheritances or divisions of property, for there is no occupation save idleness and no respect of kindred beyond the common rights of man to man; no clothing, agriculture or metal; no use of wine or wheat. The very words which signify falsehood, treachery, dissimulation, avarice, envy, slander, forgiveness, are never heard of.' ('A Man from the New World' in *Autobiography*, p. 211.) 'The effect of this commerce will be their ruin, which I suppose is well under way. I much fear we have already hastened it by our contagion and sold them our ideas and arts at a terrible price.' (Ibid., p. 215).

The Stoic Origins

munities – Plutarch of Chaeronea, Rousseau of Geneva. Municipal life still flourished in Greece and Plutarch spent most of his life in his native town, to the affairs of which he gave a whole lifetime's devoted service. The tone of his writings is municipal: he was imbued with a very strong local patriotism, which could not but make its mark on his political philosophy. The contemporary Roman Stoic – such as Seneca – lived in a great cosmopolis, the centre of a vast empire in which nationalist prejudices were beginning to disappear. The developing cosmopolitanism inevitably reinforced the basic universalism of Roman Stoicism. Rousseau's forbears had been prominent in the affairs of the city-state of Geneva and he never lost his local patriotism. 'That news', he wrote of the announcement of the award of the Academy of Dijon, 'reawoke all the ideas that had been dictated to me, it animated me with a new force and put in fermentation in my heart that first leaven of heroism and of virtue which my father and my country and Plutarch had put there in my childhood.'[43] The patriot-hero, austere, devoted and generous, would appeal to both Stoic and Romantic. Furthermore, Plutarch himself was, like Seneca, a merciful and kindly man.

2

The Nature of Man

In Rousseau, we have one of the great romantics: his life and works were a rebellion against the world of his time. All the institutions which men had accepted as integral to European civilization, he subjected to a radical criticism. His offence to the traditionalists is obvious: he condemned, at least implicitly, all the political and social arrangements of contemporary Europe and he explicitly rejected most of the fundamentals of the Christian religion. The traditionalists condemned him and invoked the law against him. But he also condemned the world of learning, which was in large part the milieu of the anti-traditionalists. Here he was on much more dangerous ground and from here he received wounds much more hurtful than any the ineffective Establishment would think of inflicting on him. The aristocratic eighteenth century permitted a remarkable latitude to the eccentric, especially if he had anything to say, and there can be no doubt that Rousseau was an eccentric. From that Sunday evening before the closed gates of Geneva to the moment of his lonely death at Ereménonville, he was 'the odd man out'. He never fitted into society. 'With Rousseau', says Madariaga, 'we are in the realm of incoherence: ardent, chaotic imagination.'[1] The nuances of his thought permit no complete systemization, but in so far as one can analyze that thought, it appears to embody the leading ideas of Stoicism, metamorphosed under the heat of imagination and brought to lengths of which the Stoics could not have dreamed.* These ideas, which run as

---

* 'In the course of writing', he tells us in a note to the *Émile*, 'I have a hundred times reflected that it is impossible in a long work always to give the same mean-

The Nature of Man

so many themes through his works, are: the natural goodness of man, the infallibility of uncorrupted instinct, the vanity of speculative philosophy, the equality of men.

Nature, to the Stoics, was God, and God was reason, the principle pervading the entire universe and, on the human plane, prescribing the behaviour of man and his relations with his fellows. God, in this pantheistic sense, might be viewed as an idea of reason, a principle which it is necessary to invoke in order to show that there is coherence in life. A highly emotional person would not be content with this. Nature, to Rousseau, was something alive, a universal spirit which pervades all matter, the mistress of life and ordainer of all movement and activity. In many of his references, he appears to substitute the impersonal 'Great Being' for the personal God, or to confuse both, as when he tells us:

> Ere Long, from the surface of the earth, I raised up my ideas to all the beings of Nature, to the universal system of things, to the incomprehensible Being which embraces all things. Then, the spirit lost in that immensity, I thought not, I reasoned not, I philosophised not; I felt myself, with a sort of voluptuousness, overwhelmed with the weight of that universe; I delivered myself up with ravishment to the confusion of these great ideas; I loved in imagination to lose myself in space; my heart, compressed within the limits of things, found itself in too narrow a place; I stifled in the universe; I would have taken flight into infinity; I believed that, had I unveiled all the mysteries of Nature, I should have felt myself in a situation less delicious than that dizzy ecstasy to which my spirit yielded itself without

---

ing to the same words. There is no language rich enough to furnish as many terms, turns and phrases as our ideas can have of modifications. The method of defining all terms and of substituting without cease, the definition in the place of the defined is beautiful, but impracticable; how escape from the circle? The definitions could be good, if the words were not employed to make them. Despite all that, I am persuaded that one can be clear, even in the poverty of our speech, not in giving always the same acceptations to the same words, but by contriving that the acceptation of each word, as often as it is employed, be sufficiently determined by the ideas to which it is related, and that each sentence in which a word is found serves, so to speak, for a definition. At one moment, I say that infants are incapable of reasoning; at the next, I make them reason with finesse. In that, I hold that I do not contradict myself in my ideas, but I cannot refuse to admit that I often contradict myself in my expressions' (*Émile*, in *Oeuvres*, VI, 141-2 note).

reserve and which, in the agitation of my transports, sometimes made me cry out: 'O, Great Being! O, Great Being!', unable to speak or to think further.*

Nature, in the particular, he appears to identify with the totality of spontaneous movements or impulses of the individual being, tending towards the good of that being. It is surprising that, out of all his writings on the subject of nature, he has left us only one text in which he gives anything like a definition of nature, in the particular:

> Nature, we are told, is but habitude. What does that mean? Are there not habits which are not contracted by force and which never stifle nature? Such, for example, is the habitude of plants, whose bent it is to grow vertically. The plant, set at liberty, preserves the inclination which it has been forced to take, but the sap has not for all that altered its primitive direction, and if the plant continues to vegetate, its prolongation regains the vertical. It is the same with the inclinations of men. As long as one remains in the same state, one can preserve these [inclinations] which result from habitude, and which are least natural to us, but, as soon as the situation changes, the habitude ceases and the natural bent reasserts itself. Education is certainly nothing but a habitude; for, are there not people who forget and lose their education, others who preserve it? Whence comes that difference? If the name 'nature', must be confined to habitudes conformed to nature, this nonsense can be put aside. We are born capable of receiving impressions, and, from our birth onwards, we are affected in diverse ways by the objects which surround us. As soon as we have, so to speak, the consciousness of our sensations, we are disposed to seek or to flee the objects that produce them; later on, according to the convenience or inconvenience which we find between ourselves and these objects, and, finally, according to the judgments we form on the idea of happiness or perfection, which reason gives

---

* *Troisième Lettre à M. de Malesherbes* in *Oeuvres*, XVII, 17; see also 'O Nature! O, my Mother! Behold me under your sole guardianship; there is here no cunning man to interpose himself between thee and me' in the *Confessions*, *Oeuvres*, XV, 488; and again: 'I have retired within myself and, living between myself and nature, I taste an infinite sweetness in thinking that I was not alone, that I was not conversing with a being insensible and dead . . .' in *Ier. Dial.*, *Oeuvres*, XVI. 78.

The Nature of Man

us. These dispositions extend and strengthen themselves in proportion to our increase in sensibility and enlightenment; but, constrained by our habits, they change themselves more or less with our opinions. Before that change, they are what I call our nature. It is therefore, to these primitive dispositions that all must be set in correspondence.[2]

Whatever one's estimate of the degree of precision attained in this definition, it is obvious that Rousseau regards education (that is to say, the training of the human mind by human agency) as non-natural and sees a dichotomy between the spontaneous or the implanted instinct and the operation of the discursive intellect. The laws of the universe (or 'nature') and the activities of man are, therefore, largely out of accord. Man, therefore, is a non-integrated being. He acts in accordance with 'right reason' only when he follows a certain implanted instinct; when he diverts his intellect off this narrow path, he is following 'reason of a sort', which is a misleader. What is this implanted (or 'natural') instinct?

The principal, or, rather, the only primitive instinct is, according to Rousseau, the *amour de soi*, that is, the desire for self-conservation. All other instincts are but modifications of this passion. Since every being wishes its own conservation, it will naturally love what tends to conserve it and abhor what tends to harm it.[3] The source of our passions, then, is good, but all that proceeds from that source is not so, for a thousand muddy streams flow in from without to pollute it. These streams are nothing else than the pernicious influence of society: they are, above all, the products of pride, from which proceed inequality, ambition and greed, the great social sins. 'All is well, coming from the hands of Nature, the Author of all things; all degenerates in the hands of man'.[4] Man, as he comes from the hands of nature, equipped by her with all the faculties calculated to ensure his conservation and promote his happiness, is good and will remain so until he ceases to be self-sufficient.

> The fundamental principle of all morality, on which I have reasoned in all my writings and which I have developed in this last with all the clarity of which I was capable, is that man is a being naturally good, loving justice and order, that there is no original perversity in the human heart and that the first movements of nature are always right. . . . I have shown that all

the vices one imputes to the human heart are not natural to it: I have told of the manner in which they were born: I have, so to speak, traced their genealogy; and I have shown how, by the successive alteration of their original goodness, men eventually become what they are.[5]

The doctrine of Original Sin Rousseau dismisses as incompatible with the goodness of God. Has God, he asks Mgr de Beaumont, created man wicked in order to have the pleasure of punishing him? With Christian teaching on the effects of baptism, Rousseau appears to have been imperfectly acquainted, for he asks: 'According to the Christian teaching, have we not all been cleansed of the effects of Original Sin by baptism and restored to our primeval health? How then do we come to fall again?' 'You attribute to Original Sin the vices of peoples whom you avow to have been delivered from Original Sin; then you blame me for having given another origin to these vices. Is it just to make it a crime in me for not having reasoned as badly as you?'[6] Again, he asks, was not our First Parent a sinner? Why cannot the sins of his descendants be explained in the same manner as his, without consideration of Original Sin?

> You lay down that, according to my principle, one loses sight of the ray of light which acquaints us with the mystery of our own hearts; and you do not see that that principle, much more universal, itself throws light on the fault of the first man, which yours leaves in obscurity. You can see only man in the hands of the devil, and I – I see how he has fallen into them. The cause of evil is, according to you, corrupted nature; that very corruption is an evil, the cause of which must be sought. Man was created good: we agree, both of us, I believe, as to that; but you say that he is wicked because he had been wicked; as for me, I show how he has become wicked. Which of us, in your opinion, goes back the further to beginnings?[7]

Whence, then, proceeds all evil?

> From our social order, which, in every respect contrary to nature whom nothing can destroy, tyrannizes over her without cease and compels her without cease to reclaim her rights. . . . It alone explains all the vices of men and all the evils of society. From which, I conclude that it was not necessary to

The Nature of Man

suppose man wicked by nature when the origin and the progress of that wickedness can be demonstrated. These reflections led me to new researches on the human spirit, considered in the civil state, and I found that the development of the intelligence and of the vices takes place, in that state, in direct proportion, the one to the other, not in the individuals, but in the peoples; a distinction which I have always carefully made and which none of my attackers has ever been able to conceive.[8]

3

Natural Man & his Downfall

❖

Having dismissed the doctrine of Original Sin as the explanation of human wickedness, Rousseau assured the Archbishop of Paris that he had shown how man became wicked.

Man's social order, he claimed, was the source of all evil. The origin and the progress of wickedness can be demonstrated. He had made his own demonstration in the *Discours sur l'Origine de l'Inégalité Parmi les Hommes*, having already given more than a hint in the earlier *Discourse to the Academy of Dijon* on the pernicious influence of learning and the arts. Contemporary society must itself have had an origin and that origin must have been evil. Man, who is naturally good, was once actually so. There was a time when 'right reason', the law of nature or providence, was spontaneously obeyed by the whole of mankind. There was a Golden Age. What interfered with the spontaneous or instinctive obedience? The answer is 'reason of a sort': human vanity, which made reason the servant of appetite. The original sin was committed by the first man who employed his mental powers for his own advancement.

Belief in the Golden Age was to Rousseau, as to the Stoics, an act of faith. There was never a question of historical proof. Before writing the *Discourse on the Origin of Inequality*, Rousseau sojourned for some time in the wooded countryside of St Germains.

> For the rest of the time, buried in the forest, I sought and found the picture of the earliest times, of which I boldly traced the history; I rejected the little lies of men; I dared to strip naked

Natural Man & his Downfall

their nature, to follow the passage of time and of things, which they have disfigured, and, comparing man as he pictures himself with the natural man, to show men at the height of their pretensions the true source of their misery. My soul, elevated by its sublime contemplations, dared to place itself near the divinity, and seeing from that place my fellowmen follow the blind route of their prejudices, of their errors, of their unhappiness, of their crimes, I called to them with a feeble voice which they could not hear: 'Mad ones, who complain endlessly of nature, learn that all your ills come from yourselves'.*

The result of this experience was a picture of man devoid of virtually every social instinct, of almost every characteristic which might be suspected as due to any measure of social experience, a product of a high flight of imagination which would have startled even Seneca: this was Rousseau's man 'of the earliest times' or man 'in the state of nature', as he had come straight from the hands of the Deity or Great Being and as providence had intended him to live.

Man in his earliest or natural condition was an isolated being; there were no institutions, political or social: no government, no family, no property, none of the usages of society. There was no need for any bond or constraint, for men obeyed instinctively the commands of that 'right reason' which providence had implanted in them. Consequently, all was peaceful and harmonious within man and in the world around him. The most outstanding characteristic of man in the state of nature was his self-sufficiency. In his every reference throughout his description of 'early man' Rousseau makes it plain that from the moment one man had need of another he left the freedom of nature behind. 'It is impossible to conceive why, in that primitive state, a man should have any more need of another man than a monkey or a wolf should have need of another of its kind.'[1] Wandering through the forests, the child of nature led the life of the healthy animal. His few wants were easily satisfied—water from the brook, food from the trees and plants around him, a bed wherever he

---

* *Confessions* in *Oeuvres*, XV, 150–1. 'Let us, then, pass over all the facts, for they do not touch the question. It is unnecessary to make those researches into which one can enter on this subject for the purpose of establishing historic truths, but only for the hypothetical and conditional reasonings more appropriate to clarify the nature of things than to show the real origin, and like those which our natural philosophers daily make on the formation of the world.' *Inégalité*, in *Oeuvres*, I, 37.

chose to lie. Instinct alone was his guide; by following its propulsions, he retained a heart at peace and a body in strength. He lived in the present: memory brought him no regrets, for his memory was short; imagination painted for him no horrors, for he had no imagination; intellectual curiosity brought him no misgivings or painful conjectures, for his intellect was dormant and unused. The physical need of the moment satisfied, he knew of on pining for what was not. His fellowmen, whenever he saw them, he scarcely recognized. He could neither love nor hate them, for he never paused even to think of them or of their way of life. Even if he wished to communicate with them, he could find no way of doing so, for he had no speech in common with them.[2] When he did come in contact with them, relations were almost invariably of a peaceful nature, for, in the pre-social state, natural pity, one of the strongest of human instincts, took the place of laws, customs and virtue, and, indeed, exercised a more effective sway, for no one was tempted to disobey its sweet voice.

Timidity, not wickedness, was the mark of these primitive beings. To preserve themselves from harm, rather than to inflict it on others, was the only preoccupation; and, knowing so little of one another, they could know nothing of those vices that spring from a life in common: vanity and ambition, suspicion and contempt, all of which are bred by competition among men. Thus, there could be no hatred of a lasting nature, nor thought of vengeance. Occasional acts of violence there may have been, but these were done solely on the impulse of a moment, and, no sooner done, were forgotten by both aggressor and victim. *Tanto plus in illis proficit vitiorum ignoratio quam in his cognitio virtutis.* [There was among them ignorance of vice rather than knowledge of virtue]* Hobbes, who portrayed natural man as 'a wolf to his kind', failed to see this; for, in denying to the primitive man a knowledge of good, he should likewise have denied him a knowledge of evil and, consequently, should have seen that inner calmness and the ignorance of vice would be quite sufficient to restrain him from deliberate wrongdoing. Man cannot do wrong when he listens to none but nature. It is the use of reason that begets the abuse of our faculties. '. . . I venture almost to affirm that the

---

* The words occur in *Inégalité, Oeuvres*, I, p. 64, without acknowledgement by Rousseau. They express accurately the sentiments of the latter part of Ep. 90, but that particular sentence does not occur. Cf. *Non erant illi sapientes viri, etiam si faciebant facienda sapientibus.* [The men of that era were not philosophers, even if they acted as philosophers are supposed to act.] *Ep.* 90, 36–7.

Natural Man & his Downfall

state of reflection is one contrary to nature, and that the man who meditates is a depraved animal'.*

Rousseau's bitter outbursts against the human reason have been remarked by all commentators. They are a conspicuous feature of that attitude of his which gives him his place in the history of thought; the idea that it is through feeling, rather than intellect, that one apprehends truth, is the characteristic of extreme romanticism. While this attitude may well appear, at first sight at least, at variance with Stoicism, some reflection may show a connection. Discounting his extravagance of expression, one may see that what Rousseau had in mind in his denunciations was the 'reason of a sort' (*ratio quidem*) which Seneca deprecated as running in disaccord with the 'perfect reason' (*recta ratio*) which Deity intends us to follow, or that he was influenced by the doctrine of the unitary personality, in which reason and passion are inseparable and simultaneously corruptible. It might not be fanciful, then, to see in these strange outbursts of Rousseau's a kind of Stoicism heavily infused with emotion: Stoicism transmuted into romanticism. Rousseau's contemporaries of the Enlightenment, in their various methods of approach, either did not make this distinction or else accepted the partition of the personality and assumed that the human reason could be so educated and developed that it would master the passions and freely follow the commands of Deity or 'laws of the universe' and proceed with its speculative and practical activities. In other words, they believed that the human reason, progressively enlightened, and strengthened by exercise, could be safely trusted to produce indefinite progress along every line, moral,

---

* *Inégalité*, in *Oeuvres*, I, 44. *Hanc philosophiam fuisse illo rudi saeculo quo adhuc artificia deerant et ipso usu discebantur utilia, non credo . . . ignorantia rerum innocentes erant. Multum autem interest utrum peccare aliquis nolit aut nesciat. Deerat prudentia, deerat temperantia ac fortitudo. Omnibus his virtutibus habebat similia quaedam rudis vita: virtus non continget animo nisi instituto et edocto et ad summum assidua exercitations perducto.* (Seneca; *Ep.* 90, 35, 46.) [And I do not believe that this philosophy was in existence in that primitive era in which technical skills were still unknown and useful knowledge was acquired through practical experience . . . The fact remains that their innocence was due to ignorance and nothing else. And there is a world of difference between, on the one hand, choosing not to do what is wrong and, on the other, not knowing how to do it in the first place. They lacked the cardinal virtues of justice, moral insight, self control and courage. There were corresponding qualities, in each case not unlike these, that had a place in their primitive lives; but virtue comes only to a character which has been thoroughly schooled and trained and brought to a pitch of perfection by unremitting practice.]

intellectual and technological; that not merely could it be so trusted, but that it was the only means to such progress. Those, such as Godwin, who thought in this way, retained their individualism to the very end of their speculation on human destiny. Rousseau did not. His pessimism drove him to take refuge in the Social Contract. Only in a solidarist society, the final product of the sentiment of sociability, could man be safe. There alone the generality of mankind would be kept immune from the workings of disastrous vanity. It was a solution reactionary in the extreme and badly received by the progressives: 'the unmeaning rant of romance', said Godwin of Rousseau's nationalist mysticism.[3] It is the paradox of Rousseau that his revolt against human reason gives him at once his place in the history of anarchism and in that of solidarism. His personal characteristics and his contempt for the institutions of contemporary society, which he condemns as products of human reason, give him the former; that same condemnation of reason place him in the latter; but even the anarchistic elements in him are non-progressive, from the same cause.

This attitude of his explains the theory of history (if one may call it that) which he unfolds in the *Discours sur l'Origine de l'Inégalité*. Human reason, far from leading us to heavenly harmony, is represented in the *Discours* as the fatal faculty which, once set in operation, shattered the ancient harmony of nature. It opened Pandora's Box.

> It would be sad for us to admit that that distinctive and almost unlimited faculty is the source of all the unhappiness of man: it is that which draws him, in the course of time and by the force of circumstances, from that original condition in which he had passed days of tranquillity and innocence: it is that which, increasing with the centuries his insight and his errors, his vices and his virtues, makes him finally the tyrant over himself and over nature.*

Of progress among Rousseau's primitive nomads, there could be none, for no one thought of it. Indeed, even if one exceptional man conceived such an idea, how could he communicate it to others whom

---

* *Inégalité*, in *Oeuvres*, I, 49–50. Expressions of this sentiment are frequent even outside the *Discours*, particularly in the *Nouvelle Héloise*, the *Confessions* and the *Rêveries*. 'Thinking', he tells us, 'has been for me a labour, painful and without charm' (*Proménade VII* in *Oeuvres*, XVII, 115).

Natural Man & his Downfall

he encountered but rarely and by chance? How could he communicate it without a common language? The invention must perish with the inventor, and the world, peopled by men without foresight or curiosity, continue in its primeval calm. 'The centuries passed and the rudeness of the earliest times remained unchanged; the race was already old and man was still a child'.* Rousseau's individual, it will be observed, was very different from the revolutionary individual of the progressivists: far from building utopias or thinking dangerous thoughts, he may be regarded as intensely, if unconsciously, conservative, for his life and being were ordered by the unchallengeable, all-pervading conservatism of the dumb animal.

The first moment of self-consciousness was the beginning of man's decline, for reflection led him to the fatal knowledge of his superiority to the other animals and of the potentiality that lay within him. Thus, came the first stirrings of human pride, man's first disobedience, of which the woes of our race down through the ages have been the fruit. Deliberately divorcing himself from tutelary nature, man became a being apart and set out to subdue the world, to advance himself in knowledge and power and to perfect his faculties by the use of his awakening reason.

> See how luxury, debauchery and slavery have at all times been the chastisement of the proud efforts we have made to break out from the happy ignorance where the eternal wisdom placed us. The thick veil with which she covered all her operations seemed to turn us away as if we were never destined for vain researches. But is it one of her lessons from which we have been able to profit, or one which we have been able to neglect with impunity? Peoples! Know that nature once wished to preserve you from science, as a mother snatches a dangerous firearm from the hands of her child; that all the secrets she hides from you are so many evils from which she keeps you, and that the trouble you find in instructing yourselves is not the least of her benefits. Men are perverse; they would be worse still if they had the misfortune to be born learned.[4]

---

* *Inégalité* in *Oeuvres*, I, 72, Cf.: 'It is absolutely certain that the learned societies of Europe are but so many schools of falsehood; and very surely there are more errors in the Academy of Sciences than in the whole tribe of Hurons' (*Émile* in *Oeuvres*, VI, 325).

Rousseau: Stoic & Romantic

Rousseau's isolated 'Man of Nature' was a figment of his own imagination; not much more so than Hobbes's compound of wickedness or Locke's compound of rationality. Each of these figments reflects something of the age in which it was invented and more or less of the personality of the inventor. Hobbes's 'natural man', a 'wolf to his kind', combined the barbarism of the mid-seventeenth century with the cynicism of the author; Locke's rational creation reflects the peculiarly abstract mode of thought and the marked complacency of the early days of the Age of Reason. They both thought in abstractions and both were products of a remarkably unhistorically-minded period. Rousseau, the last of the great abstractionists (if we except Holbach), infused much of his own personality into his 'Man of Nature': he was the lonely man who fitted into no social context. Yet, there was a germ of sociability even in the child of nature: he was possessed of a 'natural pity' for his fellows.

It is not surprising, then, that the first rift with nature arose out of man's first thought of association with others of his kind. Observation of their ways showed him how closely men resembled one another; outward similarity of habit led him to presume inward similarity of thought and feeling and inevitably led to the desire for closer relations. Hence arose the earliest attempts at community life: fortuitous congregations which could scarcely boast of organization worthy of the name paved the way for closer association and the era of family life. Thus, increasing independence of nature brought with it increasing dependence upon man.

With the development of the family arose a rudimentary notion of property. The nomadic life came gradually to be abandoned; families began to settle in groups, each in a dwelling of its own, around which a rude form of agriculture was carried on.* This stage, midway between the indolence of the primitive state and the feverish activity

---

* Cf. *Sed primi mortalium quique ex his geniti naturam incorrupti sequebantur eundem habebant et ducem et legem, commissi melioribus arbitrio . . . Nemo quantum posset adversus eos experiebatur per quos coeperat posse, non erat cuiquam aut animus in iniuriam aut causa, cum bene imperanti bene paretur, nihilque rex maius minari male parentibus posset quam ut abiret e regno.* (*Ep.* 90 (4, 6).) [But the first men on this earth and their immediate descendants followed Nature unspoiled: they took one and the same person as their leader and their law, freely submitting to the decision of a man of superior merit . . . No one tried out the extent of his power over those to whom he owed that power in the first place. And no one had either reason or inclination to perpetuate injustice, since people governing well were equally well obeyed, and a king could issue no greater threat to disobedient subjects than that of his own abdication.]

Natural Man & his Downfall

of civilization, was, despite its defects, the youth of the world, the stage beyond which man ought never to have advanced. He was still close enough to nature to need no coercive laws: the customs which imperceptibly grew in the group to which he belonged were sufficient to ensure well-being and order and were instinctively obeyed. Rousseau's picture of these earliest communities might well have been suggested by some of the more charming passages of Seneca, and so might the shadows that fell across it:

> They accustomed themselves to assemble before their dwellings or around a great tree; song and dance, true children of love and idleness, became the amusement, or rather the occupation, of the indolent men and women who played together. Each one began to observe the others and to wish himself to be observed, the esteem of all his fellows being the prize. He that sang or danced best, the handsomest, the strongest, the most skilful or the most eloquent, became the most highly considered. And that was the first step towards inequality and towards wickedness at the same time, for these first preferences produced, on the one side, vanity and contempt for others, and, on the other, shame and envy. The fermentation caused by these new leavens brought adjustments baneful to happiness and innocence.[5]

To the craving for reputation there was later added a new object of ambition and an even more fruitful cause of discord and violence. As agriculture advanced, it became necessary that the idea of property be made more exact. In the scramble for land, it was inevitable that some should fail and become dependent economically on their successful brothers. Thus, to the earlier distinctions was now added the distinction between rich and poor. The old, happy times when each man could support himself by his own unaided effort had passed away. Mutual interdependence made its appearance on the human scene. Man became the slave of his fellows, loaded with new shackles by the need to satisfy the multitude of wants which accompanied the new social structure. The servant found himself compelled to look to the master for his daily bread and the master found himself dependent for the maintenance of his new position on the exertions of his servants and on the good will of all who might be able to injure him. To those in his power he could be as merciless as he wished; to those beyond his reach it was necessary to cover his hatred and jealousy with a mask of benevolence: 'To be and to appear became two things altogether different, and, from this distinction arose the treacherous imposition, the lying ruse and all the vices that follow in their wake'.[6]

The institution of property, which was the second major step in the downward course of man, brought irreversible calamity. That stage was now reached which Hobbes mistook for the state of nature: the war of everyman against everyman. But, Rousseau maintains, so far beyond the true state of nature had we gone, that we now behold man 'with all his faculties developed, his memory and imagination at work, his *amour propre* stirred, his reason active and his mind almost at the limit of the perfection of which it is susceptible.'[7] All his newly-found ability was placed at the service of the devouring ambition which came to be the ruling passion in the heart of every member, rich and poor, of society. The natural pity which in earlier times occupied the place of laws had disappeared, and whatever beneficent customs had flowed from the goodness of primitive man were violently broken and swept aside, and the only rule that could prevail was that of force and craft. The usurpations of the rich were followed by the dreadful vengeance of the poor and universal brigandage and murder turned the earth into a desert and the once-happy villages and dwellings of men into places of death. Unable now to retrace their steps, dreading to think of what the future might bring and not knowing, in their terror, whither to turn, men might well have come to think that the end of all things was at hand.

It was then that ingenuity suggested one of the cleverest schemes that ever entered the mind of man. The rich, who had everything to lose and nothing to gain by a continuance of anarchy, conceived the plan of harnessing the forces that had hitherto been a menace to their security and employing them to establish a condition of things favourable to the possession of property. With great show of righteousness and concern for the general well-being, they appealed:

> Let us unite, to guarantee the weak from oppression, to keep the ambitious within bounds and to assure to each what is his own. Let us set up rules of justice and peace to which all may be obliged to conform, rules which may make no exception of anyone and which shall, in some measure, make up for the caprices of fortune by holding the powerful and the weak equally to their mutual obligations. In a word, instead of turning our forces

Natural Man & his Downfall

against ourselves, let us gather together to uphold a supreme power which may govern us according to wise laws, which may protect and defend all the members of the association, repulse our common foes and keep us in an everlasting concord.[8]

All too easily were simple men beguiled. The suggestion was received with acclamation. Only the proposers of the project understood what the consequences would be. The masses of the dispossessed, desiring little but relief from the terrors of strife, never paused to consider the future; even the wisest thought it a good bargain to sacrifice one part of freedom in order to ensure the rest. Thinking, then, to make their liberty safe, 'all rushed to their chains'. Thus was born the State.[9]

It is not easy, thinks Rousseau, to determine what were precisely the nature and constitution of the earliest civil governments. On one point, however, he is emphatic: whatever type of rule was set up, it was certainly not the despotism imagined by Hobbes.[10] Since no one in his senses would seek to escape the petty annoyances of foxes and jackals by delivering himself up to the mercy of a devouring lion, the Social Contract of Hobbes may, believes Rousseau, be dismissed as too absurd for consideration. The Contract was doubtless an attractive one for all, expressed in words similar to those used in the appeal. Men were to come together to agree to just laws, equally binding on all, and assuring the peace and well-being of everyone. Chiefs were to be chosen to enforce them and to protect the people against wrongdoers within and enemies without. For a brief moment, perfection seemed to have been reached.* If the elected chiefs performed their duties without fear or favour, if the strong respected the rights of the weak; if, in a word, men were what they were not, all would have been well. But the very vices that had rendered government necessary rendered the abuse of power inevitable. Those who had been placed in authority proceeded to use the public power conferred on them to advance their private aims. Election by the people disappeared; public office came to be regarded by its holders as the private preserve of their families and the law became the instrument of the aggrandise-

---

* *Inégalité* in *Oeuvres*, I, 107 et seq. *Sed postquam surrepentibus vitiis in tyrannidem regna conversa sunt, opus esse legibus coepit. Quas et ipsas inter initia tulere sapientes.* Seneca; *Ep.* 90 (6). [But with the gradual infiltration of the vices and the resultant transformation of kingships into tyrannies, the need arose for laws – laws which were themselves, at the beginning, drafted by the wise.]

ment of the powerful and the oppression of the weak. Gradually, as the lesser tyrants weakened or destroyed one another, the power of the greater ones grew. These, in their time, will fight among themselves and so, the struggle will go on until none but the fittest shall survive, when humanity shall have reached once more a condition of equality – this time, however, an equality of slavery, in which the men of every nation shall stand equal in poverty and wretchedness over against the one triumphant despot. By this time, the situation may present opportunities for successful revolution.[11]

This is Rousseau's version of the Doctrine of Increasing Misery.

> If we follow the progress of inequality in its diverse revolutions, we shall find that the establishment of the law and the right of property was its first stage, the institution of magistracy the second, the third and last was the changing of legitimate power into arbitrary power. Thus, the condition of *rich* and *poor* was authorized by the first epoch; that of *powerful* and *weak* by the second, and, by the third, that of *master* and *slave* which is the last degree of inequality and the term towards which all others move, up to the point at which new revolutions dissolve the government entirely or bring it nearer to a legitimate institution.*

---

* Ibid., 108 Cf. the anarchist, Proudhon: 'Thus, moral evil, or, in this case, disorder in society, is naturally explained by your power of reflection. The mother of poverty, crime, insurrection and war was inequality of conditions, which was the daughter of property, which was born of selfishness, which was engendered by private opinion, which descended in a direct line from the autocracy of reason. Man, in his infancy, is neither criminal nor barbarous, but ignorant and inexperienced. Endowed with imperious instincts, which are under the control of his reasoning faculty, at first he reflects but little and reasons inaccurately; then, benefiting by his mistakes, he rectifies his ideas, then perfects his reason' (P.-J. Proudhon, *What is Property? First Memoir*. Vol. 1, ch. V, 244).

4

Émile, or the Natural Man in Society

❖

Deterioration has been the lot of the generality of mankind, but not necessarily that of the individual. The development of individual intelligence need not be accompanied by a development of wickedness in any particular person. Provided it takes place under the proper conditions, it entails even a vast increase in goodness.

Under what conditions, one may ask? How can man develop his intelligence without injury to his soul? In other words, how can he develop his reason so that its operations shall always be directed towards moral ends and be untinged by unworthy motives? How can man be trained to follow the *recta ratio* and ignore the *ratio quidem*, or rather to bring the latter under complete control?

Only two kinds of men are truly autonomous: the primitive man in isolation and the virtuous man in society. The former, since he has no relations with others, has but to follow his instincts without restraint. Following the impulses of nature, he must be good, and, being immune from the knowledge of evil, he must be happy. Inclination and duty are, for him, coincident: he is an amoral animal.[1] 'Happy the people among whom one can be good without effort and just without virtue.'[2]

To live rightly and happily in contemporary society, man must have the strength to combat evil. He must have virtue; that is, he must obey the dictates of conscience, which are developments under the operation of 'right reason' of the fundamental passion implanted in us by nature or providence: the desire of self-conservation or the *amour de soi*.

> ... Man is not a simple being: he is composed of two substances. ... The being agreed upon, it will be seen that the *amour de soi* is no more a simple passion, but has two principles, namely, the intelligent being and the sensitive being, of which the well-being of each is not the same. The appetite tends to that of the body, the love of order to that of the soul. This latter love, developed and made active, takes the name of conscience; but conscience does not develop and become active except with the intelligence of the man. It is only through the intelligence that he comes to know order, and it is only when he knows it that his conscience brings him to love it. ... [3]

So says Rousseau in his defence of *Émile*. Elsewhere, the conception of conscience is frequently something much more nearly approaching of the romantic: conscience is conceived of as 'independent' of the reason, anterior to it and operating with immediacy, although its conclusions will always coincide with those of 'right reason':

> Conscience, conscience, instinct divine, immortal and celestial voice: assured guide of a being who is ignorant and limited, but intelligent and free: infallible judge of good and evil, making men like to God: it is you who make the excellence of his nature and the morality of his actions.[4]

The intellect takes a subordinate place in this scheme of things. Its findings must be in conformity with the promptings of the heart, with the 'inner voice': otherwise, it becomes a misleading and mischievous thing. The primacy belongs to sentiment: '... to exist is, for us, to feel: our sensibility is uncontestably anterior to our intelligence and we have had sentiments before ideas'.[5] All the wisdom we need is within us; the only true book is the human heart; whoever reads therein will learn 'to judge with more sentiment than science, and by effects rather than by rules'. 'I have often', says Julie, 'found myself at fault in my reasoning, but never in the secret impulses that inspire themselves in me, with the result that I have more confidence in my instinct than in my reason.'[6] The errors of reason can be rectified only by consulting conscience. Instinct, sentiment, conscience: this is the voice of God. Human reason can do little but come between man and the truth.

Émile, or the Natural Man in Society

This appeal to the deeps in man, to the elemental things in human nature, is the feature that distinguishes the libertarianism of Rousseau from the intellectualist libertarianism of the Enlightenment. It is also the secret of the success of the former: the poet will succeed where the mere logician leaves no impression; the man of emotion will exercise a deeper and wider influence than the scholar. Intellectualism is essentially aristocratic: comparatively few possess brains. Emotionalism is essentially democratic: everyone possesses feelings. On the other side, too, a recollection of Rousseau's reliance on sentiment will help to supply one of the bridges between the anarchistic individualism encountered in him and the solidarism or *étatisme* of such works as the *Contrat Social*, the *Projet de Constitution pour la Corse* and the *Considérations sur le Gouvernement de Pologne*: 'We gladly will that which the folk we love will' (*Économie Politique*, p. 189). Submission under the Social Pact is made, not to the will of a despot, but to the General Will, and obedience to the latter is to be secured by awakening the '*sentiment* of humanity', the *feeling* of patriotism, 'the most important of all (laws), which is engraved, not in marble or in bronze, but in the *hearts* of the citizens; . . . which, when the others grow old and enfeebled, reanimates them or substitutes itself for them, keeps a people in the spirit of its institution and *substitutes insensibly the force of habitude for that of authority*' (*Contrat Social* in *Oeuvres*, II, 51). Hence, the insistence on the Civil Religion and the cultivation of the 'sentiments of sociability' (Ibid., p. 158). Hence, too, the emphasis on the need for moulding the character of the young by a system of universal national education which will keep forever before their eyes, as a palpable, living thing, the figure of the Fatherland. This is the other facet of romanticism. As these ideals depend for their attainment on the strength of brotherly feeling among citizens, the perfect State is so small as to permit all to know one another and to meet as a legislature.

From his denunciation of civil society as it existed in his time, one might expect to find in Rousseau an advocate of radical revolution, but, while the logic of much of his thought is obviously revolutionary, Rousseau was no Bakunin, and in fact resented the charge of being anti-social. 'What, then? Ought we to destroy society, annihilate *mine* and *thine*, and return to live in the forest with the bears? That is the conclusion at which my adversaries would wish me to arrive.'[7]

A return to the state of nature, he says, is now neither possible nor desirable. Once we abandon that state, we compel all our fellows to do likewise, since we render it impossible for anyone in the midst of civil society to live the life of primitive isolation. Any attempt at a turning back would, by destroying the social bonds and presenting to men an unlimited licence, result in a defeat of its object. The men we see around us are unfitted by their weakness and their vices for freedom. Liberty is a heady wine which only the wise and strong can taste with safety. To present it to those who are unworthy of it is to make them free only in appearance: their liberty will be nothing more than that of the slave whose master has forgotten to give him a command. Let them try to cast off their bonds, and they will but succeed in drawing them tighter than before. Nor, as has been said, is a return desirable, for the primitive man in his forest, although happy and free, is not the highest object of emulation. His higher nature is undeveloped, and those characteristics which are the mark of a man, reason and conscience, are dormant; he is a creature of appetite. In the letter to Mgr de Beaumont, Rousseau discusses the moral condition of the isolated savage:

> Conscience is nought in the man who has made no comparisons and has never known relationships. In that condition, man knows nothing but himself; he does not see his well-being either opposed to, or in conformity with, that of anyone else; he neither hates nor loves anyone; limited to physical instinct alone, he is nothing, he is a beast: that is what I have shown in my *Discours sur l'Inégalité*.[8]

In this same letter, having reaffirmed his original thesis that man is good but men are wicked, he goes on to speak of his purpose in writing the *Émile*: 'It is to discover how to prevent them from becoming thus (wicked), that I have devoted my book. I have not affirmed that, in the existing order, the thing was absolutely possible; but I have strongly affirmed, and I still affirm, that there are, for the achievement of that end, no other means than those I have proposed'.[9]

Nature gives us all the power we need to make ourselves virtuous and happy and it ultimately reveals to us all we can know about God. It is sufficient for all our purposes: the implied rejection of the Christian doctrine of Grace was the chief feature of the *Émile* which brought the ecclesiastical condemnation on the work. It is the first of many

Émile, or the Natural Man in Society

large schemes of naturalistic education, a plan for the training of a Stoic.*

Since there is no original perversity in the human heart, and no wickedness therein which cannot be shown to have entered from without, the whole problem of evil may be disposed of by the simple process of closing the entries of vice thereto. If these be kept closed, the harmony of nature will assert itself within and the only lessons learned from the external world will be good and will ultimately enhance the virtue and happiness of the learner, who will in his own private sphere relive the life of the Golden Age. The early education of Émile, then, is purely negative. It consists, not in the inculcation of idea of truth and virtue, but in protecting him from error and folly. A role of masterly inactivity is assigned to the tutor; his function is but to assist nature and supply the deficiencies of circumstances. 'Think of yourself', Rousseau bids him, 'as the minister of nature, and you will never become her enemy.'[10] He must practise the negative virtue: 'Do no evil', rather than the positive one: 'Do good'.

> The only lesson in morality suitable to infancy, and the most important for all ages, is never to do evil to anyone. Even the precept: 'Do good', if it be not subordinated to that, is dangerous, false and contradictory. For who does not do good? Everyone is doing it: the wicked as well as the others: it gives happiness to one man at the cost of misery to a hundred, and, from this proceed all our calamities.[11]

With these cryptic aphorisms echoing in his ears, our tutor proceeds to the task of educating Émile, or, rather, of watching Émile educate himself by following his own inclinations. The freedom of Émile is that of the young savage, except that, in the course of his games, he learns to think and to use his initiative in solving the problems that confront him. Becoming accustomed, thus, to employing his native intelligence in judging of all matters, he never becomes the slave of habit; what he does today forms no precedent for tomorrow; he is uninfluenced by example and knows not the meaning of human authority. His dependence is on things: the only authority

---

* 'Rousseau is first to look in human history itself, in the immanent world of man, for that totality which men had hitherto found in transcendental worlds in divine providence.' 'The totality in which Rousseau seeks to compensate for an abstract historical society is still an immanent one.' (Lionel Gossman, *Time and History in Rousseau*, Vol. 30, 345, 346.)

to which he yields is that of necessity. He thus becomes both free and disciplined.

> There are two kinds of dependence: that on things, which means on nature, and that on men, which means on society. Dependence on things, being amoral, does not infringe on liberty and engenders no vice; dependence on men, being not ordained by nature, engenders them all, and, by it, the master and the slave deprave each other. . . .[12]

This curious distinction between dependence 'on men' and dependence 'on things' runs also through the rationalistic anarchism of Godwin. Both philosophers assume that 'general justice', the 'system of the universe' and 'necessity of nature' are interchangeable terms: each in his own fashion assumes that there is a pre-ordained harmony of 'things', which in fact operates, and a pre-ordained harmony of men, which does not. Each assumes that the development of man has been an exception to that of the entire remainder of the universe. Each assumes that the harmonious 'things' are entirely unaffected by the activities of imperfect man. Neither philosopher tells us what precisely those 'things' are. The origin of the dichotomy, according to Godwin and his fellow hedonists, is human ignorance; according to Rousseau, it is the abandonment of ignorance. Yet, the dichotomy remains: man is still the exception to the rest of the entire universe. The only thinking being is the only erring one. To Godwin, the solution was a simple one: make man think more. To Rousseau, it was equally simple: make him think less and feel more.

Evil has come to us mainly through the acceptance of other men's opinions ('dependence on men') and the most widely influential of these opinions have come to us from books. Books, then, must play no part in the early education of Émile and all forms of instruction, other than that of necessity, must be avoided. The tutor must command nothing; he must avoid, under every circumstance, giving his pupil the least impression of a pretence at authority over him. Thus, no promises ought ever to be exacted, since their fulfilment may impose restriction on his freedom of action; the truth ought never be demanded of him, lest he be tempted to lie; and even in the event of his lying, he ought to be punished, not directly for the falsehood, but indirectly, by having it demonstrated to him in practice that the person suspected of being untruthful is disbelieved even when he tells

Émile, or the Natural Man in Society

the truth.[13] Similarly, when his tutor wishes to make a convention or pact of any kind with him, he must so contrive it that the initiative seems to come from Émile. Once engaged, he must be given an immediate and evident interest in keeping the contract on every occasion on which he might be tempted to break it; and, should he fail to keep his word, his punishment must seem to proceed from the natural order of things, and not from the vengefulness of his tutor. 'From nature herself must be drawn the instruments to regulate her.'[14] In this submission to the laws of nature, Émile finds the true liberty of man. 'You have made me free by teaching me to yield to necessity', he tells his tutor in later years.[15] The shackles of opinion have never fettered him; the bonds of nature he cheerfully bears and will gladly continue to bear to the day of his death, for submission to them is the mark of a man. The discipline of nature inculcates the only true resignation, for it shows man the real measure of his power and the limits beyond which it would be foolish for him to stray. 'It is thus you make him patient, temperate, resigned and peaceable, even when he shall fail to obtain what he has wished, for it is in the nature of man to bear patiently the necessity of things, but not the caprice of another.'[16] Even the awful thought of death presents little terror to the child of nature, as, in Rousseau's experience, it presents little to savages and lower animals.[17] Throughout this period of purely negative education which continues up to Émile's twelfth year, the tutor's intervention must be restricted and surreptitious.* His role is that of a

---

* Émile, in Oeuvres, VI, 99: '. . . let us distinguish the *penchants* which come from nature from those that arise from opinion. There is a thirst for knowledge which is the product only of the desire to be esteemed learned; but there is another which is born of a natural curiosity respecting everything of interest, immediate or remote. The innate desire of well-being and the impossibility of satisfying this desire completely compel him to seek without cease for new means to contribute to it. . . . Let us, then, exclude from our early studies those attainments the taste for which is not natural to man, and confine ourselves to those which instinct drives us to seek' (ibid., 253-4). This exclusion can be achieved only by means of the 'negative education'. 'Émile has only natural and purely physical knowledge. He does not know even the name of history, nor what metaphysics and ethics are. He knows the essential relations of man to things but nothing of the moral relations of man to man' (ibid., 331). The study of ethics is beyond the ability of childhood. It must therefore be excluded throughout the early period, if the *amour de soi* is not to be perverted into *amour propre* or vicious vanity; mere affectation of knowledge is symptomatic of this perversion. By following 'instinct', we ensure that the *amour de soi*, the 'primitive notion', develops as nature intended it to develop, and the adolescent retains the true sense of direction, the true or 'natural' humility. He continues to be his 'real' or

providence to the young Robinson Crusoe: to protect him from any grave evil to which he may unwittingly expose himself, to contrive that he shall be placed, as constantly as possible, in those circumstances that 'will inculcate the "primitive notions", and to create those circumstances for him whenever they do not exist'.[18]

His twelfth year thus finds Émile a vigorous, healthy young animal, ignorant of the ways of men, of good and evil in any metaphysical sense, of his own soul and of God.[19] Divested of all morality in his actions, he can do nothing which is morally wrong, and which merits either chastisement or reprimand.[20] His education has been achieved through the knowledge of things, not of words. The lessons he has learned have been impressed indelibly upon him by his own experiences; his mind, which has not been choked by a mass of verbiage that could convey nothing to him, remains free and fresh and open to the reception of the useful lessons to which he must henceforth apply himself. His natural curiosity and unprejudiced mind will enable him to learn quickly and to the greatest advantage during the short period of formal instruction that lies before him.

> Give me a child of twelve years who knows nothing whatsoever, and, at fifteen, I warrant you to have made him as learned as he whom you have instructed from his earliest years, with this difference: that the learning of your pupil will lie but in his memory, while that of mine will lie in his judgment.[21]

The next three years of Émile's life are spent in acquiring, through practical experiment, a knowledge of such useful subjects as suit his tastes. There must be no attempt at forcing him to study: his attention must be drawn through the stimulation of his curiosity; his industry must be the result of a genuine pleasure in equipping himself with knowledge which he considers useful. It is preferable that he learn nothing than learn against his inclination.[22] 'Never command him to do anything whatever, not the least thing in the world. Never allow him to imagine that you assume to have any authority over him.'[23] His teacher, then, ought rarely propose what he ought to learn: it is for Émile 'to desire, to seek and to find'. The duty of the tutor is to allow him to follow his bent, to awaken in him the right

---

'authentic' self, as distinct from the 'inauthentic' or 'social' self into which our corrupt society would make him.

Émile, or the Natural Man in Society

desires and supply him with the means of satisfying them. That he should learn to read is of little importance. The child who reads does not instruct himself: he learns words. Émile's education must make him enlightened, self-reliant and happy by stirring within him such ideas as enable him to know where his permanent well-being lies, to enlighten himself on his duties in life, and, so, to regulate all his affairs in a manner 'agreeable to his being and his faculties'. Instead, then, of wasting his youthful years in the study of abstruse subjects which he cannot understand, he learns a trade, acquires a knowledge of the physical world around him; he comes to know things, not by their nature, but in their relation to himself. Abstract knowledge means nothing to him; metaphysics, morals, history and such matters he neither knows nor cares about. It matters not to know what *is*, but only what is *useful*.[24] He knows nothing of science, but he can invent. He is the centre of his universe, and judges all things according to their usefulness to himself. The opinion of others matters not in the least to him. 'He demands nothing of anyone and thinks himself under obligation to none. He stands alone in human society and counts on himself alone.'[25] Authority, convention, obedience, are words whose meaning is foreign to him. He will extend assistance to another on the understanding that his exertions will be recompensed: never in compliance with a command. No respecter of persons, he ignores the arbitrary distinctions of rank and caste which other men hold sacred. 'He would give the whole Academy of Sciences for the smallest confectioner in the Rue des Lombards.'[26] He is the Economic Man. 'What is the use of that? Behold, henceforth, the consecrated word.'*

Thus stands Émile at the end of his fifteenth year. The first step towards making him a man has been taken. One side of his nature is now fully developed: his *amour de soi*, or self-preservative instinct, has been given free rein, but has been prevented, by his isolation from the world and by the purely amoral training which he has received, from degenerating into *amour propre*. He knows his place in the world of *things*; he must now be taught to find it in the world of men, for he can no longer remain outside society. How to enable him to play his

---

* Ibid., 276: 'Of what importance is it to a scholar to know how Hannibal proceeded in order to prevail upon his soldiers to cross the Alps? If, in place of these magnificent harangues, you tell him how to proceed in order to induce his master to grant him a leave of absence, you may be sure he will be more attentive to your rules' (ibid., 410).

part in the social world, without degenerating through the evil influences that will henceforth surround him, is now the problem.

The *amour de soi* is no mere selfish thing, for it includes within itself the 'sentiment of sociability'. The legitimate desire for self-conservation drives us to seek and follow the rules of 'right reason' or natural morality, which command us to seek also the good of others. The desire for one's own happiness and that for the happiness of others are but two constituents of the same implanted, natural instinct. The second follows naturally from the first, and if the first be kept inviolate, the second will follow in fact. Émile has, so far, been very fortunate: not only has his *amour de soi* been kept inviolate, but it is in a vigorous condition owing to the free exercise which his negative education has allowed him to give it. He is therefore in a very strong position to deal with the moral problems that arise out of relations with men. So, he steps out of the isolated world of 'things' and into the world of 'men'.

With this second step in the making of Émile into a man, we leave the narrowly utilitarian sphere and enter into the moral order. Progress in this order will consist in developing the second constituent of the *amour de soi*: the instinct to love and to feel pity. 'We have made a being who can act and think; nothing now remains for us, in order to make a man, but to make a being who can love and feel: that is to say, to perfect reason by means of sentiment.'[27] The sentiment of pity, 'the first relative sentiment that touches the human heart, according to the order of nature', must, therefore, be stirred in Émile by the spectacle of human misery, in order that he may come to love those around him.[28] By cultivating his capacity for love, by reflecting deeply on his own sentiments and on those of others under his observation, he will come in time to develop the notion of humanity in the abstract and to embrace it with a general love which will identify him with it. Thus he becomes a social being, with a morality made for humanity. This humanist religion, austere product of conscience and reason, will preserve him from the weaknesses to which a sensitive nature is prone: it will check misplaced pity and indulgence towards the unworthy; it will make him at once benevolent and stern.[29] The first promptings of conscience come from the heart, since 'the first movements of nature are always right';[30] our notions of good and of evil, then, have arisen from the primitive sentiments of love and hate. By the exercise of reason, man comes to know of order; once known,

Émile, or the Natural Man in Society

conscience compels him to love it. Thus, he comes to discover for himself the eternal laws of nature which are 'written at the bottom of his heart by conscience and by reason'.[31]

To complete and crown his religion, Émile must now be taught to know God. The approach to this knowledge, as to all other, must be made, not by the teaching of dogma, nor the study of books, but through the senses of the pupil and the working of his conscience.

In this part of the *Émile*, Rousseau gives us one of the clearest expositions of his religious ideas, one that is highly individualistic, anti-authoritarian and marked with pantheistic overtones. Religion, to Rousseau, is a purely private matter, a tête-a-tête with God. All communication between man and God is direct between the individual and the Deity. There is no place for a visible link, a principle of religious authority or for religious organization: 'My own mind is my own Church', as Thomas Paine put it. These notions explain Rousseau's antipathy towards the Catholic Church, which represents religion in its most authoritarian and most highly organized form. Natural reason ('right reason') and natural sentiment alone point the way to God; they also provide us with the means (and the sole means) to perfection and salvation, and they are readily available to us. This is the doctrine of naturalism in its clearest form, the doctrine of human self-sufficiency which placed Rousseau directly at variance with the Catholic Church in respect of some of the most fundamental tenets of Christianity. In so far as Rousseau would allow religious belief to be regulated externally at all, he would have it done, not by a Church (and certainly not by a supra-national Church), but by the Sovereign People in his ideal State.

Atheism, Rousseau detested. The regularity and order of the material universe, he firmly believed, demonstrate the existence of a Supreme Intelligence. The beauty and wonder of all creation, the beneficence of nature, the voice of conscience, proclaim His greatness and His goodness. Our true liberty consists in obedience to His laws, for these are the laws of necessity, and the happiness which we feel when we obey is the surest indication of His love for us. To follow conscience is to fulfil His commands; to look within oneself, to consult the heart, is to discover the guiding maxim: 'Be just and you will be happy'. He speaks directly to us, having no need of Moses or of any other man to tell us what our duty is.[32] Beyond what conscience and natural reason tell us, we can know no more about Him.

Rousseau: Stoic & Romantic

'I perceive God everywhere in His works', says the Savoyard Vicar, 'I feel Him in myself; I see Him universally around me. But, when I would seek where He is, what He is, of what substance, He glides away from me and my troubled soul discerns nothing.'[33] These, then, are the essentials of the natural religion: that there is a God, that He is good, that He speaks directly to the individual man through conscience. Beyond this, no further belief is asked of Émile, for it contains all the articles of faith that man needs. Should he desire to join himself to any particular Church or religious association, that is a matter for himself: '. . . With what particular sect shall we associate the man of nature? The reply is very simple, it seems to me: we shall not associate him with this nor with that, but we shall place him in the state in which he can choose that towards which the best use of his reason ought to conduct him.'[34]

The education of Émile is now complete and he takes his place as a fully developed man of nature in the midst of society, fully equipped to withstand all the temptations to which others, not trained as he has been, inevitably succumb. Egoism and altruism are perfectly balanced in him; all his natural good qualities are so highly developed that little need be feared for his future. He is stronger than the world, master of his destiny. His self-sufficiency enables him to move about the busy haunts of men with the detachment of a Stoic; he is in society, but not of it, a spectator rather than a participant, and the eminence upon which he stands enables him to understand the problems that weary and baffle those who are so deeply immersed in the petty, daily commerce of the town as to be incapable of seeing things in their true proportion, of raising their eyes to seek the great and permanent things of life. He is not led by the passions and opinions of the crowd: he sees with his own eye, feels with his own heart and admits of no authority over him but his own conscience and reason.

> It is then only that he finds his true interest in being good, in acting rightly without thought of the applause of men, and, without being forced by the laws, in being just in all matters between God and himself, in doing his duty even at the cost of his life, and in carrying virtue in his heart, not alone for the love of order, to which each one at all times prefers his *amour de soi*, but for the love of the Author of his being, a love which he confounds with that same *amour de soi*, to find finally the durable

Émile, or the Natural Man in Society

happiness which the repose of a good conscience and the contemplation of that Supreme Being promise him in the other life, having acquitted himself well in this. . . .*

Émile is a post-Christian Stoic, for he has added to the ancient principles of morality the belief in personal immortality different from the Stoic in conception and in rewards and punishments in a future life, a belief to which Rousseau and the generality of eighteenth-century Deists subscribed.

It is not difficult, then, to see that a community of Émiles would realize the anarchist dream of a free society of perfect men – a stateless and classless society of Stoics. The frailties of man overcome, the evil and the unhappiness, legacy of ages of tyranny and misdirection, rooted up and cast out, the need for human authority would pass away; necessity, the true lawgiver, would reign sole and supreme and 'government by men' would be replaced by the 'administration of things'. The Golden Age would have come again, virtue now taking the place of innocence.

Alternatively, such a community might constitute itself into the ideal State or Sovereign People of the *Contrat Social*, whose General Will, being always right (because it is the will of uncorrupt and undeceivable beings), constitutes the sole law, moral and positive. Such a social reorganization would entail no loss of freedom, for its General Will would be in accordance with no other principle than the *recta ratio*, which the Stoic already obeys: in 'obeying all', he would be 'as free as before'. Again, the Golden Age would have come; again, with virtue taking the place of innocence.

---

* Ibid., in *Oeuvres* VII, 106. Cf. 'The hell of the wicked is to be reduced to living alone with himself; but it is the paradise of the good man and there is for him no spectacle more agreeable than that of his own conscience' (*Mon Portrait*, in Streckeisen-Moultou, p. 286).

To discover the natural man, it is necessary to 'remove the rust' which hides the primitive traits: i.e. to divest oneself of prejudices, of selfishness, of vanity (*amour propre*) and all the factitious needs that flow from it, 'to count for nothing the opinion (estimation) of others, to conduct oneself solely in accordance with one's own *penchants* and one's own reason, regardless of public approval or blame'. (*Dial.*, in *Oeuvres*, XVI, 341).

5

The Return to Nature

For the men of his times, who had not received the boon of a naturalistic education, there yet remained a way of salvation: the return to nature.

Throughout his life, Rousseau preached the sweetness of the 'simple life' amid rustic scenes. The People alone, he tells us in the *Lettre à d'Alembert*, are governed by nature, for they are exempt from the vices of their social betters:[1] and, by the People, he means the peasantry, not the urban rabble. To study a people, one must go to the backward provinces, 'Where the inhabitants yet have their natural inclinations',[2] and 'the simple customs of earliest times'.[3] The countryfolk come 'almost directly from the hands of nature';[4] their lives are spent in close communion with her, for 'the natural condition of man is to cultivate the soil and to live by its fruits'.[5] 'Adieu, Paris, city of noise, smoke and mud!' Far from the crowded streets and the gilded salons, out in the broad fields and in the homely cabins of the peasantry, men come to understand one another; close to nature, they are good, for there the clash of interests seldom occurs; ambition, the begetter of all strife, is absent, *amour propre*, the desire to excel, can find no place, for men have few needs and but little desire for comparison with others. Man, when self-sufficient, free and happy, is good, for he becomes wicked only through unhappiness.[6] The self-sufficient man has but to follow his inclinations in order to be happy; the man who is not self-sufficient has to change, not his inclinations, which is impossible, but his circumstances, if he is to place himself within reach of happiness.[7]

The Return to Nature

The only change which can ensure the permanent happiness of man consists in reversing the tendencies of contemporary France:

> . . . to forsake all the things of institution, to bring everything back to nature, to give to men the love of equality and the simple life, to rid them of the fantasies of opinion, to give them the taste of the true pleasures, to make them love solitude and peace, to keep them at some distance from one another, and, instead of inciting them to huddle together in the town, bring them to spread themselves equally over the land, that they may give life to every place. . . .[8]

That is the way of salvation. In the book of nature are all the lessons that man needs: all other learning is but vanity. Whoever reads therein will learn true humility; problems of public affairs that vex the great ones of the earth are not for him; his wish and care are bounded by his own vicinity. Of governments and laws, says Julie:

> Obliged as I am to love the government under which it has pleased heaven that I be born, I trouble myself little to know if it is the best. What would it serve me to know them, with so little power to establish them? And why should I sadden my soul with the contemplation of such great evils which I can do nought to remedy, when I see others around me whom it is permitted to succour?[9]

Discard the non-essential things, then: cast off the useless lumber that burdens our minds and return to the lasting happiness which the rural life gave to our fathers and holds in readiness for us. To gaze across the peaceful woods and fields, to watch the scattered groups at work or at rest, to listen to the far-off sound of song, to feel the quiet of it all, is to soothe the spirit and transport one back to the Golden Age:

> We forget our century and our contemporaries, we are transported back to the days of the patriarchs; we would lend a hand to the work, share in the rustic toil and the happiness which we see joined with it. O! times of love and innocence, when women were tender and modest, and men simple and content: O! Rachel, charming daughter, and so faithfully loved, happy he, who, to obtain thee, regretted not a slavery of fourteen years!

Rousseau: Stoic & Romantic

O! sweet pupil of Naomi! Happy the good old man whose feet and heart you warmed. No! Never does beauty reign with fuller sway than in the midst of rural cares. It is there the Graces are upon their thrones, there that simplicity adorns them, that gaiety gives them life, there that one must adore them.*

This is the idyllic Rousseau of the *Nouvelle Heloïse*, the writer who supplied the high society of the Ancien Régime with a new hobby and sent Marie Antoinette and her courtiers to play at milkmaids and shepherds on the lawns of Versailles. As is invariably the case with the reformer who writes charmingly, his immediate effect was to give delight to the very classes of whose ways the author disapproved. The garlands of flowers which Rousseau wove through all his romances captivated a whole society; few of the fashionable pondered over the underlying message, fewer still took it seriously.

* *Nouv. Hel.*, in *Oeuvres*, V, 111–12. '. . . one of the examples the good ought to give to others is that of the patriarchal and rustic life (*la vie patriarcale et champêtre*), the first life of man, the most peaceable, the most natural and the sweetest to him whose heart is incorrupt. Our regrets for it are always vain. . . . How to bring it back? To love it. (*Émile* in *Oeuvres*, VII, 401–2).

6

Jean-Jacques, the Man of Nature

Whatever characteristics Rousseau shared with the Stoics, the calm which we associate with that school was not one. The eccentricity of his manners, the strangeness of his opinions, his morbid sensitiveness, all tended to separate him from the crowd. Such a man makes many enemies, and the evidence or appearance of hostility towards him begets a deeply felt resentment towards whole classes of men. This resentment is clearly illustrated in the Swiftian outbursts of the early *Discourses*, in the romantic effusions of the *Confessions* and the *Rêveries* and, indeed, in the fashion of a recurrent theme, throughout his entire works. He was a wanderer among men. The condemnations of Church and State, the decree of arrest, the flights from country to country, the poisoned pens of his philosophical adversaries, all the censures which he failed to understand, marked him out in his own mind as a man who is not as other men, a being of another world whom this corrupt and fallen generation would not understand, whose message was jeered at, disbelieved or ignored.

But if men, in disregard of his pleas and admonitions, persisted in the old and evil ways, Jean-Jacques would, nonetheless, give them the example of a man living the life that nature had intended:

> I form an enterprise which has never yet had an example, the execution of which will have no imitator. I will show my fellows a man in all the truth of nature, and that man shall be I. I, alone. I know my heart and I know men. I am not made like any of those I have seen: I dare to believe, unlike any of those that

exist. If I am not better, I am, at least, different. If nature has done well or ill in breaking the mould in which she cast me, it can be judged only when I have been read.*

Sorely wounded by the evidence of governmental and ecclesiastical disapproval and driven well-nigh to distraction by the gibes of his literary adversaries, he came to despair of the world around him. Finding that others had none of the good sentiments that he had expected to find in them, he would retire from the world and live within himself. He would be the modern Timon: '. . . when I no longer looked on men, I ceased to despise them: when I no longer saw the wicked, I ceased to hate them'.[1] Away from the haunts of men, he would be the real Jean-Jacques, as nature had made him, unmodified by education, free from all artificiality. This reversion would not be a difficult task for him, for he had always been the man of instinct, the man 'with the heart like crystal', so different from others that it would require far greater effort on his part to become like them than unlike them.[2]

For Jean-Jacques, the simple life is no pose: '. . . it is but natural, since it is the work of no effort, nor that of reason, but a simple impulsion of temperament determined by necessity. The sole merit of him who surrenders himself to it is to have yielded without resistance to the *penchant* of nature and not to be deflected by a mischievous shame nor by a foolish vanity'.[3] He is the complete quietist: 'Rebel to all other will, he knows not to obey his own, or, rather, he finds it so fatiguing even to will, that he loves better, in the routine of his life, to follow an impulsion purely mechanical which sweeps him along without pains on his part to attempt to direct it'.[4] The indolent man, although not virtuous, is not wicked, for wickedness implies effort. He has not the germ of a shameful passion in his heart, for he has no *amour propre*: so indifferent is he to the malice of others, that he can overlook all human vices and embrace the whole world with a benevolence that is wholly disinterested. He is what he has been made: that is as it ought to be.

---

* *Confessions* in *Oeuvres*, XIV, 3. Rousseau's place in the tradition of self-advertisement is a capital one. Maritain discusses this aspect of the Rousseauite literary vogue with memorable eloquence in his *Three Reformers*, and Georges Sorel, from a very different point of view, in his *Reflections on Violence*, deals very sharply with the literature of romantic self-pity.

Jean-Jacques, the Man of Nature

> In a word, he is sensual, more so, perhaps, than he ought to be, but not so much so as to be nothing else. Those that are thus are called evil: nevertheless, they follow in all its simplicity the impulse of nature who prompts us to seek that which pleases us and to flee that which is repugnant. I do not see what evil produces that *penchant*. The sensual man is the man of nature: the man who reflects is the man of opinion. It is the latter who is dangerous: the other can never be, even when he falls into an excess. . . .[5]

Leaping on to the back of nature, he knows that he is safe. His sins will be overlooked, because he believes implicitly in everything he does and is; that he is good is everything; what he does matters little.[6] Sentiment, then, being the arbiter of good and evil, who is better than Jean-Jacques? Is he not the unique man, one who appears to come 'of another race of men'?[7] If all men were like him, how sweet would human society be, how tranquil the world!

So, in the long hours of solitary meditation, when past and future are alike out of mind, when the waters on which he drifts and the blossoms that fill the air with perfume and the sky above into which he gazes have entered into him, then the vision of such a world as never existed arises before him:

> Picture an ideal world, like to ours, but, for all that, very different. Nature there is the same as on our earth, but the way of life is more sensible, the order more marked, the scene more admirable, the forms are more elegant, the colours more vivid, the odours more suave; all objects are more interesting. All nature there is so fair that her contemplation, inflaming the souls of men with love for so affecting a picture, inspires them, together with the desire to fly to so beautiful a system, with the fear of troubling its harmony; and from all that is born an exquisite sensibility which gives to those who are gifted with it immediate joys, unknown to the hearts whom these same contemplations have not enkindled.[8]

In the *Confessions* Rousseau has introduced us to this Elysian dream-world of his:

> Forgetting altogether the human race, I make me societies of perfect creatures, as heavenly in their virtues as in their beauty,

of firm friends, tender and faithful, such as I have never found here below. I take such delight to float thus in the empyrean, amidst the charming objects with which I have surrounded myself, that I have passed, there, the hours and the days without count; and, losing the memory of all other things, I have scarcely delayed to swallow a morsel of food; for the haste that tore me away to rush back to my groves.[9]

Alone with an imagination which can drift whithersoever it will, Jean-Jacques can compensate himself for all that life has denied him. He can see lake and wood and mountain and the heaven above in a light which other men have never known: he can see all things with the eye of one who looks upon them for the first time. He can be the perpetual pioneer, the first among mortals to have seen things as he sees them. This is the significance of the Armenian costume: 'I have seen him', says one of his interlocutors, 'more alone in the middle of Paris than Robinson on his isle.'*

The *Nouvelle Heloïse*, together with those latest works of his life, the *Confessions*, the *Dialogues* and the *Rêveries*, show us Rousseau in his most extravagant mood. Although not typical of all his thought, they reveal his true bent – that of the extreme Romantic. The cult of instinct which they proclaim, the underlying assumption that harmony is to be attained through universal individual autonomy, have a place of the first importance in the creed of anarchism. Could the attributes of the 'Man of Nature' be transferred to whole communities, we should then have the ideal State. In such a society, the will of the people would be infallible, and would therefore need no check. Perhaps the connection between the 'natural man' and the 'sovereign People' lies in a transfer of attributes? To transport the *moi* into the Common unity – the *moi commun* – and to produce a psychic organism possessing the characteristics of the Man of Nature, may be the means to political and social perfection.

* *Dial.*, in *Oeuvres*, XVI, 199; 'The solitaries all have the romantic spirit; I am full of that spirit . . .' (*Lettre au Maréchal de Luxembourg*, in *Oeuvres*, XVIII, 245).

7

Rousseau, the Étatiste

It is difficult to conceive the author of the *Confessions* and the *Rêveries* as recognizing any kind of authority, and the self-sufficient Émile would not, one feels, very gladly accommodate himself to the demands of other men less perfect than he.

Nevertheless, the constant denunciation of inequality, the professions of faith in the goodness of the simple, common man and the ever-repeated lament for the degeneration of society through ambition and avarice and the arbitrary exercise of power by individuals, do give us some hint of what we may expect Rousseau, as a constructive political theorist, to demand. His admission that unrestricted liberty is now impracticable, the implication that, had the anti-social particular will been held in check or annihilated, society would have remained happy and harmonious, ought to forwarn us that, on his positive side, he would advocate not the abolition of authority as a preliminary to progress, but its complete reorganization, on an entirely new basis, as a preliminary to the re-establishment of human unity and general happiness. Rousseau, it must always be remembered, looks back; his ideal society, like that of the Stoics, was that early one of primitive hunters and agriculturists whose striking features were general solidarity and fraternity. With the progressive ideas of the utilitarian school he could have no sympathy; a static community of simple, contented human beings was to Rousseau quite sufficient. He never looked forward to scientific or technological progress. Equality, fraternity, contentment with the simple things of life were the constituents of happiness and the demands of 'right' reason

Rousseau: Stoic & Romantic

in the Senecan sense of the words. How could society be organized to ensure the fulfilment of these demands?

The 'Discours sur l'Économie Politique' as an Introduction to the ideas of the 'Contrat Social'

Foremost of Rousseau's political works comes the famous *Contrat Social*, a book which may well be numbered amongst the most powerful influences on the political thought of the period that has lapsed since its publication. Rousseau tells us that he began to think upon the project of a comprehensive work on political theory about the time of his sojourn at Venice in the early forties of the century, and he worked sporadically upon it for many years. Not until 1762 was the book published under the title *Du Contrat Social, ou Principes de Droit Politique*. Its effect was profound. The first immediate result of publication was the issue of a Decree of Arrest which Rousseau evaded by fleeing to Switzerland, thereby beginning a long and unpleasant series of conflicts with established authority, of those continual wanderings and quarrels with former friends, all of which contributed much to the disturbance and final overthrow of the mental balance of this unusual man. Meantime, the doctrines of his book attracted ever-widening attention throughout a great part of western Europe and the American Colonies.

Before the publication of his *magnum opus*, however, he had prepared his philosophic friends for the reception of its doctrines by giving them, in 1756, some of the fruits of his meditations in an article for the *Encyclopaedia* entitled *Discours sur l'Économie Politique*.

The opening statements of the article are obviously inspired by Locke's *First Treatise on Civil Government* and present a viewpoint close enough to that of the general philosophical radicalism of the day to attract comparatively little attention. There is an examination of the analogy which divine right theorists had made between the natural family and the State, followed by its rejection. The family being a natural institution, says Rousseau, the authority of the father possesses the full sanction of nature; his power over all its members is essential to the welfare of all and his natural love for his children may be trusted to ensure that that power shall never be used to their detriment. Furthermore, the head of the family possesses a strength superior to that of any of his children – the latter possess no material

Rousseau, the Étatiste

benefits save those they have received from him. He is equipped with an intimate knowledge of the requirements of all: his interest is identical with theirs. He may, therefore, be trusted with all power, short of that of life and death, over his children. The State is an institution of an entirely different kind, founded, not by nature, but by human convention, and composed of members who are, therefore, all natural equals. The nature of the convention which Rousseau had here in mind is obviously similar to that which he outlined in the *Inégalité des Conditions*: an agreement of equals to establish just laws binding equally on all and to select chiefs to enforce them and to protect the people from harm. The head of the State cannot possibly be informed with a solicitude for the masses of men subject to him, comparable with that of a father for his own natural children; his private interest cannot be identical with that of the community, nor can any one man possess as much knowledge of the needs of every one of his subjects as does the head of a household of those of his immediate dependents. The State, again, is founded to ensure the security of the person and protect the right to property of each member. The analogy of Filmer and his fellow-apologists, then, breaks down completely, and their 'odious system', based on claims of a paternal authority, is roundly denounced.[1]

The State, being founded, thus, upon convention and having for its object the preservation of the persons and property of its members, must be guided in accordance with the requirements of the general welfare.

> In the great family, of which all the members are naturally equal, political authority, purely arbitrary in its institution, can be founded only upon conventions, nor may the magistrate utter command to others save by virtue of the laws. The power of the father over his children, based upon their particular advantage, cannot, of its nature, extend to the right of life and death; but the sovereign power, which has no other object than the common welfare, has no bounds but those of the public utility well understood: a distinction which I shall explain in due course.[2]

The logical consequence of this, believes Rousseau, is the rejection of all forms of government irresponsible to the public. If the supreme office be hereditary, a people may find itself often subject to a child; if it be filled by election, the situation is not vastly better. Whatever the form of government, if it be irresponsible, men will find themselves at the mercy of persons who have little reason to love them. The private interest of individuals is, in most particulars, opposed to the interest of the community: the members of a government inevitably tend to promote their own interests at the expense of those who entrust them with power. To discover a means of destroying this mischievous tendency ought to be the quest of the political thinker.[3]

So far, Rousseau speaks in a language quite familiar to the radicals of his day. Nor could he fail to be understood by many when he speaks of the authority of government as merely executive and places the sovereignty, or supreme legislative authority, elsewhere.[4] It is when he comes to the term 'law' that he begins to diverge from the conceptions of society hitherto prevalent.

The body politic, he tells us, resembles the human organism, every part of which fulfils a function essential to the life of the whole. The sovereign power is the head; the laws and customs are the brain or nerve centre of the State, the seat of the understanding and the will. Of this understanding and will, the members of the executive or administration are the organs. Agriculture is the mouth and stomach by means of which the physical life is preserved. The public finances are the blood, and the citizenry are those members which endow the body with movement and the ability to work and to live. The whole is thus an integral unit, informed by a common life, possessing a common interest and a common will whose sole object can be nothing other than the preservation of the life and well-being of the whole and the health of every organ and member, This *'moi commun'* is the life of the State and all its parts. Should these parts cease to work in harmony, the health of the body is weakened; should internal interaction cease, 'The man is dead, the State dissolved'.* Internal co-

---

* Ibid., 175 et seq. Cf. *Émile*: 'The natural man is complete in himself; he is the numerical unit, the absolute whole, who is related only to himself, or his fellow-men. Civilized man is but a fractional unit that is dependent on its denominator and whose value consists in its relation to the whole, which is the social organization. Good social institutions are those which are the best able to de-naturalize man (*dénaturer l'homme*) and to take from him his absolute existence in order to give him one which is relative, and to transport the *moi* into the common unity, in such a way that each individual no longer feels himself one, but a part of the unit, and is no longer susceptible of feeling, save when forming a part of the whole' (*Émile*, in *Oeuvres*, VI, 14–15). The emphasis on 'feeling' will not escape notice.

Rousseau, the Étatiste

hesion and co-operation is the will of the whole, or the General Will, whose object is the preservation and well-being of the body or State, and to this Will the activities of every organ and member must conform.

> The body politic is, then, also, a moral being which has a will; and that General Will, which tends always to the conservation and well-being of the whole and of each part, and is the source of the laws, is, for all the members of the State, in relation to them and to it, the rule of just and unjust.[5]

The General Will, or will of the body politic, ought thus to be the will of every member. In relation, however, to other States and their members, it is but an individual, alien will, depending for its justice upon the law of nature, that is to say, the law of universal reason. As each State has a will of its own to which the will of every one of its members ought to be subject, we find that the world is peopled, not by individual men, but by great moral beings called States, each one possessed of all the attributes hitherto ascribed to the natural, individual man: life, intelligence, will, physical strength and self-sufficiency. The natural individual disappears and the Super-Individual or State takes the centre of the stage. And the relations subsisting among these 'Mortall Gods' are governed by the law of nature.

> It is important to remark that that rule of justice, trustworthy in relation to all the citizens, can be faulty in relation to foreigners; and the reason for that is obvious, for the will of the State, although general in relation to its members, is not so in relation to other States and their members, but becomes for them a will which is both particular and individual, which has its rule of justice in the law of nature: a conditions which accords perfectly with the principle just established, the great City of the world being, thus, the body politic of which the law of nature is always the General Will and of which the different States and peoples are but the individual members.[6]

Turning again to internal concerns, he devotes the remainder of the article to an endeavour to give precision to his idea of the 'will of the body politic', or 'General Will', and to define the duties of government in relation to it. In this connection, the views of this portion of the *Discours* may most profitably be discussed in conjunction with those of the main work, the *Contrat Social*.

The 'Contrat Social'. False Conceptions of the Social Contract and the True

Like the early *Discours sur l'Économie Politique*, the famous *Contrat Social* opens in a tone which seems to promise an impassioned vindication of radical individualism. 'Man is born free, but everywhere he is in chains.'[7]

The only natural society is the family; all others are founded upon human convention, and even the family is but a passing institution, since the authority of the father over his children ceases to exist as they become capable of self-support. All men are, by the law of nature, equal and entitled to personal freedom:

> That common liberty is a consequence of man's nature. His first law is to look to his own conservation; his first duties are those which he owes to himself, and as soon as he reaches the age of reason, he, being the sole judge of the appropriate means of self-preservation, becomes, accordingly, his own master'.[8]

No portion of that natural liberty may be alienated by the members of society, save whatever ought to be surrendered to ensure their own well-being. There can, thus, as Rousseau has already pointed out in the *Discours sur l'Économie Politique*, be no true analogy between the father of the family and the head of the State. The authority of the former possesses a natural sanction; that of the latter is a trust given him by society. Government exists for the governed, and the sophistries of apologists for despotism must be rejected.

In whatever terms one may attempt to justify arbitrary rule, the task is vain, for such domination can have no ultimate basis but in superior strength. As 'force does not create right', we must recognize the natural equality and right to freedom of every member of society and look elsewhere than to force for a basis to legitimate political authority.

Submission to government ought to be a civil act; that is to say, the act of a people who have already formed themselves into a society. The fundamental problem, therefore, is to discover, not how a government came to be a government, but how a people became a people.[9]

Mankind, in the state of nature, must have reached a stage at which

Rousseau, the Étatiste

the strength of individuals ceased to be a sufficient protection for their rights and it became a matter of urgent importance to discover a means whereby a sufficient degree of order might be established to enable each and every individual to enjoy his rightful personal liberty and property in peace and security. This, at first sight, is no easy problem: for how can men place themselves under an external coercive authority without surrendering personal freedom? In other words, how can any form of a contract whereby freedom is even curtailed escape objection? This is the problem with which men wishing to leave the pre-civil stage were faced: 'To find a form of association which defends and protects with the whole force of the community the person and property of each associate, and, by means of which, each one uniting himself to all, obeys, nevertheless, only himself and remains as free as heretofore.'*

The difficulty is overcome by the terms of a Social Contract which has two salient characteristics. In the first place, the terms of the pact are such that the slightest subsequent infringement of the rights of any associate causes the whole pact to become void; so soon, therefore, as the terms of the original contract are departed from in the least particular, every individual is released from his obligations:

> The clauses of the contract are so determined by the nature of the act, that the slightest modification renders them void and of no effect: in such a manner that, although they may well never have been formally enunciated, they remain always the same, tacitly admitted and universally recognized until, the Social Pact being violated, everyone regains his natural rights and resumes his natural liberty.[10]

The natural liberty of the associate may, therefore, be said to be held only in abeyance and the individual's power loaned to, or deposited with, the community, to be resumed once the remainder of the body commits the slightest abuse of power. It is, then, no unconditional surrender. (The anarchistic implication of this conception is barely disguised, leaving as it does the individual as the arbiter of society's obligation towards him.† In the second place, the contract is made,

---

* *Contrat Social*, in *Oeuvres*, II, 16. The anti-authoritarian inspiration of this conception of a contract is evident.

† Cf. Burke: 'No government could stand a moment, if it could be blown down with anything so loose and indefinite as an opinion of misconduct' (*Works*, Vol. II, 301).

not between a mass of individuals, of the one part, and a man, or body of men, of the other, but by the agreement among all the members of the community to submit themselves to the community. The associates, as individuals, contract with themselves as a body. Every individual, so to speak, contracts with himself and finds himself contracting in two different capacities: as an individual with the public and as a part of the public with the individual. So far, then, from producing a relationship of inequality between ruler and ruled, the Social Pact produces identity. The people place themselves under the sovereignty of the people: sovereign and subjects are one and the same. All members of the community find themselves accordingly in a state of perfect equality both as subjects and as participants in the sovereignty.[11]

This equality among subjects and identity of sovereign and subjects subsisting, there need be no thought of reserve in the transfer of individual powers under the terms of the Social Pact. The surrender of each individual must be complete.

> These clauses, when thoroughly understood, reduce themselves to one alone, namely: the total alienation of each associate with all his rights to the whole community; for, in the first place, each one giving himself entirely, the condition is equal for all; and the condition being equal for all, no one has an interest in making it onerous for the others.[12]

This complete surrender is, indeed, believes Rousseau, logically necessary. Should reservation be made to individuals of certain rights, each man would find himself his own judge in certain particulars and the anarchy which the contract was designed to remedy would continue to subsist. From being one's own judge to constituting oneself the judge of others is a short step; thus, the advent of arbitrary rule could not long be delayed. Reservation of rights and consequent lack of finality and precision in the terms of the contract would thus ultimately render the new association either an instrument of despotism or leave it devoid of meaning.

It is notable that, on this very same page, Rousseau speaks of a resumption of natural liberty in the event of a breach of the contract and also of a 'total alienation'. It is difficult to reconcile these two conceptions of the contract. If no one is to be his own judge, the question arises: who is to judge when the contract has been violated?

Rousseau, the Étatiste

Rousseau defines slavery as subjection to the will of another man. Total alienation to the whole community, including oneself, is not slavery, since 'each one, in giving himself to *all*, *gives himself to no one*'.[13] All submitting on exactly the same terms, there is no master, and the right which each acquires over the other being reciprocal, everyone gains the 'equivalent of what he has lost and more force to preserve what he has'. Submission to the will of another is indefensible, because the other is fallible: submission to that which is infallible is a moral duty. Now, the only infallible guide to man is an agency which will ensure the true well-being of each through the good of all; and this agency is the will of the community as a whole, which, by definition, can no more will the injury of any part than can the individual will the injury of one of his organs or members. In the *Émile*, in virtually identical words, Rousseau also defines the Social Contract:

> To decide all such questions well, we must always recall that the social pact is of a particular nature, proper to itself alone, in that the people contracts only with itself; that is to say, the people as a body as sovereign, with the individuals as subjects: conditions which produce all the artifice and the play of the political machine and which alone make legitimate, reasonable and without danger engagements which otherwise would be absurd, tyrannical and subject to the most enormous abuses. The individuals being subject only to the sovereign and the sovereign authority being nothing other than the General Will, we shall see that each man, obeying the sovereign, obeys only himself and one is freer under the social pact than in the state of nature.[14]

There is no halfway between the isolation of the state of nature and the collectivity:

> That which produces human misery is the contradiction between our conditions and our desires, between our duties and our inclinations, between nature and social institutions, between the man and the citizen. Make man one and you make him as happy as he can be. Give him entirely to the State or leave him entirely to himself, but if you divide his heart, you tear him in two; and do not imagine that the State can be happy when all the members suffer.[15]

Submission under the Social Contract is made, then, to what Rousseau names the General Will, and in the following terms: 'Each of us places his person and all his powers under the supreme direction of the General Will; and we, in a body, receive each member as an inseparable part of the whole.'[16]

We have now reached the monistic conception of the ideal State, to which Rousseau has already introduced us in the *Discours sur l'Économie Politique*. The new association is not to be confused with any loosely-bound aggregation. There is no room here for dualism of Church and State nor for traditional constitutionalism.

> Forthwith, in the place of the particular person of each contracting party, this act of association produces a moral and collective being, composed of as many members as the assembly has voices; the latter receives from that same act its unity, its *moi commun*, its life and will. This public person which is formed by the union of all the others took in former times the name of City and nowadays that of *republic* or *body politic*, which is called *state* when passive, *sovereign* when active, *power* in relation to other bodies of its kind.[17]

The society is fully organic in the psychical sense.

8

The General Will

According to the terms of the Social Contract, a principle known as the General Will is set up as the law of the State. As all legitimate authority must be based upon the law, the problem of defining the term, 'General Will', as employed by Rousseau, becomes one of central importance. What is this 'General Will'?

At the very outset, one may prepare the reader for the indecisiveness of the discussion by stating that it is disputable that Rousseau ever gave a clear-cut, final answer, or that any one of his commentators has ever answered it for him to the complete satisfaction of the others.

In one chapter of the *Contrat Social*, he comes nearest to precision by indicating that it may, under the condition that no private or selfish influence is exerted upon the citizens, be discovered in a decision by numerical majority.[1] Throughout the *Projet de Constitution pour la Corse*, he seems, too, to assume that majority-decision is *per se* the only right and legitimate one. In the *Économie Politique*, however, it cannot be said that he approaches any view so close to that of contemporary radicalism, but he gives us a fairly clear admission of the difficulty of recognizing the General Will, by remarking that to distinguish between the will of the individual or that of a limited group, on the one hand, and the General Will, on the other, one should possess such a degree of enlightenment as can accompany only 'the most sublime virtue'.[2] Again, he tells us, 'it is necessary only to be just in order to follow the General Will'.[3] It is 'right reason' in the Stoic sense: that is to say, reason untinged in its operation by any unworthy motive. This, in turn, is 'the voice of nature', since nature and reason 'never find themselves in contradiction, if man does not impose on himself needs which he is subsequently forced to prefer always to natural impulsion'.[4] It would seem, then, that the General Will cannot easily be discovered in contemporary society.

In the *Économie Politique*, Rousseau commences his consideration of this difficult problem by discussing the existence of will in bodies different in kind from the State. As men possess interests in common, the promotion of which appears to each to be of immediate or remote urgency, so they tend to coalesce into bodies or associations varying in size, force and permanence for the purpose of such promotion. These bodies vary in size according to the number of individuals possessing in common the particular interest whose promotion is principally desired; and in force, according to the importance attached by the members to the principal common interest and to the general determination and power of the united body – the *ésprit de corps* – to secure its promotion. Society is thus honeycombed with an infinitude of lesser associations, made up by all kinds of ever-changing combinations and permutations of the individual citizens.

> Every political society is made up of other societies, smaller in size and of different kinds, each of which has its interests and its maxims: but these societies which are visible to all because of their outward and sanctioned form are not the only bodies which have a real existence within the State: all the individuals whom a common interest unites form as many others, permanent or ephemeral, of which the force is not the less real for being less apparent, an acute and thorough observation of whose diverse inter-relations supplies a true and accurate knowledge of the condition of general morality.[5]

Now, in relation to the members of each such society, the will of that society is general: it tends to the promotion of the interests of each and all. But in relation to the will of the great society, which is the State, it is no more than a private or particular will which tends to promote the well-being of a part at the expense, in certain particulars, of the whole. Thus, the general will of a lesser society may, in relation to that society, be good, but, in relation to the body politic, harmful. 'Such a man can be a devout priest, or a brave soldier, or a zealous patrician, and a bad citizen.'[6]

The General Will

The greatest degree of enlightenment is therefore required to enable one to pursue the interests of the whole in preference to those of the part. Unfortunately, thinks Rousseau, men are prone to do the opposite of this: the smaller the society and the baser the objectives, the greater is the impulsion of the selfish private interest. From this, it seems incontrovertible that the wider the society, the more just is the will. The widest society being the whole community, its will is consequently the most general and the most just. Thus we have 'an unshakeable proof that the most general will is also the most just, and that the voice of the people is verily the voice of God'.[7] The State, then, or the community politically organized in accordance with the terms of the Social Contract, is the only fully legitimate society.

It is not true, though, that the genuine voice of the people can be discerned in a general assembly of the populace. For, bearing in mind the existence of these lesser associations among the members of such an assembly, we easily perceive that such public deliberation, in many important matters, consists not in the endeavour to serve the general welfare but in a struggle amongst the principal cliques or confederacies, each of which is bent on bringing about a decision in its own particular interest at the expense of that of the whole, with the result that the largest or most active element only too often succeeds in prevailing over all others and in passing its own voice for that of the whole. This was the case in the popular assemblies of Athens, which was not, believes Rousseau, a genuine democracy, but was governed by philosophers and orators who knew how to influence the populace.[8]

The solidarity and strength of an association depends upon the clearness of the realization by every member that the association stands for the promotion of important interests of his own and from the friendship which this realization begets among the associates. Not only the calculating faculty, but the passion of friendship or brotherly love in however distorted a form is involved in the generation of *ésprit de corps*. Could the reason of man be enabled to distinguish the true, universal good and the natural passion of love be directed into the right channel, so that men should love, not a relative good and a fraction of their fellows, but the absolute good and the entirety of their fellows, then we could truly say that the General Will prevails. Each would then will the true good of all and all will the true good of each. The will of the individual would, accordingly, be identical with the will of all, whose objective would be the true good of the whole and of each. The General Will is thus identical with the will of man truly enlightened and completely purged of all selfishness – the will, for example, of the Stoic or of the fully developed Émile. It is the sublime of both the reason and the instinct of man. With this idea in mind, Rousseau assures us that 'it is necessary only to be just to assure oneself of following the General Will'.[9] A little later, he speaks of the need of enlisting passion, which he never tires of telling us is good in its source, in the establishment of justice and social solidarity:

> If it be said to me that whoever has to govern men ought not to seek outside their nature for a perfection of which they are not susceptible, that one ought not to wish to destroy in them the passions and that the execution of such a project would be even less desirable than possible, I shall agree with that all the more whole-heartedly by saying that the man devoid of passion would certainly make a very bad citizen. But it must likewise be agreed that if men are taught to love, it is not impossible to direct their love towards one object rather than another, and towards that which is beautiful rather than towards that which is deformed.[10]

On the whole, it must be said that Rousseau bases his hopes on a development of the feelings of men rather than upon their capacity for intellectual improvement. Although he often defends obedience to the law in terms of an enlightened self-interest, it becomes evident to the reader that he is never sanguine about the capacity of unaided intellect to introduce and maintain improvement in human affairs.

That which is good and conforms to order is so by the nature of things and independently of human conventions.

> All justice comes from God: he alone is its source. But, if we knew how to receive it from so high a source, we should need neither government nor laws. Without doubt, there is a universal justice, emanating from reason alone: but that justice, to be admitted among us, should be reciprocal. Humanly speaking, the laws of justice, failing a natural sanction, are vain among men; they wreak only the advantage of the wicked and the misfortune of the just, since the latter observes them in his relations with everyone, while no one observes them towards him.[11]

The General Will

This passage is one of the most significant in all the writings of Rousseau, rejecting, as it seems to, traditionally-held conceptions of authority, temporal and spiritual, and pointing the way to his own thinking on the subject.

The Stoic identification is: God, Nature and Reason. This seems to be Rousseau's also. Man in society, and not God or man in the state of nature, is responsible for the development of evil. Has the entire human personality, then, become diseased by our membership of society as it has existed? That is to say, have our reason and our passions alike become diseased? This recalls the ancient dispute among the Stoics as to the nature of the personality: has it two components, the reason and the passions, often at war, the former always right, but losing because of the corruption of the latter in the case of most men? This was the view of the 'rationalists' or more optimistically-minded. Or is the personality a unitary thing, reason and passions the same phenomenon, both corruptible, the reason no more than the passions being reliable in man as we know him in contemporary society? Rousseau would seem to accept the latter view. When men got together, they developed false systems which did not square with the facts. Hence, the defective systems, moral and juridical, in which men have sought to imprison us. The conscious reason of men as we know them can devise systems that would put us only in a straight-jacket. Rousseau, proponent of the life-sciences, believed that the universe is changing all the time: we cannot know all the ways of Nature (i.e. of God), so our conscious reason cannot tell us all about them.[12] Our tendency to rationalize, then, only too often leads us away from the truth, since our very personality has become corrupted. Naturalism or uncorrupted instinct is the sure guide to truth. And uncorrupted instinct is the well-spring of the General Will in the ideal State.

This rejection of traditional conceptions of authority and this diffidence in the powers of reason which he endeavours to supply with a reliance on the potency of sentiment could not fail to have a far-reaching effect on Rousseau's political thought. The laws of justice require a sanction, and this sanction lies in human convention. Reciprocity must be enforced and the strongest guarantee of such enforcement lies not so much in the reason as in the sentiment of men: men must be made to *feel* their interest in the fulfilment of the law; they must *experience* the beauty of equitable dealing and a love of their fellows in order to make the practice of virtue a source of the deepest pleasure. In brief, the enforcement of the law must depend upon the sentiment of humanity among men. In any community in which this sentiment is very strong, the laws of justice will prevail. 'They would feel that the greatest court of appeal of the public authority is in the hearts of the citizens.'[13] Everyday experience shows us that concern for the well-being of our fellows depends for its depth upon the degree of our intimacy with them. The misfortunes of faraway lands mean little to us; the most dreadful cataclysms on the other side of the globe fail to impress even the best of men with the fulness of their horror, whereas we may feel the sorrows of those whom we know intimately and love as keenly as if they were our own. The important part which our senses play in the generation of fraternity and solidarity among men makes, therefore, the existence of a universal human will unthinkable and precludes a universal convention – even in idea.

> It is apparent that the sentiment of humanity evaporates and becomes enfeebled in stretching itself all over the earth and that we are less capable of being touched by the calamities of Tartary or Japan than by those of a European people. It is necessary that interest and commiseration be in some manner bounded and compressed within limits in order to give them activity. Since, therefore, that *penchant* within us can be of use only in relation to those with whom we have to live, it is good that humane feeling, concentrated among fellow-citizens, should take on a new force through their being continually in sight of one another and by the common interest which unites them.[14]

This, it may be remarked, is probably the nearest approach we find in Rousseau to a rationalization of the principle of nationality and it will be noted that the arguments of Godwin and many others of the philosophical radicals of later times in favour of political decentralization were based upon a very similar idea. Even John Stuart Mill found himself compelled to give a limited approval to the principle of nationality for a similar reason.[15]

However, Rousseau's treatment of sentiment took him far away from the universalism of the Utilitarians and from their somewhat mechanistic conceptions of human organization. Justice and interest, believes Rousseau, must not remain lifeless abstractions; we must be

The General Will

made to *feel* them and our passions must be enlisted to enforce their demands. The Social Contract, to be effective, must therefore be confined to a group sufficiently small to ensure such community of ideas, tastes, views and interests as will tend to make the body of associates think and act as one in all fundamental matters. 'How can it be brought about that they obey and no one commands, that they serve and have no master . . .? These prodigies are the work of the law.' 'The most absolute authority is that which penetrates right down into the interior of man and exercises no less compulsion upon his will than upon his actions.'[16] And this solidarity must be felt as a living thing among men. Thus, transcending all merely utilitarian considerations of community of interest and above the brotherly love and natural benevolence of member for member and pervading the whole life and being of the society, there must be that imponderable sentiment of patriotism or devotion to the Fatherland. In this love, the evil sentiments of the old self-seeking individual are extinguished; man is elevated and inspired to think and act socially, public spirit is maintained and strengthened and all men become truly one.

> If, for example, they are exercised early enough in life never to regard their individuality save in its relation to the body of the State and never to see their own existence, so to speak, but as a part of the existence of the body politic, they will come finally to identify themselves in a certain manner with that greater whole, to feel themselves members of the Fatherland, to love it with that exquisite sentiment which every isolated man has only for himself, to elevate perpetually their souls to that great object and to transfer, thus, into a sublime virtue that dangerous disposition from which are born all our vices.[17]

For examples of the 'prodigies of virtue' which patriotism is capable of producing, Rousseau untiringly draws upon the histories of Greece and early Rome, while lamenting the inability of his sophisticated contemporaries to understand what love of country means. It is a proclivity which he shares with that other great admirer of antiquity and exponent of patriotism, Machiavelli, although Rousseau's democratic and humanitarian sentiments do not allow him to accept Machiavelli's grim view of the State as naturally expansive and aggressive and, beyond a certain small degree, the Florentine's admiration of the ancient civic religion as an adjunct to the strength of the State.

This new conception of State and individual must be borne in mind if we are to form any approximately accurate idea of what Rousseau has in mind when he speaks of the General Will. The Lockeian State, which was external to the individual, was a mere device of convenience, a mechanical contrivance which was reluctantly admitted to be necessary but could never become an object of devotion. According to Rousseau, a community of this kind would be devoid of any keen public spirit and incapable of strong communal life; there could exist among such a people no discoverable public will, since each member would will primarily his own particular good and desire the good of others only in so far as it would conduce to his own. The gap between egoism and altruism would be unbridged. With Rousseau, the individual loses himself in the State. The latter is the true source of morality and law; to it the individual owes those qualities that make him human. This transformation of the individual is the result of the Social Contract:

> This passage from the state of nature to the civil state produces in man a very remarkable change, by substituting in his conduct justice for instinct and in giving his actions the morality they had previously lacked. The voice of duty succeeding to physical impulsion, and right succeeding to appetite, it is thus alone that man, who had hitherto looked to no one but himself, finds himself compelled to act on other principles and to consult his reason before listening to the voice of his own desires.[18]

So vast, indeed, is the debt of the individual to the State, that in any tolerably well-regulated society, he 'ought unceasingly to bless the happy moment which had snatched him forever from it [the state of nature] and which, from a stupid and limited animal, made of him an intelligent being and a man'.[19] In this sense, it may be said that in a good polity the only real existence is that of the State; the individual can be known only as a member of it. Its power is all-pervasive because it 'reaches down into the hearts of men' and obedience to its dictates is obedience to a truly self-prescribed law, which is the true moral liberty. The conscience of this organized body is the only standard of right and its will, consequently, is the only will which is necessarily just and right and merits the title of General.

9

How the General Will is recognized

That a corporate will exists in all societies Rousseau is in no doubt; from the mere fact that a number of men organize themselves into one body for any purpose, it follows that the organization has but one will: the preservation and welfare of the group and, through that, the well-being of every member. This being so in the case of small associations, it must follow that such a will exists in the body politic or State. In a homogeneous society of simple and honest men uncorrupted by the diseases which inequality brings with it and enjoying the blessings of peace, the corporate will needs nothing but 'good sense' for its discovery: the requirements of the common welfare are so evident to all that when new laws become necessary, 'the first who proposes them does no more than speak what was already in the minds of all'.[1] In such a society, truth is so plainly and universally visible that there can be no place for intriguing cliques and no possibility of the deception of any part of the people; public affairs will be managed in a simple open fashion in accordance with reason and commonsense. As in the ideal communities of William Godwin and the philosophical anarchists, the 'sober consensus of opinion' would regulate all things and the charlatanry and affectation of mystery in government which results from inequality and disunity would be unheard of.[2] An uncorrupt and simple people cannot be deceived: their very simplicity enables them to detect speciousness. It is only pride and the false values which it engenders among the over-civilized peoples of contemporary Europe that blind men to truth and render them gullible. 'When one sees among the happiest people in the world assemblies of peasants regulate the affairs of the State under an oak-tree and conduct their proceedings with wisdom at all times, can one avoid despising the refinements of other nations which make themselves illustrious and miserable with so much of art and so much of mystery?'[3]

With the growth of inequality, the body politic degenerates; unity and patriotism, devotion to corporate aims and purposes decrease; selfish, individual and particular interests come to occupy the minds of citizens to the exclusion of the general interest in varying degrees. The General Will ceases to be the will of all and in the endless debates and disputes that accompany the decline from equality and simplicity it becomes increasingly difficult to distinguish it. As the General Will is the will of the whole 'under one aspect' legislating for the whole 'under another aspect',[4] the interposition of any consideration of a particular person or a particular act in public deliberation necessarily precludes the possibility of a universal will in that particular, as it suspends the homogeneity of the community. Instead of one sovereign body legislating for itself, we have two parties, with two separate and perhaps opposed wills, neither of them general. 'It is a matter in which the individuals under discussion are one of the parties and the public is the other; but in which I see neither the law to follow nor the judge to decide.'[5]

A decision by the majority in such a matter could not be construed as the General Will. It would be ridiculous to profess that there could be identity with an express declaration of the General Will in such a decision, 'which could be nothing more than the conclusion of one of the parties and, consequently, nothing to the other but an alien, particular will, prompted on this occasion by injustice and subject to error'.[6] Introduction of particular consideration arouses selfishness and causes men to lose sight of the needs of the body politic.

Despite the growth of dissension which accompanies the degeneration of the State, it cannot, however, be said that the General Will, wherever it once existed, ever ceases completely to exist, for even in the most corrupt society each individual does not separate his own interest entirely from the general interest. In spite of conflicting ambition and selfishness, there do remain, even in such a society,

How the General Will is recognized

certain interests whose promotion is universally desired: otherwise the term 'society' becomes inapplicable. Thus, to the individual in the performance of a particular unsocial act, the immediate good accruing to himself from that act seems to outweigh the harm done to the common welfare; but apart from his preference in this and a limited number of other particulars, he wills the general welfare in his own interest as strongly as anyone else. Without some measure of concern in the minds of individuals for the general welfare, the idea of society is inconceivable, for such concern constitutes the social bond. The very existence of society therefore entails community of will in a certain measure: in other words, it entails the existence in some degree of a General Will.

As society degenerates, the General Will, although not destroyed, becomes increasingly difficult to discover. By what means, then, may it become known in a society fallen from perfection? Clearly not, as Rousseau has already emphasized, by means of public deliberations which are influenced by the pressure of particular associations and individuals. Each man wills his own good, but he does not always see it; 'the people are never corrupted, but are often deceived, and it is thus alone that they seem to will what is bad'.[7] Despite this weakness of the people, they may often be stirred by a blatant injustice or by some pressing universal need and the General Will then becomes evident. 'Often', we are told in the *Économie Politique*, 'when it is too openly flouted, it makes itself appear, in spite of the terrible bridle of the public authority.'[8] And in the same passage we are assured that such guarantees against misgovernment as general assemblies of the nation are unnecessary 'when the government proceeds in good faith'. Again, in the *Contrat Social*, we are told that in many situations for which the government takes it upon itself to prescribe, an absence of protest implies that the procedure is in accordance with the wishes of the people: 'In such a case, from the universal silence, the consent of the people ought to be presumed'.[9]

Such expressions as these seem to indicate that Rousseau had in mind something closely akin to the Benthamite 'public opinion' as the source of morality. However, a closer examination will show that he was not as easily satisfied in his search for a sound foundation to government as were his Utilitarian contemporaries. According to the latter, public opinion was easily and infallibly to be discovered in the opinion of a simple majority by means of a referendum or general canvass. Such a procedure would have been accepted by Rousseau with reservations: the will of all is not, he believes, necessarily and in all circumstances to be identified with the General Will. In the large territorial State, the individual in expressing his will has in mind only his own selfish interests; the result of a universal canvass is nothing more than a statement of the wills of so many separate individuals, each one differing in some respect from that of the next. Nevertheless, it is possible to deduce from such statements the real General Will, which consists of those elements which all the particular wills have in common.

> There is often a great difference between the will of all and the General Will. The latter considers only the common interest; the former considers only the private interest and is but the sum of particular wills. But take away from these same wills the more and the less which cause them to cancel one another out, and from the sum of the differences emerges the General Will.[10]

However, a very important condition is here inserted: there must be no attempt on the part of associations to influence the judgement of the individual citizen, for the intervention of cliques in public deliberation means that the votes given are not the votes of men, but those of associations. 'If, when the people, sufficiently informed, deliberate, the citizens have no communication among one another, then from the great number of slight differences there will always emerge the General Will and the deliberation will always be good.'[11]

The obvious remedy for the imperfections which have hitherto prevented the emergence of the General Will from public deliberation lies therefore in the suppression of all associations, so that nothing shall stand between the individual and the State. 'It is essential, then, in order to obtain a clear expression of the General Will, that there be no partial society within the State and that each citizen speak nothing but his own mind.' Should the suppression of such societies be impracticable, their number should be so multiplied as to prevent such growth in any as would secure for it the domination of the rest and, consequently, of the whole State.[12]

We have to await the chapter, 'Of Suffrages', near the close of the *Contrat Social*, to find Rousseau's mind made up, to gather together into a synthesis the *obiter dicta* thrown out in the earlier parts of the

How the General Will is recognized

work on this subject of discovering the General Will, and to approach closest to the position of majority-rule advocacy.

In this chapter he returns to the problem of discerning the General Will in societies according to the degree of solidarity among the citizens. And here again he deplores the effects of lesser associations within the State:

> The greater the degree to which harmony prevails in the assemblies, that is to say the closer the opinions expressed approach unanimity, the more does the General Will dominate. But long debates, dissensions, tumult, proclaim the ascendency of particular interests and the decline of the State.[13]

The complete destruction of the State is marked by unanimity again, but this time it is the unanimity of slavery, when men have so forgotten their dignity as to cease to think for themselves on any subject. In this final state of degradation, 'there is no more deliberation; men either adore or curse'. Such was the condition of the Roman Senate in the days of Otho. Under such conditions, it is quite impossible to discover the General Will, since the will of one man or of one clique has been imposed on all.

As the General Will becomes less easy to distinguish with the degeneration of the body politic, it is very important, Rousseau thinks, to devise maxims upon which one may judge the degree of its emergence from public deliberation.

In the first place, unanimity is essential to the enactment of but one law: the Social Contract. This by its very nature is the most freely performed of all human acts, since no man may be compelled to subject himself to external authority. The refusal of an individual to enter society does not invalidate the Social Pact: it simply means that he remains a foreigner among the citizens. However, if he continues to reside among them, his residence implies adherence to the contract and consequently a promise on his part to conform to the General Will: when the State has been instituted, consent lies in residence. To dwell upon the territory of the State is to submit oneself to its sovereignty. Rousseau hastens to meet the anticipated objections to this condition by uttering the qualification that it can apply only in 'a free State', but goes no further than Locke in explaining the epithet 'free' in this instance.

Once the contract is made, unanimity is no longer necessary to secure an expression of the General Will. How then is it to be discovered? Rousseau promptly replies that it lies in a decision by the majority: 'Outside of the original contract, the decision of the greatest number always obliges the other: this follows from the contract itself'. To the objection that submission by the dissenting minority to the will of the majority is the negation of freedom, Rousseau answers that the question, 'How can the opponents be said to be free and subject to laws to whose enactment they have not consented?', is 'badly put' (*'mal posée'*). Adherence to the contract involves consent to obey the laws: this consent is the 'constant will' of the citizens and the 'constant will of all the members of the State is the General Will; it is thereby that they are citizens and freemen'.[14] The citizen, by the fact of his citizenship, promises to obey the laws. Without this consent, there could be no civil society and no authority among men.

In a very remarkable passage, Rousseau describes the situation of the dissenting citizen:

> When a law is proposed in the assembly of the people, that which is demanded is not precisely whether they approve the proposition or reject it, but whether or not it conforms to the General Will, which is theirs. Each one in giving his vote, gives his opinion on the latter question and from the reckoning of the votes emerges the General Will. When the opinion contrary to my own prevails, that proves nothing else than that I had been in error and that what I had thought to be the General Will was not so. Had my counsel prevailed, I should have done something other than I had willed, and it is then that I should not have been free.[15]

This much-criticized passage, taken from its context, would constitute a conclusive proof that Rousseau, at the time of writing it, was as wholehearted an advocate of government by majority-decision as any of the philosophical radicals. By itself, it clearly states that the will of the majority is the General Will. But here, again, he affirms his belief that the General Will is expressed by a majority only in the absence of associations within the State and upon the condition that public deliberation takes place among equal and independent citizens.

As society declines from this ideal condition, the proportion of votes required to express the General Will becomes necessarily greater. 'The difference of a single voice destroys equality: a single

How the General Will is recognized

opponent destroys unanimity; but between unanimity and equality there are many unequal divisions to each of which one can fix the number according to the condition of the State and the needs of the body politic.'[16] With these considerations in mind, Rousseau proceeds to lay down two general maxims for application to the decisions of public assemblies. First: the more important and grave the matter under discussion, the nearer ought opinion approach unanimity. Secondly: the speedier the decision required, the smaller need be the majority, whilst 'in deliberations which require to be concluded on the spot, a majority of one ought to suffice'. The first maxim applies to the enactment of laws, the second to the regulation of day-to-day business.[17] As the enactment of laws appertains only to the General Will, it is obvious that something considerably more than a mere majority is normally required. Only with both maxims in mind, however, can we be enabled to estimate in any given circumstances the degree to which the General Will may be said to emerge from a public discussion.

On the whole, then, it is clear that Rousseau regards mere numbers as an unsatisfying criterion in the discovery of the General Will. With this dissatisfaction in mind, he tells us in the chapter on 'The Limits of the Sovereign Power' that 'that which generalizes the will is less the number of voices than the common interest which unites them'. Again, in this same chapter, he emphasizes another most important qualification which he reiterates throughout the *Contrat Social*: 'That the General Will, to be truly such, ought to be general in its object as in its essence: that it ought to spring from all, to apply to all'.[18] The General Will therefore must proceed from the people as a whole and have for its aim the welfare of the people as a whole. It cannot, then, proceed from an individual or an association within the State, nor can it refer in its enunciation to a particular person or a particular matter. 'Thus, just as a particular will cannot represent the General Will, the General Will in turn changes in nature when it has a particular object and cannot, as general, make any pronouncement upon a particular man or a particular fact.'[19] Speaking of the law, which is the expression of the General Will, Rousseau says that it 'considers the subjects as a body and actions in the abstract'; never such-and-such a man or such-and-such an action. For example, the law may decide that privileges shall exist, but may not proceed to confer them upon any particular individuals; it may declare that society shall be divided into classes, but may not make the actual division among the citizens; it may declare that a monarchy shall be set up as the form of government, but may not nominate any particular man to be king. The law, in short, must be an act of 'all the people' binding on 'all the people'; the whole under one aspect legislates for the whole under another aspect and the matter of the enactment is as general as the will which enacts.[20]

Under such conditions, all selfish or unsocial considerations are excluded from the minds of all the participants, since all being equal and possessing the same interest in the general matter under discussion, each will unfailingly desire the general welfare in his own interest. Accordingly, the conditions being the same for all, each individual, in giving his vote, acts with an entire absence of selfish bias and gives the judgement which seems the fairest and most equitable. 'How comes it that the General Will is always right, and how can all be said to will constantly the happiness of each, except in this way: that there is no one who does not apply to himself that term, "each", and thinks not of himself in voting for all?'* The problem of bridging the gap between egoism and altruism which so exercised the Utilitarians is, thus, according to Rousseau, solved by the evolution of the General Will: '. . . equality of right and the notion of justice which it produces derive from the preference which each gives to himself and, consequently, from the nature of man'.[21] The General Will is thus the outcome of 'enlightened self-love'. It is a proposition on which Rousseau comes remarkably close to the Utilitarian maxim that 'love of country is ultimately love of oneself'. But, unlike the optimistic rationalists, Rousseau will not leave the development of the higher morality to the unaided or loosely-organized individual (the 'economic man' of the Utilitarians): only when thinking as part of the mass can the individual be trusted to act equitably and impartially, to 'do as he would be done by'; society has snatched him from the condition of 'a stupid and limited animal' and made him 'an intelligent being and a man'. In submitting himself to the General Will, man is submitting his lower to his higher self, conquering appetite and obeying conscience.

* *Contrat Social*, in *Oeuvres*, 33. That this proposition is of unvarying applicability is open to question.

10

The State & Individual Rights

The 'public person' of whom all the associates are members and whose voice is the General Will is set up, as we have seen, as the Sovereign under the terms of the Social Contract.

On entering into the contract, every associate makes a total alienation of his rights and powers to the community. The sovereignty of this body is complete and subject to no conditions or restrictions. To suggest, therefore, that the individual possesses rights which may not be violated by the State is to misapprehend the relationship of State and individual and to show a failure to comprehend the nature of sovereignty: for the individual, being an integral part of the State, cannot logically be said to possess a right against the whole body of which he is a member, any more than a limb or organ of the human body can be said to possess a separate will from the body of which it forms part.

> If the State or City is but a moral person whose life consists in the union of its members and if the most important of its needs is that of its own preservation, it requires a universal and compulsive force to move and dispose of every part in the manner most agreeable to the whole. As nature gives to every man an absolute power over all his members, the Social Pact gives the body politic an absolute power over its own. And it is this same power which, directed by the General Will, bears, as I have said, the name of sovereignty.*

* *Contrat Social*, in *Oeuvres*, vol. II, 32. The question whether this 'absolute power' is moral as well as physical here presents itself.

Rousseau: Stoic & Romantic

This is not to say that the individual possesses no rights. He does possess them, but he possesses them as a member of the State, and as that alone. To speak, therefore, of an individual's right against the State is to speak an absurdity: it is equivalent to speaking of a man's right against himself. The individual, in a word, possesses such rights as are compatible with his membership of the State:

> It is agreed that all which each one alienates in virtue of the Social Pact of his powers, his material possessions and of his liberty consists only in the portion of all these things whose use is of moment to the community. But, it must be agreed, also, that the Sovereign alone is the judge of that importance.[1]

The power of the Sovereign over the individual is limited to the promotion of the good of the whole. It cannot of its nature do anything injurious to the body politic even in the person of the least of its members, since such an act would be one of self-mutilation.

> All the services that an individual can render the State, he owes to it as soon as the Sovereign demands them: but the Sovereign on its part cannot impose useless restrictions on the community: it cannot even will such a thing, since by the law of reason nothing is done without cause, any more than under the law of nature.[2]

That the logical inability of the Sovereign to harm its members could be construed as a limitation on the sovereign power is thus an unsustainable proposition. By definition, the Sovereign can do no wrong. There can therefore be no fundamental law binding on the Sovereign, since the latter is always right and just in relation to the subject:

> Now, the Sovereign, composed as it is only of the individuals who make it up, neither has nor can have an interest opposed to theirs. Consequently, no safeguards are needed by the subjects against the sovereign power, since it is impossible that the body should wish to injure all its members; and we shall see later on that it can injure no particular member. The Sovereign, by the very fact of being such, is always everything that it ought to be.[3]

The State & Individual Rights

The key to Rousseau's mental process as he wrote these passages is provided by his attribution of moral self-sufficiency to human agency. His natural man was morally self-sufficient: he obeyed instinct alone, and his instinct being infallible, he always acted rightly. This quality of moral self-sufficiency Rousseau transfers from natural man to his ideal State. Both are infallible, both can be trusted absolutely, and neither can lawfully be restricted, since both are wholly good. The transfer bridges the gap between Rousseau the rebel and Rousseau the *étatiste*.

The relation of subject to Sovereign, conversely, is one of complete subjection. As obedience to the General Will is the true moral liberty, everyone should be compelled to comply with it and the whole force of the community should be directed towards ensuring this obedience. This compulsion is in the highest interest of both community and individual, since it is essential to the former that the general interest be safeguarded and to the latter that he be delivered from bondage to his own selfish appetite, which is slavery, and from dependence upon any other individual, which is also the negation of freedom.[4]

> In fine, that the Social Pact be not reduced to a vain formulary, it includes tacitly this engagement, which alone can give force to the others: that whoever shall refuse to obey the General Will shall be compelled to do so by the whole body. This signifies nothing other than that he shall be forced to be free.[5]

This conception of sovereignty cannot but give rise to the consideration of two all-important questions: those of the right of property and the right of life and death.

The Right of Property

Many of Rousseau's references to property may prompt the belief that he was by no means consistent in his attitude towards it, and the opinion has often been expressed that some of his outstanding passages on the subject have been inspired by hostility. Certainly, his judgement in the *Discours sur l'Inégalité* on the first man who proclaimed 'This is mine' over the piece of ground he had fenced shows no excessive reverence for the institution, nor does his summing up of the contributory factors in the progress of inequality: 'If we follow the progress of inequality in its different revolutions, we shall find that the establishment of the law and of the right of property was its first term'.*

Indeed, his clear emphasis on the totality of the surrender under the Social Contract by the individual to the body politic of his person, powers, faculties and material possessions seems to indicate that Rousseau was a wholehearted Socialist – an advocate, that is to say, of State ownership and control of all wealth. All these references, especially if taken in conjunction with his outflow of lyric lament for the long-gone, happy times when the human race was young and enjoyed a large measure of primitive communism, his indignation at the usurpations of the rich and the sufferings of the poor, his insistence on the recognition of the equality of all men as the condition of political justice and his advocacy of such measures of economic regulation as would tend to an approximate 'mediocrity of fortune' for all, have been interpreted as indications that Rousseau was never very far from the socialist position. Babeuf, for instance, at his trial, named Rousseau as one of his mentors and predecessors.[6] On the other hand, we find him frequently assuming the justice and even the sacredness of the institution. In a passage towards the end of the *Économie Politique* he makes as explicit a profession of reverence as any *laissez-faire* liberal could desire: 'It is necessary here to recollect that the foundation of the Social Pact is the institution of property, and its first condition that every man be maintained in the peaceful enjoyment of what belongs to him'.[7]

A close examination of his references to property throughout the entirety of his works will show that he nowhere makes a clear and unequivocal recommendation of its abolition in favour of State ownership. Indeed, on the whole, it must strike the reader that Rousseau's so-called socialistic passages represent little more than moral indignation at the greed of the few who deny or usurp the property-rights of the many – a sentiment by no means peculiar to Socialists.

---

* *Inégalité*, in *Oeuvres*, I, 108. 'The first who, having enclosed a plot of ground, said "This is mine" and found a people simple enough to believe him, was the true founder of civil society. How many crimes, wars and murders, what misery and horrors, would not the human race have been spared, had someone, plucking up the stakes or filling in the ditch, cried to his fellow men: "Do not listen to this imposter! You are lost if you forget that the fruits of the earth belong to all and that the earth belongs to no one".' (Ibid., p. 77.)

The State & Individual Rights

There remain the references to the alienation of the individual's material possessions under the terms of the Social Contract. The individual must lose himself in the community, he must change his very nature, he must annihilate himself in the State and be reborn as a cell in the body politic. Even the chapter in the *Contrat Social* on 'Real Property' opens with the apparently uncompromising declaration that 'Every member of the community gives himself to it at the moment it is formed, in the exact condition in which he is found, his person and all his forces, of which the goods in his possession form a part'.[8] It would be difficult to find a loophole in such a profession. If nothing of his material goods be retained by the individual, are not the last vestiges of private ownership logically swept away? And if the will of the Sovereign decree that all goods be administered by public authority, have we not got complete State Socialism? The General Will is always right: if it decree public ownership, then public ownership there ought to be and the private administration of wealth becomes immoral. In a well-ordered State anyone who defied such a mandate by endeavouring to cling to what he misguidedly considered his own would be 'forced to be free' by being stripped of everything.

But, the question arises: *can* the General Will decree public ownership and control? '. . . but the Sovereign, on its part, cannot impose useless restrictions on the community; it cannot even will such a thing. . . .' By the term, 'useless', in this context, one may assume that Rousseau means not merely unprofitable in the material sense, but morally undesirable. The crucial question thus emerges: Is it good for the community that all private ownership be prohibited? If the answer be 'Yes', then the Sovereign may retain everything and the subject be propertyless. If it be 'No', then State Socialism cannot be the will of the Sovereign. The question is thus not one of utility to the individual in the narrow, materialistic sense, but of the moral good of the community.

Now, if it can be shown that Rousseau in any one of his references to property expressly declares that the public ownership and control of all the wealth of the community is for the moral good of the community, we are forced to admit that, at least at the moment of making that reference, Rousseau was a Socialist. Such a declaration cannot be discovered throughout the length of Rousseau's writings. He cannot then be said to have subscribed to the creed of Socialism and, so, it must be assumed that in speaking of the 'total alienation', he had in mind as the economic ideal some system other than that of State ownership. In the *Projet de Constitution pour la Corse*, he would not destroy property, but keep it always sobordinate to the public welfare. In the *Émile*, he speaks of property as 'inviolable and sacred' in so far as it remains a particular and individual right, but as soon as it is considered as common to all the citizens, it is submitted to the General Will and that will can annihilate it.[9] What he means by this is that the Sovereign cannot interfere with the property of particular individuals, since that decision would be particular, and not general, in its scope; it may, however, as a result of a general decision, bring a category of property within its possession. A general property tax is thus legitimate. The confiscation of the property of certain individuals would be illegitimate, but logically the confiscation of all property would be lawful.

In the chapter on 'Real Property' in the *Contrat Social*, he gives what is probably the clearest and most succinct definition of his views on the question of authority in the economic sphere. Referring to the surrender made under the Social Contract, he says:

> This is not to say that by this act possession changes its nature by changing hands and becomes property in the hands of the Sovereign, but that the powers of the State being incomparably greater than those of an individual, public possession is also in fact stronger and more irrevocable without being more legitimate, at least towards foreigners. For the State, in relation to its members, is master of all their goods by virtue of the Social Contract which, in the State, forms the basis of all rights; but it is in relation to external powers master only by right of first occupant, which it holds of its own members.[10]

The individual is in natural justice entitled to hold such an amount of wealth as is necessary to his subsistence. 'Every man has a natural right to all that is necessary to him.'[11] In the pre-social period, the most respectable right to possession was the right of first occupant. In surrendering to the Sovereign all his material possessions, the individual alienates to it all those natural rights to the possession of such goods, of which this right of first occupant is the most deserving of respect. This right of first occupant over all the material wealth within the territory occupied by the community is thus vested in the

The State & Individual Rights

State, of which all contracting parties are members, and the security of all is thereby immeasurably strengthened against the danger of appropriation by any force external to the contracting community. Now, in exchange for these surrendered rights, which the individual in the state of nature is often powerless to enforce, the State returns to him all the possessions which he had hitherto held or was justly entitled to hold and confers them upon him as property.*

Now, as every man has a natural right, not merely to all that is necessary to the support of his existence, but to all that is necessary to his moral good, and as the Sovereign cannot injure any of its members, it follows that the possession of that minimum cannot be denied him. One must go further, on recollecting that the Sovereign is set up to promote the good of every member, and affirm that the terms of the Social Contract positively secure and guarantee such possession to each and all. And it is precisely by virtue of this undertaking on the part of the Sovereign that the individual holds, or is entitled to hold, the amount of wealth necessary to his moral good. By means of this beneficent institution, all men are made economically independent of one another in essentials:

> Every man has a natural right to all that is necessary to him, but the positive act which makes him proprietor of some wealth excludes from the use of that portion all the others. His share having been marked out, he ought to confine himself to it and has no further claim on the community. See thus why the right of first occupant, so feeble in the state of nature, is respectable in every man in civil society. By virtue of that right, it is less what belongs to others that demands respect than that which belongs not to oneself.[12]

The proprietory rights of the individual exist only *vis-à-vis* other individuals and in this respect are sacrosanct and guaranteed by all the force of the community. The State is the source, donor and guarantor of all right.

It is precisely this exclusion of others from all that is requisite to

---

* *Contrat Social*, in Oeuvres, II, 24–5. The conditions to establish the right of first occupant are: 1. The territory claimed must have been previously unoccupied. 2. That no more than is requisite to subsistence be occupied. 3. That possession be taken, not by mere assertion of the claim, but by work on and improvement of the land.

the individual that secures his proprietory right. And since this exclusion is guaranteed by the Sovereign, it is evident, Rousseau maintains, that, far from abolishing property rights, the act of association serves but to give them birth and sanctity. 'What is singular in that alienation is that, in accepting the material goods of the individuals, the community, far from stripping them of them [their goods], merely assures them legitimate possession, changes usurpation into a veritable right and enjoyment into property.'[13] The possessions of the individual are thus secured by the State against the only two dangers that can beset them: seizure or usurpation by foes from without and from within. For the State, as possessor of the right of first occupant, becomes charged with the duty of warding off external encroachment and is armed with the authority and power of the whole community to keep all individual citizens in such a state of dependence on it that none can with impunity disturb the equitable distribution of wealth made by virtue of the Social Contract. The individual possessor is thus the repository of a certain amount of the public wealth and as such he is entitled to demand for his right the respect of all. In yielding everything to the State, the members merely ensure that the just rights of each and all shall be guaranteed in perpetuity through the beneficent ultimate control of the State over all material goods within the territory of the community.

Summing up his considerations on the institution of property, Rousseau says

> It can be concluded that men begin to unite themselves before possessing anything and that, in taking possession of an extent of territory sufficient for all, they enjoy it in common or they divide it among themselves either equally or in proportions established by the Sovereign. Whatever the manner in which this acquisition is made, the right which each individual has over his own wealth is always subordinate to the right which the community has over all, without which right there would be neither solidarity in the social bond nor real force in the exercise of the sovereignty.[14]

Thus, Rousseau would have us find that what he condemns is not the institution of property but the extremely individualistic ideas respecting it which were so prevalent in his day. There is no such thing as absolute ownership: property is a trust and as such is

The State & Individual Rights

amenable in its use to the surveillance of the State. And the most important pre-requisite to the social use of wealth is equality, or the nearest approach to it practicable, in its distribution, for the object of the Social Contract is to make up for inequalities in physical and intellectual strength by the establishment of moral or conventional equality.[15]

The degree to which the ideal of absolute equality ought to be approached in practice is a matter which may be more advantageously discussed later in connection with the maxims which Rousseau lays down for the conduct of a legitimate government.[16] For the present, he satisfies himself by remarking that in a well-ordered society no one shall be left in want and no one in possession of much more than he needs.[17] Under the existing order, even an approach to the requirements of the Social Contract is not attempted. The laws that now prevail, he insists, are merely the instruments whereby inequality and its attendant evils are stabilized:

> Under the bad governments, this equality is but apparent and illusory; it serves but to keep the poor in their misery and the rich in their usurpation. In fact, the laws are always beneficial to those who possess and hurtful to those who have nothing: whence it follows that the social state is advantageous to men only in so far as all have something and no one has something over and above.[18]

Much of Rousseau's language on the subject of injustice might well have been used by Christian moralists, but the fundamental difference between the traditional Christian doctrines on the subject of rights must be kept well in mind if we are to see where Rousseau stood. To the Christian, rights are the obverse of duties; they are the means to the performance of duties. The latter being laid upon us by the Creator, the former must be taken as adhering to them and therefore divine or God-given in origin. This is the meaning of 'natural right' in the Christian context. The duty of the State is to promote the enforcement of right. The right to a means of livelihood springs from the duty to preserve life and to fulfil its diverse obligations. It is therefore antecedent to the State or any other human agency. With Rousseau, right originates in the State (in his ideal State, that is to say). This being so, one cannot resist the conclusion that the embryo of Socialism was present in his thought. 'Of his socialist tendencies', says Faguet, 'he did not wish or dared not to draw all the consequences.'[19] The consequences were soon to be drawn by Babeuf and others, as the highly complex history of early Socialism very clearly shows.[20]

It is interesting to compare Rousseau's position with those of the two schools of radical liberalism which were more or less contemporary with him: the Utilitarian and the Natural Right.

Basically, Rousseau bears a closer affinity to the former than the latter. The Utilitarians, in postulating the object of government to be the procuring of 'the greatest happiness of the greatest number', admit the competence of the State, or government set up by the majority, to regulate economic affairs in any manner which the realization of this 'greatest happiness' may appear to it to demand, even to the extent of establishing complete State ownership and control of all the national wealth, should such a measure appear the most beneficial to a democratically-elected government. Socialism is latent in their thought, as it is in all forms of positivism. 'Natural rights', said Bentham, 'is nonsense – nonsense on stilts.'* The only reason for the opposition of the Utilitarians, not only to socialistic measures, but to governmental interference in economic matters generally, lay in their premise of an underlying 'natural harmony' which would unfailingly come into play if the principle of *laissez-faire* were universally applied. Thus, according to the Benthamites, lasting economic health can come to the community and the individual in only one way – through the free operation of the economic laws which are inherent in the nature of things. Any attempt on the part of government to establish a measure of economic equality is not only doomed to failure, but, as an attempt to defy the laws of the universe, can bring nothing in the wake of its failure but the disastrous consequences which are nature's retribution for foolish rebellion against her laws. Hence, according to the Benthamites, although the State is competent in theory to interfere in economic matters to any extent, it is extremely inadvisable for it to do so. Allegiance to the principle of *laissez-faire* can easily be seen as essentially unconnected with the democratical teaching of the Utilitarians; the Benthamite State,

* An action is 'conformable to the principle of utility' when the tendency it has to augment the happiness of the community is greater than any it has to diminish it: 'When thus interpreted, the words *ought* and *right* have a meaning: when otherwise, they have none' (Jeremy Bentham, 'An Introduction to the Principles of Morals and Legislation' in *Collected Works*, Vol. I, p. 180).

The State & Individual Rights

omnicompetent by implication, bears an affinity with the Sovereign of Rousseau.

The affinity lies in a common positivism, but the positivism is based on two very different suppositions. Rousseau's positivism is based on the thesis that, in the ideal State, the General Will is morally right and consequently morally binding on all individual members. Bentham's positivism is based on the ascertained fact that governments exist and the probability that, without them, there would be no order; they are, in a word, useful. It is highly desirable that they become, or be made, more useful: that is to say, that they permit the general increase of happiness (excess of pleasure over pain) and ultimately the harmony of individual happiness with that of society as a whole. But, as there are no natural rights, so there is no juridical relationship between the individual and the legislature of his country save that determined by the law of the land. This may be very undesirable and counterproductive of happiness, but it cannot be objected to on the basis of any formal ethic, since there is no such ethic outside the positive law. Utilitarianism is universalistic in the sense that it postulates a body of rules outside the State or community, valid for all men at all times. Utilitarianism is, in this sense, beyond the State and applies to all States in a way that Rousseau's theories do not.

Utilitarians, then, belong to a natural law school in a way in which Rousseau does not, but also in a way in which the classical Natural Right school does not. The Utilitarian uses the term 'natural law' in the scientific sense of a theoretical principle deduced from particular facts, a statement of what happens when certain conditions are present. To Rousseau and to the Natural Law school, a natural law is a moral imperative. In Rousseau's ideal State, the General Will is both moral imperative and positive law and expresses the requirements of natural-moral law in that particular State. To Bentham, Utilitarian theory is antecedent to all States, but is not morally binding on them in the traditional sense. It is desirable that States should permit Utilitarian theory to be implemented, but no formal ethic binds the legislature.* Should a constituent part of the theory fail to stand the test of experience, one's recommendations

---

* It is true that the term, 'laws of nature', employed in the scientific sense, has often carried moral overtones, suggesting commands imposed by the Deity on matter and consequently binding on mankind.

concerning State policy might require alteration. Without faith in the 'natural harmony', Bentham might well desire an authoritarian socialist legislator to bring about the 'greatest happiness of the greatest number'.

The whole conception of omnicompetence is abhorrent to the theorists of the Natural Right school, which in many important respects stands in the Christian tradition. Characteristically Christian (or post-Christian, in the case of many of the eighteenth-century thinkers) is the insistence of this school that morality is antecedent to the State. Property rights inhere in the individual and are inalienable. In this connection, however, it is necessary to separate two strands of thought which lie side by side and are often almost inextricably interwoven in the writings of the Natural Right thinkers. These two strands consist in (1) the affirmation of the reality of natural rights inhering in the individual and demanding respect in all circumstances and (2) the Utilitarian premise of a natural harmony and the affirmation of the beneficence of the *laissez-faire* principle in operation. There is no essential connection between the two, but they both happened to be fashionable throughout a great part of the eighteenth century. The idea of natural right, which was a heritage of Christian thought, tended to lose its appeal towards the end of the century, partly in face of the growing interest in the historical approach to political and social questions and partly owing to the growing appeal of Utilitarian considerations. From the early nineteenth century onwards we find radicalism becoming less doctrinaire and more pragmatic, speaking more the language of Bentham and Mill than of Thomas Paine. In time, the faith in the economic 'natural harmony' was to go and radicalism was to take varying forms of Socialism and of pragmatic democratic politics.

Paine, who is one of the best-known defenders of Natural Right, paid tribute to the virtues of free trade but clearly held misgivings on the existence of a perfect economic 'natural harmony', and in his pamphlet 'Agrarian justice' and elsewhere very vehemently advocates governmental interference in economic affairs with the object of assuring a comfortable livelihood for all. This interference, argues Paine, far from involving a violation of the right of property, is essential to its universal vindication, since it will address itself to securing to the less fortunate the protection of the property right which is as real in the poor man as in the rich.[21]

The State & Individual Rights

In this respect, the position of Paine, as of all others who held that natural right cannot be maintained save by governmental surveillance, is apparently close to that of Rousseau. In reality, however, they are far apart, for according to Rousseau the individual surrenders all his rights to the State – he enjoys only civil rights: that is, rights conferred on him by the State. According to Paine and those who think with him, the right of property inheres in the individual and cannot be surrendered to the State or to any other agency. The State is a mere external device of convenience, set up for the purpose of preventing men from violating the natural rights of others. To Rousseau, the individual cannot be said to have a right against the State, because State and individual are morally identical. To Paine, the right of the individual is invincible against all comers: the individual is the point of reference; his welfare is the end and the State is only a means. The deep gulf between Rousseau and Paine lies therefore between two opposed conceptions of the State. Rousseau, on the one hand, and the Natural Right theorists, on the other, are thus opposed in fundamentals: the element of objectivism in the latter marks the gulf.

The Right of Life and Death

The right of the State to inflict capital punishment for certain transgressions is one which secured affirmation generally until it came to be challenged by Beccaria and subsequently by Godwin, Bentham and other liberal critics of traditional notions.[22] Rousseau, who affirms the right, discusses the question in the *Contrat Social* and anticipates two serious objections. The first is the well-known objection so often proposed to contractualists: Has man ever a right to destroy his own life? The second is one which might be considered appropriate with reference to his own organic conception of the State: Can a man 'cut off an arm or tear out his own eyes' without injuring himself? The State, we have been assured, cannot injure the least of its members: how then may it destroy one of them?

In reply to the first objection, he admits that on no condition does a man have the right to take his own life. How then can men 'transmit to the Sovereign that same right which they have not got'? The question, replies Rousseau, is, like the earlier one 'How can men be free and forced to obey others?', (see p. 82), 'badly put (*mal posée*)'. 'Every man has a right to risk his own life in order to save it'. Thus, the man who breaks his neck in jumping from a burning house cannot be deemed a suicide, nor does the sailor's constant awareness of the perils of the deep make it a crime for him to drown in a storm. The man who enters civil society in order to enjoy its innumerable benefits renders himself amenable to the laws which make these benefits real. 'He who wills the end wills also the means.'[23] Man must choose between the unbridled but precarious freedom of the state of nature and the order and security of society. If he choose the latter, he must accept the conditions which society holds necessary to its conservation; in committing himself to the protection of the law, he commits himself to its mercy. Such being the condition of the Social Contract, it is clear that every citizen incurs risk in order to enjoy the amenities of society.

> He who wishes to conserve his life with the assistance of others ought also to give it for them when necessary. For the citizen is not longer judge of the peril to which the law wishes that he expose himself; and when the prince says to him, 'It is expedient to the State that you die', he ought to die, since it is only on that condition that he has hitherto lived in security, his life being no longer a benefit from nature alone, but a conditional gift from the State. . . . It is in order not to be the victim of an assassin that a man consents to die should be become one.[24]

The second objection, based on the organic conception of the State, presents the difficulty of reconciling the destruction of a member with the health of the body politic. Rousseau's answer to this is that, by his defiance of the law, the offending individual ceases to be a member of the body politic and becomes instead an external enemy. 'He ceases to be a member of it, on violating its laws, and even makes war on it.' In breaking his contract with society, he returns to the state of nature and now finds himself, *vis-à-vis* the society he has just quit and struck at, a separate being and a standing threat. The relationship between him and State is that of natural enemies.

It remains true then that the State cannot injure a member, but is bound by all the laws of its nature to protect itself against all who would injure or destroy it. In taking the life of a criminal, the State, far from injuring one of its members, destroys an external foe.

11

The 'Prince' or Government

Sovereign authority lying, according to Rousseau, in 'all the people', legislating for 'all the people', it remains to be seen what place he allots to government.

The Social Contract sets up the whole body of the people as the sole legislative power. This sovereignty is unlimited, inalienable and indivisible.[1] Any subsequent instrument or development purporting to give government a measure of autonomy is invalid, since it must connote a division of sovereignty and consequently a partial alienation of it and a limitation on the rightful authority of the people, which would entail the violation of the Social Contract and the dissolution of the body politic. 'In the first place, the supreme authority can no more modify than alienate itself: to bind itself to obey a master is to return all to the State of complete liberty.'[2]

To suppose that there is a contractual relationship between government and people is to fail to advert to the nature of the body politic which the Social Contract establishes. The State is a moral being, essentially one and indivisible, composed of all the associates of the original pact. Now, the body cannot contract with a member or organ of itself. To set up a number of individuals (henceforth to be called a government) for the purpose of arranging a contract between themselves and the remainder is clearly a violation of social unity, and the resulting instrument or development cannot conceivably be termed an act of the General Will, since it represents, not a decision of the whole people legislating for the whole people, but an agreement between two morally and physically distinct bodies. The whole quality of generality is thus absent from the transaction, for the will is general neither in its source nor in its application. 'Furthermore, it is evident that this contract of the people with such or such persons would be a particular act: whence it follows that this contract would not be a law or an act of sovereignty and, consequently, that it would be illegitimate.' Government, then, cannot be said to be founded on contract, since such a conception is irreconcilable with the terms of the Social Pact. 'There has been but one contract in the State: that of association; and that excludes every other. One cannot imagine any public contract which would not be a violation of the first.'[3]

In thus denying to government a contractual basis, Rousseau is at one with Locke and the whole body of eighteenth-century theorists, Utilitarian and other, who were agreed on at least this one point: that some other basis than contract must be sought for the institution.

To understand the nature of government, we must bear in mind, believes Rousseau, the organic conception of the State. This body, like the individual human being, possesses the two faculties that render it capable of engaging in free activity: the will and the physical power. The will dictates the act and the power carries out the decision. In so far then as any act is freely performed, the physical power of the body is merely the agent of the will and does nothing save at its bidding.

The will of the body politic or State is called the legislative power, and its physical strength the executive or governmental power. The functioning in perfect unison and harmony of these two faculties is essential to the health of the State. Thus, a State without executive power may be likened to a paralytic, whilst a State in which the executive power is exerted without the guidance or consent of the legislative power (the will of the body) resembles an imbecile. Of the two, the legislative power is infinitely the more important, for it is the very will and life of the State: destroy it, and the body politic is no more. The executive power is necessary to the functioning of the body politic: its extinction leaves it immobile and helpless, but not dead.[4]

Now, the legislative power belongs to the whole people alone, and can neither be transferred in whole nor in part, to any other body. Will cannot be transferred.[5] But the will of the State can express itself only with reference to a general object; how then are its decisions to be applied in administrative details? This application is the function

The 'Prince' or Government

of the executive power. The two cannot, therefore, in principle be identified, whatever may be thought of the wisdom of uniting them in practice (as in the case of a perfect democracy, in which the whole people both legislate and administer). Sovereignty and government cannot be confounded. The decisions of the General Will cannot be applied in particular cases by the Sovereign, as such; it must, for this purpose, enlist the services of a body called government. In principle then government is a distinct body within the State and its *raison d'être* is the fulfilment in administrative details of the mandates of the Sovereign.

> What then is government? An intermediary body, established between the subjects and the Sovereign for their mutual connection, charged with the execution of the laws and with the maintenance of liberty, civil as well as political.[6]

It will readily be seen, then, that, although a distinct body, government occupies a position of complete subordination to the Sovereign. The Sovereign People is always master; government is merely its agent or minister. From the highest to the lowliest of its officials, its duty lies in carrying out the decisions of the General Will. Government is accordingly a trust or an employment which the Sovereign is at perfect liberty to terminate whenever it deems such a source advisable.

> The members of this body are called *magistrates* or *kings*, that is to say: *governors*, and the whole body takes the name of *prince*. Thus, those who profess that the act by which a people submits itself to chiefs is not a contract are perfectly right. It is absolutely nothing more than a commission, an employment, in which, as simple officers of the Sovereign, they exercise in its name the power of which it has made them the depositories and which it can limit, modify or withdraw when it pleases, the alienation of such a right being incompatible with the nature of the social body and contrary to the end of the association.[7]

What steps, then, are necessary to the setting up of a legitimate government? The first is the legislative step whereby the Sovereign enacts that a government of a certain form shall be established. The second consists in the nomination by the people of the individuals who are to be entrusted with the task of governing. This second decision of the people is, even if unanimous, not a law; made as it is in favour of particular, named individuals, it is simply an implementation of the law or an administrative decree.

Here, however, there crops up an objection which Rousseau does not ignore: Is not this execution of the law by the people an act of government? Are we not, then, speaking of a logical impossibility: the performance of a function of government before a government has been constituted? Must it be supposed that government is set up by the first, or legislative, step? Otherwise, how can the original law be executed? The Sovereign, as such, cannot nominate officers of government. How is the gulf to be bridged?

The explanation which Rousseau offers is that, for the purpose of executing the law, the Sovereign constitutes itself a democracy and thus places the whole people in a position to carry out the executive act of nominating the officers of the government whose establishment had already been enacted.

> Here again is discovered one of those astonishing properties of the body politic, by which it reconciles operations which are apparently contradictory. For this reconciliation is achieved by a sudden conversion of the sovereignty into a democracy in such a manner that, without any sensible change, and solely by a new relation of all to all, the citizens, having become magistrates, pass from general to particular acts and from the enactment of the law to its execution.[8]

The analogy which Rousseau draws with the procedure of the House of Commons in going into committee to discuss a bill and reporting, in its capacity as a committee, to itself in its original capacity as a legislative chamber, has often been jeered at. However happy the analogy, Rousseau is aware that its insertion neither advances nor retards proof of his basic contention that an act of the General Will can set up a democratic government: 'Such is the advantage proper to democratic government, that it can be established in fact by a simple act of the General Will'.[9] His justification of this contention, although he does not expressly give it, probably amounts to this: that the establishment of a democracy in fact possesses all the characteristics of an act of the General Will, since the decision is taken by all and the object is the conferring of an equal amount of magisterial power on all, without exception. Such an act is general in its source and in its

The 'Prince' or Government

object: it is an act of the whole people under one aspect legislating for the whole people under another aspect. Whether this contention involves a confusion of principle and practice is a debatable point; at any rate, its maintenance cannot fail to impress one with the fineness of the distinction which must often subsist between the 'general' and the 'particular', between 'legislation' and 'execution', and it supplies with a prima facie case those who contend that Rousseau's logic leads inevitably to the thesis that government by majority-decision is the only form ultimately justifiable.

Again, there arises the objection that, if the General Will declares that a form of government other than the democratic be established, by what right does the provisional democratic executive exist? Its establishment even for the shortest interlude being unauthorized by the Sovereign, how can it ever legally exist or perform any executive act? And if the acts of such a body be illegitimate, what of the polity which it purports to establish?

The only solution of the problem seems to be that the decision of the General Will is twofold. It enacts that first a democracy be set up and that secondly this democracy shall proceed to establish that other form of government originally desired: the prolongation of the life of the provisional democracy is, then, legitimate only for such period as is necessary to the setting up of the machinery of the government which is to follow. Thus, whatever way we seek out of the *impasse*, it seems to be Rousseau's logic that democratic government, or in practice government by majority, is the essential prerequisite to the establishment of political justice. As the legislative authority (that is to say, supreme authority) belongs to the whole people, so all legitimate executive authority is derived from the choice and maintained by the consent of the majority.

12

The Best Form of Government

The first government known to mankind was, according to Rousseau, democracy in its purest form; the first magistracy, that of everyman. No legitimate political activity was possible in the earliest stage of human society without the equal participation of every member of the newly-formed association. That the democratic form should continue to subsist was not, however, the General Will. In other words, democracy is not in all circumstances the form of government most suitable to the body politic.

The legitimacy of a government depends on the degree of its obedience to the General Will.

> There is this essential difference between these two bodies: that the State exists of itself and that the government exists only by the Sovereign. Thus, the dominant will of the prince is not, or ought not to be, anything but the General Will or the law; its power is but the public power concentrated in it: as soon as it wills to take upon itself the performance of any arbitrary and independent act, the social bond begins to relax. Should the prince come to possess a particular will more active than that of the Sovereign and should it use the public force which is in its hands in order to procure obedience to that particular will, so that there come to exist, so to speak, two sovereigns, one of right and the other in fact – at that instant the social union vanishes and the body politic is dissolved.[1]

The best, and the only completely legitimate, government is the

The Best Form of Government

government whose will exactly coincides with, or identifies itself with, the will of the Sovereign. There can be, thus, in any community only one truly legitimate kind of government, but the form it should take depends on the circumstances of the community. He who wishes to decide for himself upon the type of government best calculated to maintain the sovereign authority of the people in any given State must descend from the plane of abstract speculation to study the concrete, historical condition of that State.[2]

Dependent on the will of the Sovereign as government is, its existence nonetheless must be viewed as a real thing. Being the agent of the Sovereign, it must be clearly distinguished from it; it is a moral being with a life and will of its own, distinct from the Sovereign whom it is meant to serve and from the subjects whom it is meant to govern. '. . . let us content ourselves to consider government as a new body within the State, distinct from the people and the Sovereign and intermediary between the one and the other'. Only by being distinct can it usefully perform its regulative function. To preserve this distinctness, it must be allowed the means of self-preservation:

> This particular existence supposes assemblies, councils, a power to deliberate, to resolve, rights, titles, privileges, which appertain exclusively to the prince and which render the condition of magistrate the more honourable in proportion as it is fraught with responsibility.[3]

It must be a little society in itself, possessing all the characteristics that distinguish an association from an aggregate. Like the great society for which it exists, it must possess a will which is general in relation to all its members, tending to the good of the whole and of each; in its own sphere, the whole body of its members must be sovereign on the one hand and subjects on the other and, like the great society without, it must possess an executive within itself, to enable the will of that Sovereign to be carried out amongst the subjects. This latter executive may be called the 'supreme magistrate' – an executive within an executive, as it were. The position of the 'supreme magistrate' is interesting. He is the mean proportion of a mean proportion; his function is to maintain the equilibrium of the body whose function it is to maintain the equilibrium of the whole State; he is at once the servant of servants and the master of masters;

the gravity of his responsibility cannot be exaggerated, for upon him in the greatest degree the fulfilment of the law, or will of the State, ultimately depends. This supreme magistrate may be styled 'king' or given any other title which it pleases the citizens or the lesser magistrates to bestow on him.

In the concession of this real power to the government, the greatest of all political problems arises: that of preserving the equilibrium of the State. Deny to government its necessary measure of power, and the result is anarchy. Give it more than its share, the result is despotism. In the latter case, the General Will cannot be implemented because the will of a lesser body has superimposed itself upon it and usurped in whole or part the Sovereign power. Of the evils of anarchy, man has had but little experience; despotism, which has hitherto widely followed the establishment of government among men, is by far the greater danger. Better were it that the public power should lie unused, as it does under a weak executive, than that it be actively misused when the prince usurps the sovereignty. While it is a good and necessary thing that the executive possess power and a clearly distinct existence, it should be prepared to surrender rather than misuse them; in the event of a clash of interest with the community, it should 'always be ready to sacrifice the government to the people and not the people to the government'.

Usurpation, however, is not to be guarded against by moralizing on the duties of government; the only sure precaution is to place the executive in such a position that it cannot usurp. The best form of government in any particular State is that which exists when circumstances bestow on it the fullest possible power to implement the General Will, but not one degree of power over that. And the most important of the circumstances affecting the power of an executive are two: the size of the population and the moral qualities of the people.

All the associates in the Social Pact are equal partakers in the sovereignty. The greater the number of associates, then, the smaller the fraction of authority that attaches to each, and vice versa. The greater the population, the less influence has each citizen in the enactment of the laws and in the formation of opinion. This is the ground of Rousseau's objection to the large State. The smaller the State, the greater is the individual citizen's power. Furthermore, the General Will of a small community is always more evident than that of a large one; there is always a greater degree of understanding among the

The Best Form of Government

citizens and a clearer perception of the true interest of the whole, and this latter factor helps more than anything else to produce among the members of the State the essential moral qualities of unselfishness and devotion to the common good. The structure of the small community is simpler, its life calmer and more harmonious than that of the large State. On the other hand, it will readily be seen that the larger the State, the greater is the necessity for coercion in the interest of the whole. A strong executive is needed to preserve order and enforce the law, while, to counterbalance the power of the executive and so maintain the equilibrium of the State, a correspondingly great degree of control over the executive by the people is essential. Of the possibility, in a very large State, of maintaining this degree of control, Rousseau is more than doubtful.[4]

The clearness of the General Will in the small State and the greater degree of spontaneous compliance with it demand a corresponding degree of inactivity on the part of the executive. The factor determining most constantly the activity or strength of a government is the number of individuals which comprises it. In any community, the governmental body is entrusted by the people with the whole force of the State for the purpose of implementing the General Will. This amount of force, in proportion to the size of the population, is thus always the same. However, the amount at its disposal for exercise on those outside its own ranks – the people, let us call them – will vary according to the numerical strength of its own membership. The larger that membership, the greater the amount of its strength has the government or executive to spend upon the regulation of its own internal concerns and the less has it left to exercise on the people. The more numerous the executive in proportion to the total population, the weaker the government in relation to the sovereign power. 'The more numerous is the magistracy, the more feeble is the government.' In a pure democracy, then, the executive power is at its weakest and the Sovereignty at its strongest; the possibility of usurpation is therefore virtually non-existent. So it would seem in theory, but in practice Rousseau fears such a condition would lead to the opposite of usurpation – anarchy.

To illustrate his contentions on the relationship of the numerical strength of executive and people, Rousseau considers the condition of the individual member of the government. The magistrate, he says, is possessed of three different wills. In the first place, as a human being he possesses a will particular to himself and tending to ensure his own well-being. Again, as a member of the executive body he is informed with the *esprit de corps* which biases him in favour of that body. Finally, as a member of the State he tends to concur with the General Will. It goes without saying that the individual or particular will ought to be absent and that the will of the executive body ought to be subordinated to the General Will. In other words, a member of the government ought to be first and above all a citizen, secondly a magistrate and, last of all things, a self-willed individual. (The whole history of government, laments Rousseau, shows that rulers have been the reverse.) When the whole executive power of a State is entrusted to one man (that is, when the government is monarchical in the pure sense), the individual or particular will of this person is united with the will of the executive body, since he is at one and the same time both an individual man and the executive body. Thus, the two stronger species of will are united in him. Moreover, since the will of the body (*corps*) is now identical with the particular will of the individual, it assumes the greatest degree of intensity and activity possible. The strongest and most active of all governments is that of one man. Consequently, the risk of usurpation is at its greatest under such a régime. Turning to the other end of the scale, Rousseau considers the pure democracy: that is, the polity in which the government is composed of all the citizens. In this case, the will of the executive body loses itself in the General Will and ceases to possess any more intensity or activity than the latter – which, as we know, is the least potent of the three species. The particular wills of all are, then, left throughout the State with the least possible check upon them. Thus, a State which unites the functions of prince with those of Sovereign possesses the feeblest of all governments: only the most favourable of circumstances can prevent it from falling into anarchy.[5]

The strength of a government, however, Rousseau is careful to emphasize, has nothing in itself to do with its rectitude, which depends entirely upon its preserving the equilibrium of the State, or in other words on the loyalty and efficiency with which it carries out the General Will. Failure to discover the exact point of balance between the strength of the government and the strength of what lies outside it – the particular wills of the populace – results either in a measure of tyranny or of anarchy, corresponding to the extent of the error made

The Best Form of Government

in the computation. However small that degree of error be, the inevitable tendency will be either towards usurpation of the sovereignty or towards the disappearance of government.

> Thus, what can be gained on the one side is lost on the other, and the art of the Lawgiver consists in knowing where to fix the point at which the force and the will of the government, remaining in reciprocal proportion, combine themselves in the relation most advantageous to the State.[6]

It might seem from this outline of what Rousseau terms 'the principles constituting diverse forms of government', that he pins his faith for the discovery of political perfection on a formula of mechanical simplicity. But, whatever Rousseau's faults, crudity is not conspicuous among them, and he was at all times alive to the certainty of the jeers with which intelligent critics would fall upon a panacea.

> If, to turn this system to ridicule, it be said that, to find the mean proportion and so form the executive body, all that need be done is, according to me, to find the square root of the number of the people, I should reply that I here take number only for an example; that the relationships of which I speak are not measured solely by the number of men, but in general by the quantity of action which combines itself out of a multitude of causes; that, for the rest, if in order to explain myself in the least amount of words, I borrow for a moment the terms of geometry, I do not for all that overlook the fact that geometrical precision has no place in the moral qualities.[7]

Unlike so many of the early radical doctrinaires to whom the universal prescription for good polity consisted in the adoption of parliamentary government elected on a wide, if not universal, suffrage, Rousseau never omits to emphasize the need for high moral qualities – honesty, selflessness, patriotism – among a people as an essential condition for good government. A corrupt and degenerate community, whatever its numerical strength, will make all good government impossible. It is a constant theme in his writings, as it is in Machiavelli's. He despised the urban classes of France and England, as Machiavelli despised the ruling classes and the canaille of Italy. To Rousseau, the corruption of his time was beyond practical political remedy; to Machiavelli, the remedy was the Prophet Armed, the dictator-prince. Both looked back to the simple *pietas* of antiquity and the civic pride which it bred. Rousseau found the virtues among the peasantry and he found the material for practical reform among the remote and rugged Corsicans and the distant gallant Poles.

13

The Types of Government

Governments may be almost infinite in their variety. It has been customary, however, to speak of them as divided into three or four different types. Up to the nineteenth century, the régime under which all the citizens constituted the legislature was called a democracy. At the other extreme, the government of one man was called monarchy (or, in ancient times, tyranny – with or without the pejorative overtones). In between lay aristocracy, or government by a small number of the citizens.

In practice, it has never been possible to draw dividing lines. As the membership of an aristocracy increases in proportion to the whole population, it comes to assume many of the features of a democracy, while a shrinkage in the membership of a democracy marks the reverse tendency. In between the two clearly defined conditions of the very wide and the very limited magistracy, democracy has passed over into aristocracy and vice versa, while, in or about the middle of the scale, there have been polities which might have been referred to indifferently as either. The distinction between aristocracy and monarchy was generally regarded as more clear; nevertheless, history shows us many examples of what is called 'partitioned' or 'divided' kingship whose features resemble closely those of an aristocracy of very small membership. Again, under any of these régimes, the work of government might be divided up amongst sections of its own membership and its different functions performed after various manners. Thus, one part of the administration may be carried out on monarchical, another on aristocratic and another on democratic lines, each part of the administration enjoying a greater or less measure of freedom from the control of the supreme magistrate. This is called a mixed government and has been, as an examination of the administrative system almost everywhere will show, virtually universal in practice, for so complex a task as the regulation of affairs in any but the smallest community demands a corresponding complexity in the machinery of government.*

> Strictly speaking, there is no such thing as a simple government. A single head must have his subalterns; a popular government must have a head. Thus, in the sharing of the executive power there is always a gradation from the great number to the less, with this difference: that sometimes the great number is dependent on the small and sometimes the small on the great.[1]

Simple government has, thus, merely a theoretical or ideal existence.

For the sake of convenience, however, government has been described as democratic, aristocratic and monarchic, according to the simple, ideal type to which it approximates.

On the basis of his contention that the numerical strength of a government is in inverse proportion to the numerical strength of the population, Rousseau grades governments in ascending degrees of power as the democratic, the aristocratic and the monarchic. The smaller the State, the weaker or less active ought the executive to be. Democracy, therefore, is the type of government best suited to the small State, aristocracy to the middle-sized and monarchy to the very large.

> If, in the different States, the number of magistrates ought to be in inverse ratio to that of the citizens, it follows that, in general, democratic government is best suited to the small States, the aristocratic to the middle-sized and the monarchic to the great. This rule derives immediately from the principle. But how can be

---

* Cf. Thomas Paine: 'That Civil Government is necessary, all civilized Nations will agree; but Civil Government is republican Government. All that part of the Government of England, which begins with the office of constable, and proceeds through the department of magistrate, quarter session and general assize, including trial by jury, is republican Government. Nothing of monarchy appears in it, except the name which William the Conqueror imposed upon the English, that of obliging them to call him "Their Sovereign Lord, the King".' (*The Rights of Man*, Pt II, 79.)

The Types of Government

counted the multitude of circumstances that can furnish the exceptions?[2]

It is clear that Rousseau has no objection to any form of government in the abstract. Provided that the people ruled is an association and not an aggregate and that the executive unfailingly respects the General Will, the description of the executive is a matter of indifference. Compliance with the General Will is the sole criterion of the legitimacy of a government.

Turning to the concrete, however, he comes to express decided condemnation of the stronger governments, tempered with misgivings as to the viability of the weakest, but leaving no doubt where his sympathies lie.

Democracy

There is no question that democracy, as the eighteenth century understood it, is the polity towards which Rousseau leaned. The entire spirit of his works is democratic and egalitarian.

At first sight, his chapter on the subject in the *Contrat Social* may come as a surprise, for here he regretfully puts democracy aside on the ground that it is impracticable.[3] His central objection to pure democracy in practice is based on his theory that the General Will, which is the Law, must be general in its source and in its object: that it cannot relate to 'a particular man or a particular fact'. When the Sovereign absorbs in itself the function of prince or executive (as it does, by definition, in a pure democracy), the people are exercised with concrete, particular problems in addition to the abstract and general: the introduction of the former can bring only disunity, indifference to the claims of justice and partisan passion which chokes solicitude for the general welfare. The resulting corruption may weaken the social bond to breaking-point.

> It is not good that he who makes the laws should execute them, nor that the body of the people turn aside its attention from general views to bestow it upon particular objects. Nothing is more dangerous than the influence of private interests in public affairs; and the abuse of the law by the government is less an evil than the corruption of the legislator, which is the inevitable consequence of particular views.[4]

Rousseau: Stoic & Romantic

There has never been a true democracy; the tendency of the citizens in all republics whose constitutions were democratic has at all times been either to depute many, or all, of the functions of government to commissions or to submit themselves to the guidance of philosophers or orators, as they did in Athens, changing thereby the whole character of their States. It is only in circumstances of the rarest, and under conditions the most difficult to preserve that any polity approaching the democratic can be maintained; the earliest societies of simple agriculturists and herdsmen such as we have met in the *Discours sur l'Inégalité* may have known it, but the growth of civilization and the ambition and luxury which accompany it have sapped virtue and made human affairs too complex to be amenable to regulation by popular assemblies. Simplicity and virtue, the twin pillars on which a democracy must rest, have long departed from amongst the generality of men.[5]

> Moreover, how many things difficult to obtain in conjunction does not that government presume? In the first place, a very small State in which the people may easily be assembled and in which every citizen can easily know all the others. Secondly, a great simplicity of customs which prevents multiplicity in public affairs and tedious discussions. Again, a great degree of social and economic equality, without which equality in rights and authority cannot long subsist. Finally, little or no luxury, for, whether luxury be the effect of riches or whether it render riches necessary, it corrupts at one and the same time both rich and poor: the former by its enjoyment and the latter by its envy: it sells the Fatherland for effeminacy and vanity: it deprives the State of all its citizens, to enslave them one to the other and all to opinion.[6]

Nothing is more precarious than the situation of a democracy in which perfect conditions do not obtain; in no other polity is the temptation to shirk one's civic duty so great, while the very feebleness of a democratic government invites the attack of the ambitious and the unruly. Without virtue, constancy and courage of the highest order, true popular government must remain a vain dream. 'If there were a people of gods, it would govern itself democratically. A government so perfect suits not men.'[7]

He is here writing of pure or simple democracy and it must be

The Types of Government

remembered that he agrees that there is no such thing as a 'pure' polity, democratic, aristocratic or monarchic; every one is tempered by features of the others; it is in practice the dominating feature that authorizes us to categorize among existing or historical régimes. In practice, it is the spirit of a State which determines its classification. The valorous Corsicans, he believed, exhibited a temper which might well maintain a polity democratic in spirit. And not only did the democratic spirit exist in some places in Europe, but the reality of practical democracy could be found as well. In Switzerland, he remarks, the poorest cantons are democratic.[8] Patriotism is the mainstay of democracy and peasants are more attached to their soil than citizens to their city.[9]

'The voice of nature and that of reason', we remember, 'never find themselves in contradiction, if man does not impose on himself needs which he is subsequently forced to prefer always to natural impulsion.' 'For Corsica, the least costly government: that is, in general, the republican state, and, in particular, democracy.' 'No royalty, nobility, &c., &c., . . . nobility presupposes servitude and every serf which the law suffers is a citizen of whom it deprives the State. . . . Let us, then, leave to others those titles of "marquis" and of "count", degrading to simple citizens. The fundamental law of our institution ought to be equality.'[10]

Aristocracy and Monarchy

Aristocracy and monarchy are institutions which receive a degree of theoretical admiration from Rousseau, which is more than counterbalanced by his condemnation of them in practice.

Unlike democracy, they are forms of government to which the generality of mankind has been accustomed from the beginnings of our history. In theory and at certain points, they may be held to resemble the most natural or most primitive of all forms of government: the rule of the father over his children and dependents.

Amongst the early societies and amongst the tribally organized peoples of remote regions in our own time, we find the regulation of affairs carried on by councils or gatherings of the elders. Respect for age, confidence in its judgement and probity, secure firm allegiance among simple and unspoilt people to a patriarchal government; hence, we find such societies at all times enjoying all the unity and internal tranquillity which a naturally benevolent rule can maintain. With the advance of inequality among men, the aristocracy gradually became elective; leadership came to be conferred through respect for power and wealth instead of age and wisdom, and in time the political power so conferred came to be usurped by the individuals so honoured, and was transmitted to their posterity after the fashion of material goods. This is the genesis of that hereditary aristocracy with which Europe is so familiar.

Rousseau's assessment of the merits of each of these three types of aristocracy should not be difficult to gauge: '. . . there are, then, three kinds of aristocracy: the natural, the elective and the hereditary. The first is suited only to simple peoples; the third is the worst of all governments. The second is the best: it is aristocracy in the only true sense'.[11]

It need not be remarked that in this unqualified condemnation of hereditary aristocracy, he is completely at one with all the radicals of his own and later times. Interestingly, the high praise which he gives to 'elective aristocracy' has given the admirers of government by parliaments elected on a universal suffrage a plausible claim to hail him as the apostle of what is called 'Modern Democracy'. The grounds on which he lavishes this praise were quite familiar to the long line of radical liberals who demanded democratically-elected 'representative government'.

> Beside the advantage of distinction between the two powers, it has that of the choice of its members; for in a popular government, all the citizens are born magistrates, but this (elective aristocracy) limits them to a small number and they become magistrates only by election, a means by which probity, enlightenment and all the other objects of public preference and esteem are so many extra guarantees of wisdom in government.[12]

In addition, a select assembly transacts its business with more dignity and efficiency than the ignorant multitude. Regularity of election is, however, essential to the maintenance of popular control, or rather popular sovereignty, for it must be remembered that, in Rousseau's doctrine, the sovereignty of the people is inalienable and indivisible. The people remains the legislator; the 'magistracy', however appointed, is a mere executive whose measures are not laws,

The Types of Government

but decrees implementing the people's laws. This is a fundamental point on which Rousseau differs from radicals who stand in the tradition of Locke. To Locke, the legislature (that is to say, the body to whom the people has given the ruling authority) is the supreme power in the State; this power, it is true, is fiduciary in the sense of being intended to be bounded by moral and constitutional conditions and there remains in the people an ultimate supreme power to remove or alter the legislature for grievous breach of trust, a reserve sovereignty, as it were, to be exerted in the last resort against a tyrannical or a gravely negligent legislature. But normally (that is to say, so long as it fulfils its trust), the legislature is Sovereign.[13]

When Rousseau descends from the plane of principle to that of practice, his doctrine of popular sovereignty presents some unsolved problems. The decisive argument in favour of 'elective aristocracy', he clearly implies, lies in its practicability. Pure democracy is suited only to 'a people of gods' and to very small States; 'elective aristocracy', on the other hand, is suited to States of moderate size and to men who fall short of superhuman virtue. Obstacles to its establishment in the world as we know it, although in most places very considerable, are not universally insuperable. A certain reduction in the size of most European States, some moderate moral and economic reform – these conditions will suffice for the establishment of elective government in Europe. However difficult their achievement may be in many countries, these conditions are much more within the bounds of possibility than any of the reforms that should precede the establishment of democracy. The unsolved problem is: how could the population make laws in a State too big to permit of their assembling and how, therefore, could the Sovereignty of the People be preserved? And if the Sovereignty of the People is not preserved, is not the Social Contract broken and the government illegitimate?

Monarchy, one would expect Rousseau to condemn, and so he does on the same grounds as all other republican radicals. Ideally, he thinks, monarchy might have much to commend it. The public power which is entrusted to government, to be exercised in accordance with the laws, is here committed to one man, in whom are all the faculties, so difficult to unite and maintain in a collective being. The physical unity of this government should solve the problem of maintaining its moral unity. There should be no friction within it: its internal harmony is the work of nature. A properly ordered monarchy might be expected to be the best of all governments, for in it all power, the public power of the State and the particular power of the prince, lie in a single vehicle and can be used for the same object. All the levers of the great machine are in one hand, every part should work in perfect unison. 'Archimedes, seated tranquilly upon the stream and drawing without exertion a great ship in tow, is to me the figure of a skilful monarch governing from his cabinet his vast states and making all things move while appearing immobile.'[14] The language was familiar to the age of the Enlightened Despot.

But from what monarchy ought to be to what monarchy is, is, indeed, a very far cry. The first and most cogent objection to monarchy is based on our experience of the corrupting influence of power: 'Everything conspires to deprive of justice and reason a man elevated to command others'. A State over which an absolute monarch presides has no stronger guarantee of its future well-being than the conscience of the monarch. Nor can even virtue suffice in the ruler. Monarchy, being the strongest government, is theoretically the best for a very large State. But how can one man come to know the needs of even an appreciable number of a vast population? It is beyond the power of the most enlightened and virtuous. The bond between ruler and subjects is non-existent: in order to forge one, the monarch is compelled to have recourse to the services of a hierarchy of functionaries, sacrificing thereby the monarchical character of his government. What may be gained by this change is more than outweighed by the disadvantages to the State that follow the setting up of a series of classes whose character becomes in time increasingly parasitical: an hereditary nobility, a horde of self-seeking officials who tend more and more to impose their own particular wills and the corporate wills of the associations they form upon both people and monarch. A very strong king may, it is true, do much to counteract this tendency, but complete success is impossible; the assistance of the magnates and functionaries is indispensable to him and some price must be paid.

Such is the unhappy condition under a wise and well-intentioned monarch. But how many such has mankind known? The overwhelming majority of kings has been distinguished more for folly than for wisdom, for callousness than humanity. Oppression and poverty at home, savage wars of conquest abroad, cruelty and stupidity everywhere, these are the fruits of monarchical rule.

The Types of Government

Another grave defect of the monarchical system lies in the absence of real continuity of government. We are familiar with the two modes of succession that have existed in Europe: the elective and the hereditary. At a first glance, the former appears to have much to commend it: the monarch owes his crown to some of his subjects at least and the very fact of election holds the possibility that at some time a tolerably just and able man may be raised to the throne. Experience, however, has shown that royal elections have been decided, not by the convictions of the electors, but only too frequently by a mixture of corruption and fraud. The *interregna* which occur are generally periods of the greatest danger to the State. Nor need one expect a conspicuous degree of justice and impartial benevolence in the rule of a monarch who owes his elevation to force and intrigue.[15]

In the hope of avoiding the disorders attendant on royal elections, the principle of hereditary succession has been introduced into most European countries. Nothing that the reformers and revolutionaries of later times were to say on the 'system of succession by animal generation', as Paine called it, would have seemed too harsh to Rousseau.

> Crowns have been made hereditary in certain families and there has been established an order of succession which prevents all dispute at the death of kings; that is to say, by the substitution of the inconveniences of regencies for those of elections, it is shown that an apparent tranquillity has been preferred to a wise administration and the risk of having for leaders children, monsters and imbeciles has been preferred to the task of having to dispute on the choice of good kings.[16]

Elective or hereditary, monarchy is marked by instability. King succeeding king, whether by election or by hereditary right, brings a change of policy, of method and of court favourites: a revolution takes place in the whole government with each succession; the great ship of State, instead of pursuing the steady course which a wise senate would give it, is left to pitch and roll erratically under the misdirection of careless and incompetent hands. Continuity is impossible under a monarchy; the prince changes with the death of each monarch and all is at the mercy of accident. Far otherwise is the case under a republican government, in which the prince is always the same.[17]

It seems difficult to reconcile Rousseau's doctrine of popular sovereignty with his theory that monarchy is suitable to large States. How can the populace of a State legislate, if the territory be too great to permit their meeting?

> ... one of the greatest inconveniences of large States, that which above all renders liberty most difficult to preserve, is that the legislature cannot show itself, and cannot act, save by deputation. That has its evil and its good, but the evil predominates. The legislator in person cannot be corrupted, but is easily deceived. Its representatives are hard to deceive, but easily corrupted, and it seldom happens that they are not. You have before your eyes the example of the Parliament of England and, in the *liberum veto*, that of your own nation. One can enlighten him who abuses himself, but how hinder him who sells himself?[18]

The monarch or the senate is not sovereign: 'Every law that the people has not in person ratified is null: it is no law'. Monarchy, where Rousseau would admit it at all, is only a possible form of executive; it can legitimately relate only to the executive function. Sovereignty cannot be represented; it lies in the General Will, and *will* cannot be represented. Power, however, can and, indeed, ought to be represented; but power, legitimately represented, is mere executive power, 'force applied in the support of the Law'.[19] If the power exercised by the monarch or the elected assembly be more than executive, the régime is unlawful.

A possible solution, along Rousseau's logic, might be afforded by the division of the great States into tiny sovereign units, held together by the bond of a common crown or diet: that is to say, a confederation of miniature States with a common executive. 'That two or more States be subject to the same prince is in no way contrary to right and to reason. But that one State be subject to another State appears incompatible with the nature of the body politic'.[20] Such a confederation would be an extremely precarious one, since any member could at any moment withdraw: '... there is in the State no fundamental law which cannot be revoked, not even the Social Contract. For, if all the citizens assemble to break that pact in common accord, it cannot be doubted that it has legitimately been broken'.[21]

This was the insuperable difficulty of Rousseau when he came to discuss the principle of federation, which seemed to promise security

The Types of Government

for his ideal small State. Apart from this impossibility in principle, there was the practical difficulty of reforming the imperfect contemporary world:

> . . . the political State will always remain imperfect . . . it has been repaired and patched up incessantly, instead of which a beginning should have been made by clearing the air and sweeping out all the old materials, as Lycurgus did at Sparta, in order to build a good edifice on the open site.[22]

That an attempt at confederation in Europe could be successful without recourse to physical force by its authors, Rousseau disbelieved, and a league established 'by revolutions' might well create more mischief than it could remove.[23] At times, there seemed to him little scope for a Lycurgus. He announces his dislike of precipitancy and excessive reformatory zeal in the *Préface de Narcisse* and in the *Dialogues* he tells us that '. . . he has always insisted . . . on the conservation of the existing institutions, maintaining that their destruction would remove only the palliatives and leave the vices intact, substituting brigandage for corruption'.[24] The passage would not have been disowned by de Maistre, nor by the Roman Stoics, to whom the State, with all its ferocious adjuncts, was the public embodiment of reason in a degraded world and the sole check to man's descent to chaos. The existing State, in this view of Rousseau, is relatively good (in the sense that it is the alternative to worse), but basically unlawful. The Stoics could claim a consistency which Rousseau cannot: they outlined no plan of radical general improvement. They did not believe in it. To them, the universal good was a thing of the receding past. So it was to Rousseau, but it would also be a thing of the future, if only his advice were taken.

We must accept the fact that in Rousseau's work there lies, in the abstract thought, an affirmation that the claim to legitimate authority depends upon the fulfilment of the most rigid of conditions, side by side with a tendency to greater elasticity, an inclination to compromise and to rest content with the imperfect. This comparative conservatism reaches a notable degree in the *Gouvernement de Pologne*, the decidely 'Fabian' tone of which is in marked contrast with the yearning for a 'clearing of the air' which distinguishes his truly revolutionary moments.

The logic of Rousseau's theory would be the fragmentation of the great kingdoms of Europe by the establishment of an infinity of Social Contracts all over the continent, but the nearest practicable approach to this inaccessible end he sees in measures of decentralization in Poland and in Corsica. They do not take us very far. Having advised the Poles to 'withdraw within their own limits', renouncing all those territories of mixed population then included in their domains, he goes on to say:

> Failing these withdrawals, I can see only one means that may supply for them, and, happily, this means is already in the spirit of your institutions. Let the separation of the two Polands be as marked as that of Lithuania: have three States in one. I would, if it were possible, that you should have as many as there are palatinates. Form in each one so many particular administrations. Perfect the form of the dietines, extend their authority over their respective palatinates, but mark their limits clearly and ensure that nothing can break among them the bond of the common legislation and the subordination to the body of the republic. In a word, apply yourselves to extend and perfect the system of federative governments, the only system that can unite the advantages of the great with those of the small State and, by that fact, the only one suitable to you.[25]

Indeed, as if in acknowledgment of the immense difficulty of effecting so radical a change as even that sketched above, he makes a rather vague suggestion, prompted perhaps by his recollection of the Merovings or other itinerant Germanic chiefs of Europe's infancy:

> Nevertheless, if the State cannot be reduced to just limits, there still remains one resource: it is to have no capital, to have the seat of government successively in every town and to assemble there, turn by turn, the estates of the land. . . . People the territory equally, extend the same rights throughout, spread abundance and life everywhere, and it is thus that the State will become at once the strongest and the best-governed possible.[26]

It will be noticed that, far from recommending sovereignty for any of the internal units of Poland, he emphasizes the need for the common legislative bond, and that the federation to which he refers is one of governments, that is to say, of non-legislative bodies.

The advice on the diffusion of the population is similar to that

The Types of Government

given to the Corsicans. Agriculture, he told them, is favourable to democracy; it develops the virtues and the spirit of independence and it saves people from the vices of city life.[27] He wrote for agricultural Europe. Of the vast industrial revolution, even then beginning, he no more guessed the significance than did his fellow-philosophers or his followers of 1793. What he did know of it, he disliked, and it made even his most moderate suggestions for decentralization less practicable than ever.

14

The Small State

Rousseau was least influential when least logical. His advice to the Poles and Corsicans was never taken. He is remembered for his unhistorical Social Contract, whose logic, aided by powerful emotion, led to the ideal of the small State. The doctrine of the General Will, shorn of its modifications, and the sentiment with which he surrounded his conception of the small State, are the things which give him his place in political history.

Intellectually, he was inconsistent, but emotionally, consistent: he was a rebel. His disapproval of precipitancy and his disavowal of subversive intent do not disguise his dislike of the great State. Fundamentally, its government is illegitimate, since it usurps the sovereignty. Its origins, growth and development lie, not in popular consent, but in the application of force by powerful minorities on helpless majorities. It is no association, but an agglomeration of peoples. It has no life and no existence in right. Its administration is inefficient, wasteful and oppressive in its cost. It is 'too great for its constitution and sinks down and perishes, crushed under its own weight'.[1]

The crucial test of the legitimacy of any political unit lies in the existence of a General Will. The unit must be a body politic: it must be composed only of individuals who have sufficient in common, sufficient inter-acquaintance, to perceive that the good of each depends upon the good of all and that, the latter being the paramount consideration, each ought to identify himself with the whole, see clearly the essential unity of the whole and devote himself without reserve to

The Small State

public duty. The higher the degree of similarity and reciprocal understanding, the stronger and more evident is the General Will: the smaller the association, the stronger the corporate will. The smaller the State, then, the more does the General Will prevail, and only in a State whose dimensions are so small as to permit of assemblies of the people can the General Will be constantly evident and active. It has been aptly remarked that 'When Bentham scornfully said that no law of any European state would constitute a valid act of sovereignty for Rousseau, except possibly those of the Republic of San Marino, he was saying no more than was true'.[2]

At no point does Rousseau tell us how such diminutive units could be established on the sites of existing kingdoms without recourse to violence, and of this he disapproves. Yet, in the *Contrat Social*, he tells us that 'The limits of the possible in moral things are less narrow than we think; it is our weakness and our prejudices which narrow them. Base souls cannot believe in great men; vile slaves laugh mockingly at the word *liberty*'. Assemblies of the people were an historical fact in the ancient republics and even under the monarchical governments of the Macedonians and the Franks.[3] Why doubt the possibility of what has been done? Human nature has not changed, but the conditions under which men have lived since original innocence was lost have vastly done so. Centuries of despotism have done their work. How this process of degeneration may be halted and reversed, and man restored to something like his ancient stature, is the question that occupies Rousseau in all his discussions on education; it directly inspired the famous chapter on the Lawgiver. Perhaps the advent of the small State would follow a long process of enlightenment and development of sensibility?

This ideal of the small State seems to have been toyed with by some of the extreme liberals of the Gironde, against whom one of the favourite charges of the Jacobins was that of designing the dismemberment of the Republic ('One and Indivisible'). The fragmentation of the great territorial units into minute political entities, as the prelude to the development of those conditions that would cause the 'withering-away' of the State and the decay of the very principle of authority, was looked to by the philosophical anarchists as a stage in the inevitable progress of mankind.[4] It is interesting to notice the points at which Rousseau and such rationalists as Godwin approach and at which they diverge. The commendation of the small

Rousseau: Stoic & Romantic

State is expressed in much the same way. 'I reside', says Godwin,

> upon a certain spot, because that residence is most conducive to my happiness and usefulness. I am interested in the political justice and virtue of my species, because they are men, that is, creatures eminently capable of justice and virtue; and I have perhaps additional reason to interest myself for those who live under the same government as myself, because I am better qualified to understand their claims and more capable of exerting myself on their behalf. . . . Whatever evils are included in the abstract idea of government, they are all of them extremely aggravated by the extensiveness of its jurisdiction, and softened under circumstances of an opposite nature. Ambition, which may be no less formidable than a pestilence in the former, has no room to unfold itself in the latter. Popular commotion is like the waters of the earth, capable, where the surface is large, of producing the most tragical effects, but mild and innocuous when confined within the circuit of an humble lake. Sobriety and equity are the obvious characteristics of a limited circle.[5]

There is, however, the vital difference: Rousseau intended his small State to be permanent, Godwin intended his to be a mere stage on the road to universal individual autonomy. For this reason, they differed as to the means by which the affairs of the little republic should be conducted.

To Godwin, the experience of life in the small State should enlarge the faculties of the individual member, increasing the capacity of each and all for self-direction in harmony with the laws of reason, in anticipation of the time when universal free acceptance of the directions of reason would ensure universal voluntary co-operation in the regulation of all human relationships and the disappearance of every trace of constraint because of its superfluousness. Individual reason, given increasing freedom by immediacy of contact in the small social unit and freed from the inhibitions which the artificiality of communication in large societies imposes on it, would come into ever-closer contact and ultimate identification with universal reason. Reason subsumes will, and the progress of reason is impeded by the prejudices of society. The smaller the society, after a lengthy period of intellectual progress, the fewer the impediments to reason. The very

The Small State

small society of the highly sophisticated, the fine flower of centuries of gradual progress, imposes only the very last impediments and gives the final encouragement to reason. It is the penultimate to the emergence of autonomous individual reason, in perfect accord with the universal.

> The loathsome mask has fallen, the man remains
> Sceptreless, free, uncircumscribed, but man
> Equal, unclassed, tribeless and nationless,
> Exempt from awe, worship, degree, the king
> Over himself. . . .[6]

To the rationalist, reason is incorruptible and will eventually triumph over the passions. To the pessimist – to Seneca and to Rousseau – reason becomes corrupted into the *ratio quidem* and becomes the misleader. Our sentiments are given to us by Nature to reveal to us real truths and to show us the way to happiness. They cannot be exercised by man in isolation and they are corrupted in the large society. In the small company of the like-minded who know no personal ambition, the sentiments of each and all coincide and point the same way: the real will of each and the General Will are the same – they point to the moral good of each and all.

Godwin's was the ideal of the universalist (even though, as an empiricist, he could not accept the existence of universals). Rousseau was suspicious of universalism. He rejected the eighteenth-century notion of a 'universal language' of which particular languages were, ideally speaking, divagations; all true language comes from within; spontaneity of communication is 'natural' communication; the 'universals' with which we are confronted are constructions of men living in historic, corrupted societies. The instinct for truth lies within every man and, as every man is unique, every man must find truth in his own way; *sequere naturam* – do not copy others – is essentially stoic and romantic. But equally powerful in man to the instinct for truth is the instinct of sociability. Man's own reason cannot make him autonomous; he needs others to care for. Mind cannot be separated from heart and will: the individual must be embraced by a community. This need to care for others cannot be satisfied in the large, artificially regulated societies which we have known. The ideal balance of fulfilment of the need of truth and the need for others can be found only in the very small society of the simple and virtuous. Where this balance is found, where devotion to truth and devotion to others coincide, we should find a permanent home. The ideal, small society, then, to Rousseau, is no mere stage, but an end in itself.

The constitutional machinery of the small State

Membership of the body politic established under the Social Contract is the final bourn of man on earth, for man can find fulfilment, not as an individual, but only as an integral part of the group – the *moi commun*. And this destiny can be achieved only in the very small State. This is the very core of Rousseau's political doctrine.

Given the existence of his ideal union, the next question is how to preserve it. On this, he is quite explicit in the later chapters of the *Contrat Social*. It is indeed to these chapters we must look for the clearest and most definite of his ideas on the subject of legitimate authority and of the constitutional machinery for its preservation. Besides these, we must look for his ideas on the spiritual armament with which the citizen must be equipped if the good polity is to be maintained.

One might first consider the constitutional and governmental apparatus of the State.

It will be noted, in the first place, that Rousseau does not advocate pure democracy: this form of government, under which the people is not only the legislator but also the prince, is 'fit only for a community of gods'. An executive must exist for the purpose of carrying out the details of administration, but the people shall be the legislator. For the purpose of making new laws, of continuing old laws and of making a general review of the condition of the State, the people shall assemble at fixed intervals in accordance with law. This last provision is extremely important: no popular assembly ought to be considered legal, nor any act or decision of such a body valid, unless the provisions of the law on the convocation of assemblies be strictly complied with. Without this regularity, the State would be exposed to the danger of mob rule. Nevertheless, should the people decide against enacting such a measure, or rescind it if already established, there is nothing to prohibit them. The assembled people is Sovereign: there is no law it cannot legitimately enact or repeal; not even the Social Contract is sacred.[7] Thus every assembly holds all the possibilities of a 'new beginning'.

The Small State

When the Sovereign people assembles, all the authority of government shall cease and the whole future be in the hands of the assembly, which shall consider, as the first two items on its agenda, the following questions: '1. If it please the Sovereign to preserve the present form of government. 2. If it please the people to leave the administration to those now charged with it.'[8] The complete subordination of the executive to the people could not be more clearly emphasized. Every convocation would thus begin with a referendum on the constitution and a general election. Such a polity, it need not be remarked, leaves no room for a 'constitution' in the traditional sense of the word: that is to say, a body of fundamental laws binding the legislature as well as the subject. Not even the Social Contract is a constitution in this sense, because the legislature can dissolve it. A constitution intended to bind the lawmaker would be unlawful, since it would infringe the sovereignty of the people. (Curiously enough, for a very different reason, Godwin also opposes constitutions for the democratic and egalitarian policies of the future. They would impede the 'withering-away' of the State.)*

Rousseau's State would be a complete democracy, as long, at least, as the assembly continued in session, since, on the surrender of governmental authority, the assembly becomes prince in addition to Sovereign and is perfectly free to enact the continuance of a purely democratic régime. It may, then, while in session, not only enact laws, but issue decrees: in other words, it may legitimately pronounce upon 'a particular man' or 'a particular fact'. But the decisions of the people acting as prince would not have the moral significance of the General Will. The General Will is always right in a moral sense. Pronouncement on a particular fact is not necessarily so.

This leads to the question of the procedure to be adopted by the assembly in the enactment of laws and the passing of decrees. The inescapable conclusion, from all that Rousseau says on the subject, is

---

* *Political Justice*, Vol. II, 138: 'In a country where a people are habituated to sentiments of equality and where no political monopoly is tolerated, there is little danger that any national assembly should be disposed to enforce a pernicious change and there is still less that the people should submit to the injury or not possess the means easily and with small interruption of public tranquillity to avert it. The language of reason on this subject is: "Give us equality and justice, but no constitution. Suffer us to follow, without restraint, the dictates of our own judgment, and to change our forms of social order as fast as we improve in understanding and knowledge"'.

that all decisions, except one, shall be by vote of the majority. There is but one law that requires unanimity: the Social Contract. Outside the Contract, majority decision shall prevail, for this is the only method whereby, in the last analysis, free and equal men can come to a decision on any subject (other than the establishment of a Social Contract) and is logically provided for in the original Contract.[9] Nevertheless, the carrying of an important piece of legislation by a narrow majority would leave Rousseau somewhat uneasy; wherever the logic of the Social Contract may lead, he cannot view without misgiving the possibility that measures which affect seriously the whole life of the community and every citizen in it be taken against the wish of a large section of the people. This anxiety leads him, in the chapter 'Of Suffrages', to propose two general rules to provide for the making of decisions in all matters on which unanimity is lacking:

> Two general maxims can serve to regulate these relationships: first, the more grave and important the deliberation, the nearer ought the judgment approach unanimity: secondly, the more the matter discussed demands celerity, the narrower may be the difference. In deliberations which must be terminated on the spot, a majority of one ought to suffice.[10]

The first of these maxims, he tells us, 'ought to apply to laws, the second to affairs.' It may be concluded, then, that Rousseau would wish that proposals of laws should be carried by the assembly only when a weighty majority supports them, while decrees relating to the day-to-day routine of administration may be made even by the narrowest majority.

When all this has been said, however, it remains that even Rousseau's wishes need not be sacred to the sovereign people: the assembly which can repeal even the Social Pact is under no obligation to accept recommendations on any subject from any quarter.

Such is the plan for the regulation of the internal affairs of the ideal small State. Being remote from the uglier realities of life, it is comfortably general and logical. As we approach reality, the problem of the defence of the tiny haven of perfection presents itself. Herein, the smallness of the State, which is the surest guarantee of the liberty and well-being of the citizens, appears as a fatal disadvantage. Clearly, it cannot merge itself in another, for that would be the abdication of

The Small State

its sovereignty; nor can it divide its sovereignty with any other, for sovereignty is indivisible. How are independence and security simultaneously to be maintained? The advice to the Poles provides for no sovereignty in the palatinates. Rousseau refers, very briefly, in the *Contrat Social* to the examples, ancient and modern, of federations: 'But how to give small States sufficient power to resist great? As of old, the Greek cities resisted the Great King, and as more recently, Holland and Switzerland resisted the House of Austria?'[11] Federation is not the answer, much less alliances established by force. Finally, in the same work, he postpones discussion of the federative principles and announces his intention to explore the subject:

> In the last analysis, I do not see that it will ever be possible for the Sovereign to preserve among us the exercise of its rights, if the State be not very small. But, if it be too small, shall it not be subjugated? No. I shall show later on how the exterior power of a great people may be joined with the free polity and the good order of a small State. This I have proposed to do in the sequel to this work, when, in treating of external relations, I shall come to confederations: an entirely new matter and one on which the principles are yet to be established.[12]

The sequel never came. In the doctrine of popular sovereignty, Rousseau had made for himself a Procrustean bed. Godwin, to whom all government was a matter of external force, necessary in decreasing degrees as peoples progressed towards individual autonomy, was in no such difficulty; government being a mere convenience at best, there was no place for sovereignty in either the Rousseauite or the traditional sense; the degree of autonomy to be enjoyed by any ruling body would be decided pragmatically by the weight of opinion at the different stages of progress; consequently the questions of federations and confederations will answer themselves when the times comes; all such arrangements would be purely transitory and preparatory to the complete disappearance of authority.[13]

Political and economic justice in the small State

That constitutional and legal machinery alone, however perfect in itself, will maintain the good government and happiness of men, is a suggestion one would never associate with Rousseau. Not even the admirable arrangement of the small State, with its popular assemblies, its equality and its legal guarantees against usurpation will save the body politic unless the citizens be intensely devoted to the homeland. Without the true spirit of citizenship, the popular State will degenerate with perhaps more deadly results than a State whose beginnings were much less perfect, for the decay of a non-popular régime connotes chiefly the degeneration of its government: the people suffer, it is true, and do not escape taint, but they are not irretrievably lost. The decay of a democracy, on the other hand, is the decay of the people itself: the very source of the General Will is poisoned, the sovereignty is destroyed and the hope of resuscitation is remote. Anarchy is the lot of the decaying democracy, and anarchy is the breeding-ground of the worst of despotism. Liberty and equality are vain words, unless fraternity be present. This is the gist of all Rousseau's advice to Corsicans, Poles and all others. Whatever a legitimate government is authorized to do, it is authorized above all to promote fraternity by all the means at its disposal: this is the first command of the Sovereign, because the preservation of the Sovereign depends completely upon the solidarity of the citizenry, the identification by himself of the individual with the community – in a word, upon universal love of country. Where this universal devotion to the common fatherland is strong, where universal selflessness prevails, where duty is loved with a religious zeal, there will be no division among the people, no majorities and minorities, but one great unity: and in the absence of hatreds, suspicions and jealousies, those defects which logic may discover in the constitutional machinery may never come to light.

The measures which Rousseau considered essential to the promotion of this solidarity and devotion to the State are written all over his political works: the maintenance of liberty – by which is meant the condition in which each shall be independent of other individuals, but completely dependent on the whole – of absolute equality before the law, of economic security for all, of the rigid enforcement of the General Will and, lastly, but above all, the education of the youth in the atmosphere of patriotism.

The *Économie Politique* contains a notably succinct and representative summary of the maxims upon which he would have a lawful government to act.[14] The first of these lays down that the government must enforce the General Will and cause the administration to con-

The Small State

form to the laws. To ensure that this shall be done to the best of human ability, he proposes 'two infallible rules': first, in all matters in which the General Will is known, it should be faithfully followed; secondly, in matters in which the General Will has not been explained, the administration shall follow 'the spirit of the laws'. To do this latter, all that is needed on the part of government is 'to be just'. The next maxim enjoins the education of the people in all the virtues, of which the great virtue of patriotism is the head and fount. The third refers to the need for economic justice, which can be achieved only through the maintenance of conditions that tend to produce a certain levelling of fortunes.

This last maxim, already touched on in the discussion on Rousseau's ideas on property, is really of fundamental importance for the State, for, without a universally-diffused measure of well-being (the *aurea mediocritas*) and economic security, public spirit and love of country are not likely to flourish among the populace. Extremes of wealth and poverty make social betterment impossible; liberty is an empty word when one man is rich enough to buy his neighbour and the neighbour so poor as to be compelled to sell himself, for liberty requires the greatest possible measure of 'equality in fact', the nearest approach which the public welfare will allow to complete economic equality. He does not advocate the public ownership of all wealth, nor a rigid equality in its apportionment: what he does require is its distribution in such proportions that 'personal dependence' among citizens is reduced to the minimum.[15] (Rousseau, in the course of his life, found himself frequently in 'personal dependence' on others; in the eighteenth century, it was the usual fate of the man of talent without money.)

'The fruits of the earth are for all' and it is the command of the Sovereign that the fruits of the national territory be used for the common good. To ensure this, the government should rely on a fixed policy of preventing the widening of economic gaps among the citizens. Continuous meddling with the possessions of individuals can produce mischief, nor will it ever become necessary if the tendency to accumulate great wealth be forestalled:

> It is, then, one of the most important concerns of government to prevent the extreme inequality of fortunes, not by seizing the treasures from their possessors, but by denying to all the means

of accumulating them: not by building hospitals for the poor, but by guaranteeing the citizen from becoming poor.[16]

The fiscal measures he favours to this end are the heavy taxation of articles of luxury, the freedom from impost of all articles of necessity, the incidence of the greater part of the burden on the rich and the regulation of taxation in such a way as to drive all citizens into useful and worthy pursuits:

> It is by means of such taxes as relieve poverty and charge wealth that the continual augmentation of the inequality of fortunes must be prevented, the enslavement to the rich of a multitude of workers and useless servitors, the multiplication of idlers in the towns and the desertion of the countryside.[17]

Here is Rousseau's economic ideal: a community of small proprietors, peasants and modest traders, each dependent on the community as a whole, none at the mercy of another; spartan in conception, a moral rather than an economic socialism.

The control of taxation is a function of the Sovereign, since it is a communal matter. It is true that in the *Économie Politique* he speaks of the necessity for 'the consent of the people or of its representatives' to the imposition of taxes, but it is obvious from the context of all his references to the subject that the authority to tax comes from the community and that the making of fiscal decisions by public officers ought to be the exercise of a mere concession by the people, under firm legislative direction.[18] The decisions of the officials would not be infallible, nor would the adjudication of the community on a particular official decision be so. Even in the ideal community, all decisions might not be ideal.

15

The Religion of Patriotism

The ascription to the State of a creative cultural role presented the ancients with little difficulty. The political and the religious were one: the State was divine, its function was ethical as well as political and economic and, in so far as it was limited, it was auto-limited by its own ethos. The dualism of Church and State in the Christian ages left the State with a role which, directly at least, was little beyond the political and military. The directive and formative forces in the vast areas of life outside this comparatively narrow field were the Church and the traditions of the peoples. Even in the Protestant lands in earlier modern times, the control of education was vested, not directly in the civil authorities, but in the State Churches.

English radicalism of the eighteenth century became more and more closely associated with the doctrine of *laissez-faire*. Its mentor, Locke, viewed the State as a mere guarantor of the individual's natural rights, or rather as the authorized wielder of sanctions against those who trespassed upon the area sacred to the individual. Whether the logic of Locke's doctrine on the right of property leads to *laissez-faire* or not, there can be no doubt that he excludes the State from the entire field of creative cultural activity. This exclusion remained, by and large, an English radical tradition until comparatively recent times, and even today the idea of instruction by persons who are purely and simply State officials is unpalatable in the English-speaking world; while much is demanded of public authority, its role is still seen as substitutive and auxiliary and those who impart instruction at its expense enjoy a degree of distinctness, if not autonomy. Godwin's logic is un-English in its rigidity, his individualism is carried to the extreme of nominalism, and his conclusions were dismissed as fantastic, but in his negative attitude towards the State, he was a product of his milieu.

France, although it imbibed much of the radicalism of English origin, had an authoritarian tradition which inhibited full acceptance of this attitude, and the ideal of universal national education was not unfamiliar in philosophical circles. It was, however, a mere ideal, and no one thought of calling on the existing government to play any cultural role. Contemporary governments in Western Europe did not impinge directly on their subjects in this particular field.

Rousseau's view of the ideal State as a supra-personal entity, a real organism in the psychic sense, was bound to give him a conception of its cultural role which broke radically and thoroughly with the European past and which gives him so conspicuous a place in the history of romantic nationalism. Taking the group as the self-sufficient human agency, he was certain to arrive at conclusions directly antithetical to those of such thinkers as Godwin, whose unit was the individual. At first sight, too, he seems to run contrary to the Stoics, who sought for the individual a guide to morality that is outside the State or outside the particular State in which the individual lives. The Roman Stoics, in so far as they thought of the State as a voice of reason in a deteriorating world, thought of it as a check, albeit a very imperfect one, on human wickedness, a brake on the *descensus averni*. They never envisaged the State as a supra-personal entity of a real organism and they did not think of the State as a moral guide in any positive sense. Rousseau certainly never thought of the historic State as a moral guide, but the ideal State – that in which the General Will prevails – is infallible, and that which is infallible must suffer no restriction. There is no danger in power, when power can be used only for good: *tuto enim quantum vult potest qui se nisi quod debet non putat posse* [There is nothing dangerous in a man's having as much power as he likes, if he takes the view that he has power to do only what it is his duty to do]. Seneca admitted the proposition, but would never have applied it to any conceivable political authority. Rousseau conceived of an indefectible State, to which the proposition applied.

If the fatherland is to endear itself to its children, thinks Rousseau, the function of its government must be much more extensive than the

The Religion of Patriotism

merely negative one of preventing injustices and glaring inequalities. Lack of interest in the lives of their subjects is the cardinal sin with which he charges the governments of contemporary Europe. The whole function of government, they seem to believe, consists in the collection of taxes; once the people are shorn to provide their rulers with the wealth they desire, they are left to fend for themselves like a shepherdless flock. In all the important things of life, in all those things in which direction is most needed, the people are either neglected or permitted to fall into the hands of agencies whose aim is not the general welfare, but the maintenance of sectional power and influence. No attempt is made to form the character of the people, to inculcate civic pride, devotion to the community and the virtues necessary to the promotion of a vigorous communal life: the whole sphere of creative activity is left outside the care of the modern government.

> There will never yet be a good and solid constitution but that in which the law will reign in the hearts of the citizens; in so far as the legislative force will not go that distance the laws will always be eluded. But, how to reach their hearts? Of that, our institutions, which see no means but force and punishment, scarcely dream; and, to that, material rewards lead perhaps scarcely better.[1]

The result, he thinks, is plain: watery cosmopolitanism, general scepticism, the uniform meanness of individual character which the absence of an inspiring and immediate object of devotion begets in man – all these were rife in the Europe of his time, according to Rousseau. True nobility had vanished; men were conscious of themselves only as individuals or as members of a class or party; European society was divided horizontally, the wealthy of all lands united in the same easy cynicism, the same vices, the same dislike of their poorer fellow-men. 'There are today no longer Frenchmen, Germans, Spaniards, even English, whatever one may say: there are only Europeans. All have the same tastes, the same passions, the same manners, because none has received a national form by means of a distinctive institution.'[2] All this he lays at the door of what he considers the sterile intellectualism of the prevailing type of education.[3] And the prevalence of this education suits the usurping governments of the rich, for the aridity of mind and spirit which it begets is the best assurance of the continued indifference to the political and social wrongs of everyday occurrence under their régimes.

Far different from the anaemic product of contemporary civilization was the man whom the ancient institutions moulded: there was a selflessness, a devotion to home and kin, a passionate awareness that membership of the nation was life, that separation from it was death, a spirit which the temptations of the sophist and the despot could never hope to break down.

> It is the national institutions which form the genius, the character, the tastes, the manners of a people, which make it to be itself and not another, which inspire that ardent love of country, founded on habitude impossible to uproot, which makes it die of *ennui* among other peoples, in the midst of delights of which it is deprived in its own land. Do you remember that Spartan, gorged with the pleasures of the Great King's court, who was reproached for regretting the black sauce? 'Ah!', said he to the Satrap with a sigh, 'I know your pleasures, but you do not know ours!'?[4]

The Spartan in exile, the Jew by the waters of Babylon, the Roman under alien skies – these were the figures that occupied the mind of Rousseau when he reflected on patriotism.

Whoever would form a durable State must make use of the passions of the people; reason alone is utterly incapable of promoting the degree of solidarity essential to the purpose. Passion lies, ready to hand, in all men; it cannot be extinguished. Uncontrolled, it makes dreadful havoc. It is, then, the duty of legitimate government to seize on this mighty force, to harness and canalize it so that it may serve the great end of raising men above their present stature to find their fulfilment in the State. Nothing less than the transformation of human nature is the duty of government, a work truly positive and creative, demanding unremitting application and attention to every means available: nothing must be deemed beneath notice.

> By what means, then, move the hearts of men and make the fatherland and its laws loved? Shall I dare to say? By children's games, by institutions that seem idle to the eyes of superficial men, but which form cherished habitudes and invincible attachments. If I seem to rave here, I do so to good effect, for I declare that I see underneath my folly all the traits of reason.[5]

The Religion of Patriotism

Public festivals in honour of national heroes, badges of honour for deserving officials, citizen armies for the defence of the homeland are among the recommendations to the Poles, to ensure that reminders of their nationality be kept constantly before their eyes. The cultivation of everything distinctively Polish, down to the most trivial idiosyncracies, is, to Rousseau's mind, of infinitely greater ultimate value to the ancient kingdom he so admires than any ambitious scheme of military defence or constitutional reform: 'If you fashion yourselves so that a Pole can never become a Russian, I tell you that Russia shall never subjugate Poland'.[6]

Habits, however, are not to be formed at adult age: if selfishness be ingrained in a people, there is little use in appealing to their unselfishness, and all devices to arouse patriotism will be in vain. The State must, therefore, begin with the children, for these are the malleable material out of which the citizens of the future are to be made, and, as the infant, like the adult citizen, belongs to the State, the claims of the latter on the child are paramount. This leads Rousseau to assert a competency for government in educational matters, the rightfulness of which is roundly denied by the Church and directly contrary to traditional European beliefs concerning authority. To Rousseau, the State (that is, his ideal State) is the parent of all citizens, young and old: dependence upon the State being the true liberty, and dependence upon an individual being a species of slavery, it follows that the government, as the agent of the State, ought to stand *in loco parentis* to the child. Subjection to the natural parent is servitude for the child: subjection to the law, as administered by the lawful government, is the child's liberty.[7]

> If there are laws for mature age, so there ought to be for infancy, which learns to obey others; and, as the reason of each individual is not permitted to be the unique arbiter of his duties, all the less ought to be abandoned to the intelligence and prejudice of fathers, the education of their children, which is of much greater importance to the State than to the fathers: for in the course of nature, the death of the father strips him of the last fruits of that education, but the fatherland feels sooner or later its effect: the State remains, the family dissolves.[8]

Nor can the parents complain that such a system involves an abdication of authority on their part, since they merely exchange their natural authority as parents for a civil authority as citizens in the regulation of their children's upbringing; the parents' rights are thus not only respected but reinforced and the dangers of neglect and misdirection are obviated for every child in the nation. Education, then, as becomes a matter of such import to the State, should be placed in the hands of the administration, which should make thorough provision for its regulation in accordance with the expressed wishes of the people. 'Public education under rules prescribed by the government and under masters established by the Sovereign is, then, one of the fundamental maxims of popular or legitimate government.'

The nature and object of this national education being clear, additional precision and vividness may well be added by a glance at some of the more striking passages on the subject in the *Économie Politique* and the *Gouvernement de Pologne*.

Outlining the means by which the minds of the young should be orientated towards the ideal of citizenship, Rousseau tells us in the former work that:

> If the children are reared in common in the bosom of equality, if they are steeped in the laws of the State and the maxims of the General Will, if they are instructed to respect these above all things, if they are surrounded by examples and by objects which speak to them, without cease of the tender mother who nourishes them, of the love which she has for them, of the inestimable benefits which they receive from her and of the return they owe her, let us not doubt that they will learn, thus, to cherish themselves mutually as brothers, never to will anything save what society wills, to substitute the actions of men and citizens for the sterile and vain babble of sophists and to become one day the defenders and the fathers of the homeland of whom they have for so long been the children.[9]

Nowhere, however, does he stress more heavily the exclusively nationalistic character which he desires education to possess than in the chapter on that subject in the *Gouvernement de Pologne*:

> This is the important article: It is education which ought to give to the souls of men the national form and so direct their opinions and their tastes that they become patriots by inclination, by passion, by necessity. An infant, on opening its eyes, ought to see the Fatherland, and, up to death, ought to see

The Religion of Patriotism

nothing else. Every true republican will suck with his mother's milk the love of the Fatherland: that is to say, of the laws and liberty. This love makes all his existence: he sees nothing but the Fatherland, he lives for nothing but for it; as an individual alone, he is nothing, he has no longer a Fatherland, he is no more: and, if he is not dead, he is worse.[10]

In the light of this conception of the perfect State, it is interesting to seek all those passages in the writings of Rousseau in which God and the new Caesar, the Sovereign People, are placed side by side, so to speak. 'All justice comes from God: he alone is its source. But, if we knew how to receive it from so high a source, we should need neither government nor laws.' Have we, then, no means of receiving justice publicly from God? Direct contact with God is a purely private and internal affair and it does not affect public concerns. How is the dichotomy between private and public morality to be resolved? Both Luther and Machiavelli decided that it cannot be. Rousseau, loaded with his inhibitions concerning natural and democratic rights, could not leave the question unresolved. At both ends of the gap, there had to be an infallible source of right. 'Without doubt, there is a universal justice, emanating from reason alone; but that justice, to be admitted among us, should be reciprocal.' How can justice be made reciprocal, except under the conditions of the Social Contract? And as the Social Contract sets up the Sovereign People as the dispenser of justice, is not the Sovereign People the public link between the individual and God? God is infallible and the Sovereign People is infallible, since it can do no injury without injuring itself, which is impossible. The Sovereign People, therefore, stands in the place of God in relation to public affairs. Out of this process of argumentation, Rousseau filled his gap, and the filling of the gap entailed the construction of that curious compromise between the State religion of the ancients and his own quietistic and highly individualistic kind of Deism, which he called Christianity: this compromise he called the Civil Religion.

The governments of the ancient world, he reminds us, were theocratic in nature: to the pagan peoples the whole idea of government was bound up with that of direct divine intervention in human affairs: only the divine could rule the human. The human prince, be it a king or an assembly, was the mouthpiece of the divinity. Any other idea of authority was, to the ancient mind, inconceivable.

Rousseau: Stoic & Romantic

Government claimed an unlimited jurisdiction: no thought of reservation occurred to the individual subject. Thus, the idea of a two-fold jurisdiction, a temporal and a spiritual, was unknown to the pre-Christian world.

In those early times, each State devoted itself to a god or gods of its own; it was the unification which Rome imposed upon the domains she conquered that accustomed men to the idea of universalism in government and prepared them for the idea of universalism in religion. In this way, the path was cleared for the advent of Christianity. Men, accustomed to the rule of one, universal government, men who witnessed from generation to generation the decline of particularism in religion, were much readier than their ancestors for the acceptance of monotheism in some shape. Then came Christianity, which soon revolutionized the fundamental ideas on the subject of governmental jurisdiction.

Henceforth, the allegiance of man was divided. A new body, the universal Church, claimed his soul and demanded obedience in all matters spiritual: the minor role of ministering to the needs of the body and enforcing with the sword the mandates of the Church was given to the State, a role to which the latter has become increasingly unwilling to confine itself. Even when a large measure of goodwill has been present on both sides, the history of Christian Europe has shown the difficulty men have had in defining the limits of each jurisdiction and the consequent bewilderment which the conflict of claims has created in the minds of many who wished to be at once faithful Christians and loyal subjects. The result, says Rousseau, has been deplorable for human happiness and unity: '. . . there resulted from this double power a perpetual conflict of jurisdiction which has rendered all good polity impossible in Christian states, and men have never been able to discover once for all whether it was the master or the priest that ought to be obeyed'.[11]

The fact is, according to Rousseau, that the organized Church in every land is really a state within the State. Conformity to the beliefs and practices laid down by the clergy is the provision of an ecclesiastical Social Contract – a second contract, as it were, which the faithful Christian endeavours to respect, while trying at the same time to respect the original contract of civil society. Excommunication from the body of the faithful is the sanction of that second contract. It will be seen, therefore, that the body of the clergy in each land forms

The Religion of Patriotism

a particular association of very great strength and solidarity: and we know what Rousseau's views on particular associations are. So long as this organization exists, the clergy will continue to remain apart from the State, master in their own sphere, and an insuperable obstacle to complete national unity and solidarity. Thus, even in England and in Russia, the monarch, by styling himself 'Head of the Church', really makes himself its minister and acquires, not the right to change it, but rather the duty of defending it and of perpetuating its particularity and its separateness from the State. Whatever the pretentions of monarchs, the fact remains that so long as the organized body of clergy exists within their kingdoms, there are within every one of these kingdoms two powers, the spiritual and the temporal, which divide between them the allegiance of the subjects.[12] This is a condition which Rousseau deplores, and he professes to find himself in full agreement with Hobbes on this one point, an agreement which prompts him to lament that, while so much that was false and monstrous in Hobbes' ideas has survived and found favour, all that was just and true in him has been rejected and forgotten. Hobbes, accordingly, receives his praise:

> Of all the Christian authors, the philosopher, Hobbes, is the only one who has clearly seen the evil and the remedy, who has dared to propose the joining of the two heads of the eagle and the restoration of all things to political unity, without which neither State nor government shall ever be well-constituted.[13]

How would Rousseau have 'the two heads of the eagle' joined? How abolish this 'perpetual conflict of jurisdiction which has rendered all good polity impossible'? At the outset, he rejects atheism and scepticism:

> Flee those who under the pretext of explaining nature sow desolate doctrines in the hearts of men and whose scepticism is a hundred times more affirmative and more dogmatic than the decided tone of their adversaries. Under the haughty pretext that they alone are enlightened, true and in good faith, they subject us imperiously to their trenchant decisions and pretend to give us as the true principles of things the unintelligible systems they have built in their imaginations. For the rest, they reverse and destroy, trampling under foot all that men respect, they kill for the afflicted the last consolation of their misery, for

the powerful and rich the only bridle to their passions; they uproot from the bottom of mens' hearts the remorse for crime and the hope of virtue, and yet they boast of being the benefactors of the human race.[14]

Preparatory to a search for a solution, he proceeds to review the three great species of religion which the world has known: the Deism of the individualists, the ancient pagan state-religions and the third, which he calls 'Roman Christianity'.

On the last, he speaks as an advanced nationalist and a citizen of Geneva might be expected. 'Roman Christianity' he condemns and rejects. It is a religion which '. . . giving men two legislations, two chiefs, two homelands, submits them to contradictory obligations and forbids them to be at one and the same time pious men and good citizens', is harmful to men from both the spiritual and the temporal points of view. 'The third', he says, speaking of Roman Christianity, 'is so evidently bad that it is a waste of time to amuse oneself in demonstrating it. Everything that breaks the social unity is worthless; all the institutions that put man in contradiction with himself are worth nothing'.[15] On every ground, doctrinal and emotional, Rousseau was bound to be antipathetic to 'Roman Christianity': its universality, its ages-old association with the Europe of which he so disapproved, the duality of jurisdiction which it introduced, its conflict with his monistic conception of human organization, its 'particularity' within the State, his own antecedents as a member of a family which had been Protestant since the beginning of the Reformation, his own highly romantic temperament.

There remain for consideration the first two species of religion: Deism, 'the religion of the man', and pagan State-religion, 'the religion of the citizen'.

The second, the State-religion

> . . . inscribed in a single land, gives it its gods, its own patrons and tutelaries. It has its dogmas, its rites, its external cult, prescribed by the laws: outside the one nation which follows it, all is infidel, foreign, barbarous: it extends the duties and the rights of man only as far as it extends its altars. Such were all the religions of the earliest peoples, to which the name of divine right, civil or positive, may be given.[16]

The Religion of Patriotism

It is clear that this religion holds attraction for Rousseau: instead of being a source of disunity within the State, it operates invincibly in the direction of unification, sanctifying patriotism, reinforcing solidarity and ensuring for the obligations of citizenship the ingrained respect which men reserve for the commands of divinity.

> The second is good in that it joins the divine cult with the love of the laws and that, making the Fatherland the object of the citizens' adoration, it teaches them that to serve the State is to serve the tutelary god. It is a kind of theocracy in which there is room for no other pontiff than the prince and no other priests than the magistrates. Then, to die for one's country is to become a martyr, to violate the laws is to be impious, to submit a malefactor to the public execration is to consign him to the wrath of the gods: *sacer esto.*[17]

These were the considerations that commended the Roman state-religion to Machiavelli, to whom religion, together with 'good laws and good arms', constituted the foundation of 'the good life' – that is to say, the furtherance of the interests and the promotion of the power of the State. Uninhibited by Rousseau's doctrinal notions, Machiavelli quite frankly accepted the proposition that religion is of value for its 'usefulness' to the State, rather than for its intrinsic truth: that its role is that of an adjunct to State-power.* It should serve the purpose of an 'ideology' without necessarily being true. Neither did he share Rousseau's notion of an infallibly virtuous and humane (and consequently pacific) Sovereign; the nature of Machiavelli's State made morality and concern for truth irrelevant to it.

Committed as he was to certain fundamental propositions regarding man and regarding human organization, Rousseau could not avoid being concerned with truth and morality. Despite, then, the attractions of the old State-religion, he had to reject the system as a whole, for more reasons than one. His primary objection is that the falsehood of the system demolishes every argument that may be advanced in

---

* *Discourses*, I, chs XI–XV. 'It is therefore the duty of princes and heads of republics to uphold the foundations of the religion of their countries, for then it is easy to keep their people religious and consequently well-conducted and united. And therefore everything that tends to favour religion (even though it were believed to be false) should be received and availed of to strengthen it; and this should be done the more, the wiser the rulers and the better they understand the natural course of things' (*The Prince and The Discourses*, p. 150).

favour of its usefulness: it is essentially a deception and, being a falsehood and a superstition in its cardinal articles, many of the beliefs that flow from it are tainted at the source. 'As soon as people are of a mind to made God speak, each one makes Him speak according to his own mode and makes Him say what he himself wishes'.[18] Its practices also too easily degenerate into empty ceremonies; its national exclusiveness militates against international harmony, makes the people who profess it intolerant of others, bloodthirsty and cruel and leads them to live 'in a natural state of war' with neighbours and, consequently, in unceasing insecurity. Nevertheless, the elements of good which it contains ought to be kept in mind.

The private and interior religion, which Rousseau calls Christianity or 'the religion of the man', remains to be considered. Its beauties are manifold. It is a religion of love; it elevates and ennobles the soul in the contemplation of the All-Wise and Omnipotent Creator who has lavished on us miracles of generosity; it makes its devotee see his fellow-men throughout the world as brothers, members of one family whose truest pleasure lies in the worship of the one Father and in the practice of benevolence towards one another. By keeping the truth constantly before the mind of man, it helps him to see all things in their true proportion, neither to magnify nor to minimize his own importance; it makes for the true humility and enables him to root out unsocial passions within himself and check them, by his example, in others. A world of true Christians would have need of neither laws nor government.[19]

But the world as it stands is sadly in need of both. This 'religion of the man' is not a social religion; it has no organization, no centre of authority on earth, no *point d'appui* from which to exercise public influence. It gives no direct support to external political authority.

> But that religion, having no particular relation with the body politic, leaves to the laws only the force they draw from themselves, without adding to them any other, and, by that fact, one of the great bonds of the particular society remains without power. More: far from attaching the hearts of the citizens to the State, it detaches them, as from all the other things of the earth. I know nothing more contrary to the social spirit.[20]

The simple religion of Julie is all too incomplete. Not that Christianity, as Rousseau calls this creed, is positively unsocial, but that,

The Religion of Patriotism

among men as we know them, it is not sufficiently effective to social good, in his judgment.

> Christianity is a totally spiritual religion, occupied solely with the things of heaven: the homeland of the Christian is not of this world. He does his duty, it is true, but he does it with a profound indifference to the good or bad success of his endeavours. Provided that he has nothing to reproach himself with, it matters little to him whether all goes well or ill here below.[21]

Clearly, something more than this is required: a religion that will link the two infallible agents, God and the Sovereign People, and will not refuse some help from the sword; a religion that will reconcile Rousseau the Protestant with Rousseau the nationalist.

At the outset of his search for the principles on which the new religion is to be built, Rousseau takes a turn which may come as a faint surprise to the reader of the *Contrat Social*. When he prefaces his discussion with a whole-hearted approval of d'Argenson's aphorism that 'In the republic, each one is perfectly free in that which harms not others', his democratic absolutism and his nationalistic mysticism seem forgotten for the time being. Indeed, the language in which he lays down the general principles of the State's authority in religious matters was not unfamiliar to the eighteenth-century public.

> The right which the Social Pact gives the Sovereign over the subjects does not pass, as I have said, the limits of public utility. The subjects, then, owe no account to the Sovereign of their opinions, save in so far as these opinions are of import to the community. Now, it is of great import to the community that every citizen have a religion which makes him love his duties; but the dogmas of that religion concern neither the State nor its members only to the extent to which they relate themselves to morality and to the duties which he who professes it is held to fulfil towards others. Everyone may have, over and above these, such opinions as he pleases, of which it appertains not to the Sovereign to take cognizance, for as it has no competence in the other world, whatever be the fate of the subjects in the world to come is none of its affair, provided they are good citizens in this.[22]

Rousseau: Stoic & Romantic

The attentive reader of the *Contrat Social* will recollect, however, what Rousseau said before of 'The limits of the Sovereign power':

> As nature gives to every man an absolute power over all his members, the Social Pact gives to the body politic an absolute power over its members. . . . It is agreed that the portion of his power, his wealth, his liberty, which each one alienates under the Social Pact, is only that of which the use is of import to the community; but it must also be agreed that the Sovereign alone is judge of that importance.[23]

Now, the salvation of souls is not the concern of the State, but, as belief influences morality, the State is bound to be interested in belief, this interest being actuated, not by the desire to save souls, but solely by the desire to preserve order and encourage civic virtue. Such beliefs, then, as persuade the acceptor to practise this virtue are of the utmost value to the State. It is, accordingly, of the highest importance that every member should embrace at least the minimum of those doctrines, common to all the noblest religions, sufficient to promote social morality.

> There is, then, a profession of faith, purely civil, of which it appertains to the Sovereign to fix the articles, not precisely as dogmas of religion, but as sentiments of sociability without which it is impossible to be either a good citizen or a faithful subject. Without being able to persuade anyone to believe in them, it can banish from the State whoever does not hold them: as impious, but as unsociable, as incapable of loving sincerely the laws and justice and of immolating, at need, his life for his duty. If anyone, having recognized publicly these same dogmas, behave as if he did not believe in them, let him be punished by death, for he has committed the greatest of crimes: he has lied before the laws.[24]

The prescription of doctrine appertains, as we note, to the Sovereign. Rousseau, nevertheless, enumerates what he considers a sufficiency to the purpose of promoting the well-being of the social body:

> The dogmas of the Civil Religion ought to be simple, few in number, enunciated with precision, without explanation or commentaries. The existence of the divine power, intelligent,

The Religion of Patriotism

benevolent, foreseeing, providential, the life to come, the happiness of the just, the chastisement of the wicked, the sanctity of the Social Contract and the laws: these are the positive dogmas. As to the negative, I limit them to one: intolerance. It enters into the cults we have excluded.[25]

Every citizen who subscribes to these articles of the secular, national Church ought to be fully free to hold as many additional beliefs as he pleases, with the exception of such as militate against sociability. All that is not contrary to the social spirit has the right to be tolerated: all that is must be rigorously stamped out. Every religious body that pretends to exclusive possession of the truth is the enemy of society. The intolerance of a sect represents the attempt of a particular association to impose its will upon all. Theological intolerance, wherever it is admitted, destroys the sovereignty, dissolves the body politic, violates the Social Pact. Whoever says 'Outside the Church, there is no salvation', ought to be expelled from the State. The Civil Religion ought to command the allegiance of the citizens, because it proceeds from the infallible Sovereign; all that it requires is necessarily of benefit to the body politic and to every member: 'equality of rights and the notions of justice which it produces derive from the preference which each one gives to himself'.[26] To compel the adherence of the subject is to do no more than to 'force him to be free'.

16

The Lawgiver

◆

Seneca tells us that mankind, in the age of innocence, chose its leaders for their moral excellence and freely accepted the guidance of the sages. Even in the early days of its decline, when incipient corruption gave rise to tyranny, and laws were needed to check the increasing evil, the rising despots found it necessary to engage or rely on philosophers to give the State its direction. But these wise men never exercised direct political power: they were not rulers, but guides, and their guidance was accepted because it accorded with the conscience of the masses and won the support of virtuous men. *Hi non in foro nec in consultorum atrio, sed in Pythagorae tacito illo sanctoque seccesu didicerunt iura. . . .*[1]

The idea of the Prophet, the founder of the new nation or the reviver of the old, was familiar. The unresolved question was: should he be armed? The answer depended on one's view of human nature. Seneca, looking back to a golden past, saw his Lawgiver succeeding by force of character. Machiavelli, remembering the fate of Savonarola, decided that he should be armed.* Rousseau, taking the romantic view of Seneca and bound by the principles of the Social Contract, decided that he could not be armed.

Rousseau and Machiavelli, looking at the Europe of their respective times, were at once opposed and in agreement. Both saw corruption and both attributed it to the decline of civic virtue. But the meanings they attached to the term, civic virtue, were not the

---

* 'Thus it comes about that all armed prophets have conquered and unarmed ones failed' (*The Prince and The Discourses*, p. 22).

The Lawgiver

same. To Machiavelli, the natural was the actual, and the actual as far as the State was concerned was expansion and aggression.* Civic virtue, then, consisted in a readiness to do everything necessary to promote the internal order and prosperity of the State and its designs abroad, however immoral they might be from an objective point of view. There was no social contract, no equality, no question of moral infallibility: the only question was the achievement of government policy. Rousseau liked to have the best of both worlds: while embracing an absolutist conception of the State, he could not part with the old morality and so he identified its dictates with the General Will. Civic virtue, then, to Rousseau comprehended duty to the State and devotion to traditional morality: they were, quite comfortably, one and the same thing.

Machiavelli saw corruption producing particularism in the Italy of his time. Rousseau saw it producing an undesirable universalism in his. Machiavelli desired the unification of Italy, Rousseau desired the diversification of Europe, but the motive was the same: the longing for that ideal, so difficult to define, the 'self-determination of peoples'.

The necessity for a national education, according to Rousseau, implies the necessity for a planner. The fatal tendency of society to degenerate and dissolve into unsocial factions cannot be checked by piecemeal reform and uncoordinated measures. The People is 'never corrupted, but often deceived': it wishes always to do the right; but ignorance and passion and the deception so easily practised on men too often blind them and cause them to rush to decisions injurious to their own welfare. The General Will proceeds from the whole people, but how can a people fallen from its original purity undertake so stupendous a task as that of framing a code of laws? How is it to be shown the way of justice which all desire to take? How is it to be placed on guard against the blandishments of skilled intriguers? 'The General Will is always right, but the judgment which guides it is not always enlightened.' Whence can enlightenment come? The problem of the individual *vis-à-vis* society presents itself in this way to Rousseau: 'Individuals see the good they reject: the public desires the good which it does not see. All are equally in need of guides. The

---

* 'The desire to acquire possessions is a very natural and ordinary thing, and when those men do it who can do so successfully, they are always praised and not blamed. . . .' (*The Prince and The Discourses*, p. 13).

former ought to be compelled to conform their wills to their reason: the latter must be taught to know that which it truly wishes. Thus, from the general enlightenment there results the union of the understanding and the will in the social body, and thence, the exact concurrence of all parties and, finally, the greatest force of the whole.'[2]

This supreme task of enlightening a people, of 'clearing the air and sweeping away all the old material', in order to begin everything afresh, belongs to the Lawgiver.

Long before the publication of the *Contrat Social*, Rousseau had in mind the need for a prophet or nation-builder who would so win men to his gospel as to persuade them to put away the vices that had hitherto held them in slavery, to cut themselves entirely away from the evil past, to construct a new and perfect world for themselves.[3] Not, however, until he came to discuss the Lawgiver in the *Contrat Social*, did he develop the idea. In this celebrated chapter, which must certainly be ranked amongst the most influential pieces of writing of all time, he descends to the problem of effecting political and social improvement among men as history knows them, and, with an eye thrown back on classical and later times, proceeds to look into the qualities of the man who would found a nation and give it a permanent mould.

Such a man must, muses Rousseau, be one of the extremest rarity: 'It would require gods to give laws to men'.[4] The nobility and detachment of Plato himself would scarcely suffice. The Lawgiver must be a man who stands out above all others in intellect and in spiritual strength. He must be all-wise and omniscient. The minds of men must be an open book to him, the unaccountable ways of human nature a matter of intimate knowledge. Vice, passion and sin must cause him no embarrassment. He must know the lower nature of man and the incalculable capacities of his higher nature. He must know man's unhappy past and have the vision of the limitless possibilities of happiness which the future holds for a people who are directed in the right path. He must have the infinite knowledge and the immense strength that will enable him to mould men as the potter moulds clay. He must be one who has

> a superior intelligence which perceives all the passions of men without himself having experienced any: who has no resemblance to our nature, but knows it to the very root: whose

The Lawgiver

happiness is independent of ours and who, for all that, is vitally interested in ours: in fine, one who, conducting himself with an eye on a far-off glory, can work in one age and enjoy the fruits in another.[5]

Such a man was Lycurgus and such was Mahomet; nor does Rousseau forget the hero of his own native city of Geneva, 'that great man', Calvin.[6]

Between such men and the wisest of princes, there is a world of difference, for the former create societies out of the heterogeneous mass, the latter are but the creatures of the societies they rule. The Lawgiver is the builder of the social machine, the prince is merely the attendant. The initial movement of the mechanism is imparted by the Lawgiver: its subsequent force for the ages to come is, in a sense, due to the momentum which his first impulsion supplied. As this momentum decreases, society becomes less and less vigorous, until eventually the stand-still is reached and a new reform becomes essential, if the State is not to dissolve and disappear.

The task that awaits the Lawgiver is stupendous: no mere political reform, no patching up of a tottering structure, but a total revolution which will inspire men to sweep away all the institutions that corrupt society, to blot out from memory the ways of the past, to begin again as if their generation were the first to walk the earth, to accept with enthusiasm the creed of unity, solidarity and equality which he would preach and to determine that in future the welfare of the whole should stand paramount and that all attempts at selfish avoidance of duty be rigorously suppressed.

Such a revolution can be achieved only by a radical change in men's hearts. It is there, in the heart of man, that his conquest is made. In this way alone can the undisciplined individual be altered and the social man created. This is the meaning of the total revolution which the Lawgiver personifies.

> He who dares to undertake the making of a people must feel himself able to change, so to speak, human nature itself, to transform each individual who is, in himself, a complete and isolated entity, into a part of a greater entity from which that individual derives his life and his being: to change the constitution of man in order to strengthen it, to substitute a moral existence as a part of the whole for the physical and independent

existence which we have all received from nature. He must, in a word, take away from man his own faculties, to give him those which are foreign to him and of which he can make no use without the aid of others. The more these natural faculties are dead and annihilated, the greater and more durable are those acquired, the more solid and perfect is the institution; so that, if each citizen is nothing and can be nothing save through all the others, and the acquired force of the whole be equal to or greater than the sum of the natural powers of all the individuals, it can be said that the legislation has attained the highest point of perfection possible.[7]

Such an undertaking is far beyond the power of mere physical coercion; it is a task for a prophet, not for a military dictator. The Lawgiver must, therefore, be unarmed with political authority. His function is not that of magistracy nor of sovereignty: he must have no place in the constitution: alike in character and in employment he must be 'an extraordinary man in the State'.

Apart from the impossibility indicated of effecting a radical change in the minds of men by physical coercion, there are, according to Rousseau, two reasons of great weight for this refusal of political authority to the Lawgiver. The first is based on historical experience. Since the function of the Lawgiver is a unique and superhuman one, he must remain remote from the forum, untouched by the details of daily administration, unconcerned with the struggle and compromise that fill the minds of active, lesser men. He must live in the world of contemplation, undistracted by the petty preoccupations of men of affairs.

> For if he who commands the men ought not to command the laws, no more ought he who commands the laws command the men: otherwise, the laws, ministers to his passions, will serve only to perpetuate his injustices and never can he prevent particular views from affecting adversely the holiness of his work.[8]

History, from that of Sparta to that of Geneva, illustrates the importance which men have attached to the necessity for keeping separate the functions of lawgiving and of sovereignty, while the misfortunes of Rome are readily traceable to neglect of this precaution. The second reason is, to Rousseau, more cogent, being based on right. It

The Lawgiver

would be in direct contradiction of his doctrine of sovereignty if Rousseau vested legislative authority in a particular individual. The will of one man, however enlightened, cannot pass for the General Will, which cannot be alienated and cannot be represented. Every proposal of the Lawgiver must, accordingly, receive the sanction of the people before it can become law. Any departure from this strict rule of right invalidates the Social Pact and dissolves the State:

> He who frames the laws has not, or ought not to have, any legislative right; and the people itself cannot, even if it wished, strip itself of this incommunicable right, because, according to the fundamental pact, only the General Will can bind the particular, and it can never be assured that a particular will conforms to the General Will until it has been submitted to the free suffrages of the people. This I have already said: but it is not without use to repeat it.*

Legislative authority being denied him, it remains to be seen whether the Lawgiver can secure popular approval of his proposals by an appeal to the reason of the individual, in which the philosophical radicals placed such high hope. Rousseau, as we know, fails completely to share in this contemporary faith and confesses that he can see no possibility of any mass-conversion of men by the use of reasoned argument alone. The speech of the wise will forever be strange to the simple. Unaccustomed to sustained thought, incapable of self-detachment, devoid of the knowledge and unversed in the habits of the thinker, the generality of mankind follows prejudice and custom. To expect enlightened self-denial and the fortitude that suffers present discomfort in order to reap tenfold in a distant future is to overestimate vastly the powers of men, and any scheme which depends for its fruition on the strength of the unaided reason of man is founded on illusion and doomed to failure. The fundamental error of the philosophers of the Enlightenment is, believes Rousseau, their attribution to the isolated individual of faculties which are the product of the social life: altruism, love of order, devotion to common aims, are

---

* *Contrat Social*, in *Oeuvres*, II, 45: Lenin showed scant respect for 'the free suffrages of the people' and so could not logically be accepted by Rousseau. Yet, he claimed to be the mouthpiece of Marxism and not just an autocratic ruler and claimed also that he asserted the 'real will' of the proletarian masses, whom he called the People. He undoubtedly would, if he troubled to reconcile himself with Rousseau, have affirmed that he was implementing the General Will.

derived in man from the society of which he is part; to attribute them to the natural man is to beg the question and begin the quest with the assumption of what one sets out to seek.

> That a people in process of birth could know the sound maxims of politics and follow the fundamental rules required for the guidance of the State, it is necessary that the effect should become the cause: that the social spirit, which should be the product of the institution, preside at that institution, and that men be, anterior to the institution of the laws, what they ought to become through the operation of these laws.[9]

Nevertheless, one may remark in passing, it was the inexperienced 'primitive' men who drew up the very rigid and comprehensive Social Contract. Here, indeed, we have another instance of the abstract and the historic strands of thought lying very uneasily beside each other in the speculation of Rousseau: the Lawgiver, who should preside at the birth of the State, should possess no portion of sovereignty, because his possession of it would be incompatible with the sovereignty of the people; yet, according to the passage quoted above, a people in process of formation can have no General Will and consequently no sovereignty. Machiavelli, ironically enough, would have approved of the latter affirmation.

The employment of force being forbidden him and the appeal to reason little more than useless, it may well be asked: what means are open to the Lawgiver to accomplish his superhuman work? How is he 'to lead without violence and to persuade without convincing'?

Rousseau's answer is one that has intensely annoyed the rationalists, although it would have been quite acceptable to Machiavelli. The Lawgiver, if he is to win the minds and sentiments of men, must appeal to men's awe of the supernatural. He must use religion as the vehicle of his wisdom and appear to men as the mouthpiece of the gods. Acceptance of his tenets will be based upon faith, rather than upon intellectual conviction. The assurance of divine authority for the truths he teaches will secure conversion where a merely rational course would fail. He is thus, in the eyes of men, no exponent of a mere political scheme, but the inspired preacher of a new religion – a creed of patriotism, akin to the Civil Religion of Rousseau's choice.

> See then what forced the fathers of the nations to have recourse to the intervention of heaven and, in their wisdom, to

The Lawgiver

honour the gods, so that the people, obedient to the laws of the State as to the laws of nature, and recognizing the same agency in the formation of the man and in that of the State, obey with liberty and bear with docility the yoke of the public felicity.[10]

For the enduring success of such a mission, the tricks of charlatanry and the appeal to the superstitious will be far from sufficient. The religion which the Lawgiver calls to his aid must be marked by a grandeur which secures the allegiance of man's higher nature and supplies the deepest and most lasting satisfaction of his spiritual needs. If miracle be needed to impress the minds of men, then the Lawgiver himself must appear to them as the greatest miracle of all. 'The great soul of the Lawgiver is the true miracle which ought to prove his mission.'[11]

Good law is to Rousseau not only the life of the State, but its very origin: it was born of the Social Contract. Force ought to be the mere servant of law. In the ideal polity of Rousseau's imagining, law is the creator of force; it is antecedent to it in every sense. To Machiavelli, 'good arms and good laws' are the life of the body politic, but 'good arms' are necessary to the production of good laws and take precedence. The State was founded by arms, and when its purification is necessary, arms are essential. Only when arms have done their work do good laws begin their role. No General Will exists when the prophet-prince becomes necessary; he imposes his will and this will of his carries society forward to the stage at which it develops a corporate will and becomes fit to live by law. The doctrine of the Social Contract and the conception of the unarmed Lawgiver, Machiavelli would dismiss as pieces of sentimentality, as he would dismiss the conception on which all Rousseau's political theory is ultimately based: that of the natural goodness of man.

17

The Person & the Collectivity

'The cause of evil', wrote Rousseau to the Archbishop of Paris, 'is, according to you, corrupted nature: that very corruption is the evil, the cause of which must be sought. Man was created good: we agree, both of us, I believe, as to that: but you say that he is wicked because he has been wicked: as for me, I show how he has become wicked. Which of us, in your opinion, goes back the further to beginnings?' The Archbishop went back to Original Sin. Rousseau went back to romance. Even the disbeliever in the doctrine of Original Sin cannot say that Rousseau went back further than the Archbishop, or that he showed how men became wicked: evolutionists would have reversed him and dismissed the Age of Innocence. Discarding, on his own avowal, 'all the theories of the schools', laying aside 'the teachings of religion' and 'the observations of the scientists', he conjectured, again on his own avowal, 'by the use alone of logic and feeling', the nature of man and the lot of humanity. His conjecture led him at first to the figment of 'natural man', isolated and barely recognizable as human, but entirely self-sufficient morally, and later to the Golden Age of innocence, love and idleness. Conjecture led him to see the first appearance of evil in the first moment of human self-consciousness. Thenceforward, he sees the history of mankind down through the ages in the Manichaean terms of a struggle between two principles, good and evil: beneficent Nature and debased human reason. Rousseau's experience was the common experience of man: 'I do not the good; but the evil that I do not wish, that I perform'. He faced the same question: 'Unhappy man that I am! Who will deliver me from the body of this death?'

The Person & the Collectivity

The Christian answer was given by St Paul: 'And if the Spirit of him who raised Jesus from the dead dwelleth within you, then he who raised Jesus from the dead will also bring to life your mortal bodies through his Spirit who dwelleth within you'. The Christian agrees with Rousseau when he says that 'All justice comes from God; he alone is its source', but the Christian affirms that we can 'receive justice from so high a source' and yet need 'both government and laws', for the latter are, or ought to be, the human aids to justice; but the perfection of justice comes through the Grace of God and the representative of God on earth and the great channel of grace is, to the Catholic Christian, the Catholic Church. From the belief, common to all Christians, in a personal, transcendental God, stems the affirmation of the existence of an objective, God-given moral law, the acceptance of the necessity of human authority, subject to that law and restricted by it to the promotion of justice and the common good, and, on the part of Catholic Christians, of the special place of the Church in all societies as the link between God and man and the custodian and interpreter of the moral law. These are the historic origins of the principle of duality of jurisdiction and the principle of constitutionality which have played so great a part in the development of western civilization.

There is, and can be, no infallible human institution: all human agencies, from the lowliest to the greatest, are subject to the moral law. There can never be a human legislature that needs no restriction: man is subject to error and no calculation of self-interest and no development of sensibility can guarantee him from it. There is no human omnicompetence and consequently no rightful place for a monistic polity: a polity, that is, in which a single agency is visualized as possessing the right to regulate all concerns. Communities are complex things in which men work for a plurality of ends: supernatural or religious, cultural, economic and social; there is a hierarchy of ends, and so there ought to be a hierarchy of means. Plurality of ends demands plurality of means, each promoted by a distinctive form of association. Every such association, then, is entitled to the measure of autonomy or liberty requisite to the performance of its function. *Right* being the means to the performance of *duty*, its recognition is the fundamental of liberty. The State, or political authority, essential as it is, is but one form of human organization: its function is to protect and assist society and its true role is to co-ordinate the activities of other associations, never to absorb them.

Rousseau: Stoic & Romantic

The great difficulty to the interpreter of Rousseau is his chameleon-like language: 'I hold that I do not contradict myself in my ideas, but I cannot refuse to admit that I often contradict myself in my expressions'.[1] Nowhere is this quality more evident than in some of his references to God and to that providence which he calls Nature. 'All justice comes from God; he alone is its source.' This statement might have come from the most orthodox Christian and, in itself, clearly implies belief in a transcendental God. But again, we have: 'O, Nature! O, my mother! Behold me under your sole guardianship: there is here no cunning man to interpose himself between thee and me'.[2] Whatever the overtones of such expressions, there can, however, be no doubt that he rejects the principle of religious authority on earth; even the Sovereign People of his ideal State may regulate religious profession *in foro externo* only, and that for utilitarian or earthly reasons. Whatever his idea of God, there is no place for an external religious link between the Supreme Being and the individual man; there is, therefore, no place for an authoritative Church in private or in public life. Who, then, can deliver us from 'the body of this death'?

His answer is that we ourselves can do so, individually or collectively. Nature, or beneficent providence, has given each one of us the power to make himself into an Émile or a Man of Nature: it is a simple matter of closing the entries of vice and following uncorrupted instinct. The romance of *Émile* is matched only by that of the *Contrat Social*: in the former case, perfection is attained by the individual and through the individual; in the latter, by the collectivity and through the collectivity. The antithesis of anarchism and totalitarianism is much more apparent than real – one attributes moral self-sufficiency to the individual; the other to the collectivity – but once self-sufficiency is attributed to any human agency, it can easily be switched to any other; the change is simply the transfer of an attribute. 'All the philosophers', declared Bakunin, after a lifetime of anarchism, 'had gone astray through treating man as an individual instead of as part of a collectivity.'[3] This is precisely the switch Rousseau made. The generality of men could not receive the education of an Émile. Neither could they emulate Jean-Jacques, the Man of Nature. The third way was to lose themselves in a collectivity which would ensure automatic and effortless compliance with the *recta ratio* or the dictates of uncorrupted instinct, which are the same thing: this is the General

The Person & the Collectivity

Will of the ideal State. This was the easier way, since, within the collectivity, weak man could be 'forced to be free', forced to obey his higher self, and therefore freer than before. Moral responsibility would be handed over and all would be well. The spirit of man would no longer reside in the individual, but in the group. The abdication of moral responsibility would remove all tensions within the individual and so, personal happiness and general tranquillity would automatically ensue. The Stoic ideal of moral perfection and the personal happiness that accompanies it would be achieved by a method undreamt of by the Stoics. This is the romance of the *Contrat Social*.

The stoical Émile and the infallible Sovereign People are both figments that spring from a basically pantheistic or Manichaean view of life: from the view that there is an ideal harmony underlying the historic process, a harmony that lies ready to hand. We have but to remove the accretions with which the debased human reason and the perverted passions have covered it ('our social institutions') and it will emerge: the millennium will be here. It will be here on earth, and mankind will be spared all further struggle. The only question is one of means: shall it come through the assertion of individual autonomy or through collectivization?

The fundamental distinction among political thinkers is not that between democrat and authoritarian, for a man may be either of these through force of local circumstances or for psychological reasons and yet entertain the Christian conception of authority and maintain the Christian belief in the objectivity of law; nor is it that between extreme libertarianism or anarchism, on the one hand, and the most abject of despot-worship, on the other, for there is a pessimistic as well as an optimistic naturalism. The fundamental distinction is between transcendentalist and immanentist: between him who would seek the source and sanction of authority in a principle outside and above humanity and him who would not.

Anarchism is incompatible with the recognition of the naturalness of social and communal life and of the essential, and not merely substitutional, function of authority: a recognition based on the belief in a personal God, in the objectivity of law, the rationality of man, the freedom of the will and the greatness of the part which contingency plays in the world. Authority can never take the form of an impersonal necessity; coercion is but an instrument of authority and cannot be identified with it as such. The notion of the existence of social 'laws' immanent in the course of social events and compulsive on the human will as soon as evident to the reason is irreconcilable with the principles of any non-determinist system: an anarchist paradise wherein automatic obedience to determined laws takes the place of the acceptance by the individual person of the guidance of divine or human agency would be one from which human freedom, and consequently human worth and dignity, are excluded. Where obedience is automatic, there is no freedom, and therefore no responsibility and no moral worth. Likewise, supra-personal conceptions of society, issuing in collectivism, and the arbitrary conceptions of authority that flow, or, rather, are wrenched from them, cannot be reconciled with any of the traditional principles of belief or morality. Anarchism and collectivism have at least one feature in common: the rejection of personal moral responsibility, which is the quality on which human freedom rests.

It is an irony that Stoic thought, even in modified form and received in large part indirectly, should have been so metamorphosed by Rousseau; but Stoicism was a naturalistic system and, given a change of circumstances, a naturalistic system may well undergo a metamorphosis. It encountered the temperaments of Montaigne and Rousseau in the course of its passage from the old to the modern world; what was basically more significant, it passed into a new world – a world in which its explosive content was likely to be released.

References

Please see p. vii for list of abbreviations used.

Introduction

1. Georges Pire, 'De l'influence de Sénèque sur les théories pédagogiques de J.-J. Rousseau.' *Annales de la Société Jean-Jacques Rousseau* (1953–5), Vol. 33, pp. 86, 87.
2. Peter D. Jimack, 'La genèse et la rédaction de l'Émile de J.-J. Rousseau.' *Studies in Voltaire and the Eighteenth Century* (1960), Vol. 13, pp. 350–3.
3. Rousseau, *Discours* in *Oeuvres*, tome XIII, pp. 17, 56, 117.
4. Seneca, *Ep.* 90 (4).
5. *Émile* in *Oeuvres*, VI, 14, 15.
6. *Contrat* in *Oeuvres*, II, 16.
7. Ibid., 100–1.
8. *Écon. Pol.* in *Oeuvres*, I, 178.
9. Ibid., 179.
10. Ibid., 178.
11. Ibid., 189.
12. *Contrat* in *Oeuvres*, II, 39.
13. *Émile* in *Oeuvres*, VII, 279.
14. *Gouv. Pol.* in *Oeuvres*, II, 225.
15. Godwin, *Political Justice*, Vol. I, p. 181.
16. Joseph B. Mayor, *M. Tullii Ciceronis: De Natura Deorum*, Vol. I, pp. xxx, xxxi.
17. Godwin, op. cit., p. 24.

Chapter 1

1. Rousseau, *Inégalité* in *Oeuvres*, tome I, p. 38.
2. *Summa Theologica*, Vol. 7, p. 22; Aristotle, *Physics*, Bk II, ch. 1 (pp. 23–6 in W. Charlton's translation); Aristotle, *Metaphysics*, Bk V, chs. 4 and 30 (Tredennick, 219–23 and 291).
3. Aristotle, *Metaphysics*, V, chs. 4–30 (McKeon, 755–11); *Physics*, I and II (McKeon, 218–52).
4. *De Ente et Essentia*, c. I (*Opuscula Omnia necnon Opera Minora*, ed. J. Perrier (Paris: Lethielleux, 1949), p. 26.
5. *Summa Theologica*, 7, pp. 22, 49.
6. Ibid., 7, pp. 29, 155–6 and 450.
7. Cicero, *De re pub.*, Bk III, p. xxii; *De nat. deorum*, Bk II, pp. xxxv, 90, *etc.*
8. *De re pub.*, III, xxii; Seneca, *Ep.* 124, *etc.*; Cicero, *De leg.*, II, iv, 8, 9, 10, *etc.*

References

9. Cicero, *De leg.*, V, *et seq.*
10. Seneca, *Ep.* 44, 47, 117, 121, 124; Cicero, *De leg.*, I, xvi, xvii; Cicero, *De nat. deorum*, II, xii, xiii.
11. Seneca, *Nat. Quaes.*, Bk II, pp. xxxv–xxxviii.
12. Seneca, *Ep.* 107, 11–12.
13. 'Spirit of Nature, all-sufficing Power, Necessity, Thou mother of the World.'
Shelley, 'Queen Mab', Part VI, ll. 197–8. (*The Complete Poetical Works of Percy Bysshe Shelley*, ed. Thomas Hutchinson, Oxford University Press, p. 786.)
14. Cicero, *De nat. deorum*, II, xiv.
15. Seneca, *Ep.* 75, 18.
16. Seneca, *Nat. Quaes.*, II, xxxviii.
17. See editorial note to p. xxxviii, *Nat. Quaes*, ed. P. Oltramare (Paris: Collection Budé, 1929), t. I, p. 88.
18. Cicero, *De nat. deorum*, II, xiv.
19. Rousseau, *Sur le luxe*, in Streckeisen-Moultou, p. 250.
20. Seneca, *Ep.* 90, 4.
21. Ibid., 5.
22. Ibid., 16.
23. Ibid., 44.
24. Ibid., 38.
25. Cicero, *De leg.*, I, xxiv, 62; III, 2–3; and *De re pub.*, I, xx, 33, *etc.* Seneca, *Ep.* 66 (10), 73 (2).
26. Seneca, *Thyestes* in *Thyestes-Phaedra*, ed. H. Moriocca, ll. 877–9.
27. Seneca, *De Ira*, livre II, ch. xiii (quoted by Rousseau in epigraph to *Émile* in *Oeuvres*, VI).
28. Rousseau, *Lettre à Christophe* in *Oeuvres*, VIII, 55–6.
29. Cicero, *De nat. deorum*, II, liii, 133, *etc.*
30. Seneca, *Ep.* 104; 116, 7; 117; 124, *etc.*
31. Ibid., 48 (2).
32. Rousseau, *Pensées détachées* in Streckeisen-Moultou, p. 351.
33. Seneca, *Ep.* 90, 4.
34. Diderot, *Essais sur les règnes de Claude et de Néron* in Diderot *Oeuvres Complètes*, III, 233–4.
35. Ibid., 196.
36. Montaigne, 'The days when I read', *The Autobiography of Montaigne* transl. and ed. Marvin Lowenthal (London: Routledge, 1955), pp. 140, 141.
37. 'The Life of Plutarch' in Plutarch's *Lives*, p. xx; K. M. Westaway, *The Educational Theory of Plutarch*, pp. 12, 168, *et seq.*; Plutarch, *Select Essays*, Vol. II, pp. 136, 146, 147, 264, 266, 285.
38. Ernest Seillière, *Les Origines romanesques de la morale et de la politique romantique*, p. 167.
39. Pierre Villey, *Les Sources et l'évolution des essais de Montaigne*, Vol. II, pp. 522, *et seq.*
40. Ibid., 218, 219; *Autobiography*, 332, *etc.*; 'A man from the New World', *Autobiography*.
41. Émile Faguet, *Rousseau Penseur*, p. 27.
42. Villey, op. cit., II, p. 111.
43. *Confessions* in *Oeuvres*, XV, 107.

Chapter 2

1. Salvador de Madariaga, *The Fall of the Spanish-American Empire*, p. 222 *et seq.*
2. *Émile* in *Oeuvres*, VI, 12–14.
3. Ibid., 336 *et seq.*
4. Ibid., 9.
5. *Lettre à Christophe*, in *Oeuvres*, VIII. 14.
6. Ibid., 18.
7. Ibid., 19–21.
8. Ibid., 55–6.

References

Chapter 3

1. *Inégalité* in *Oeuvres*, I, 61.
2. Ibid., 50 *et seq.*
3. Godwin, *Political Justice*, Vol. II, pp. 70 and 71.
4. *Discours Dijon*, in *Oeuvres*, XIII, 18–19.
5. *Inégalité* in *Oeuvres*, I, 84.
6. Ibid., 91, 94–5, 99; and 'There could be no injury where property is unknown.' (p. 85).
7. Ibid., 91.
8. Ibid., 94–5.
9. Ibid., 95.
10. Ibid., 99.
11. Ibid., 107 *et seq.* and 112, 113.

Chapter 4

1. *Inégalité* in *Oeuvres*, I, 62 *et seq.*; *Dial.* II in *Oeuvres*, XVI, 197, etc.
2. *Émile* in *Oeuvres*, VI, 305.
3. *Lettre à Christophe* in *Oeuvres*, VIII, 15.
4. *Émile*, in *Oeuvres*, VII, 59.
5. Ibid., 57.
6. *Nouv. Hel.* in *Oeuvres*, III, 343.
7. *Inégalité* in *Oeuvres*, I, 134.
8. Lettre à Christophe, in *Oeuvres*, VIII, 15.
9. Ibid., 16.
10. *Émile* in *Oeuvres*, VII, 110.
11. Ibid. in *Oeuvres*, VI, 135.
12. Ibid., 97. Cf. *Dial.* II in *Oeuvres*, XVI, 224. Of Rousseau himself: 'He bears without reluctance the yoke of the necessity of things, but not that of the will of men.'
13. *Émile* in *Oeuvres*, VI, 130, 131.
14. Ibid. in *Oeuvres*, VII, 130.
15. Ibid., 397.
16. Ibid. in *Oeuvres*, VI, 109.
17. Ibid., 244, 332.
18. Ibid., 98–9.
19. Ibid., 104, 105.
20. Ibid., 110.
21. Ibid. in *Oeuvres*, VII, 130.
22. Ibid. in *Oeuvres*, VI, 262.
23. Ibid., 108.
24. Ibid., 275.
25. Ibid., 332.
26. Ibid., 293.
27. Ibid., 322.
28. Ibid., 375.
29. Ibid., 375 *et seq.*
30. Ibid., 111; *Lettre à Christophe* in *Oeuvres*, VIII, 14; *Dial.* I in *Oeuvres*, XVI, 11, *etc.*
31. Émile in *Oeuvres*. VII, 399.
32. Ibid., 23 *et seq.*, 43, 65, 66 *et seq.*
33. Ibid., 33.
34. Ibid. in *Oeuvres*, VI, 426; in VII, 67, 165, 229.

Chapter 5

1. In *Oeuvres*, IX, 74 *et seq.* See also *Narcisse* in *Oeuvres*, IX, 215.
2. *Nouv. Hel.* in *Oeuvres*, III, 322.
3. Ibid., 264.
4. Ibid. in *Oeuvres*, V, 4.
5. Ibid., 18.
6. *Émile* in *Oeuvres*, VI, 67; *Dial.* II in *Oeuvres*, XVI, 197.
7. *Nouv. Hel.* in *Oeuvres*, IV, 93n.
8. Ibid. in *Oeuvres* III, 23–4.
9. Ibid., 407–8.

Chapter 6

1. *Confessions* in *Oeuvres*, XV, 188.
2. *Lettre à Duclos* in *Oeuvres*, XIX, 95; *Dial.* in *Oeuvres*, XVI, 164, 170 *et seq.*
3. *Dial.* II in XVI, 229.
4. Ibid., 224.

References

5. Ibid., 175–6.
6. *Nouv. Hel.* in *Oeuvres*, IV, 45, etc.
7. *Lettre à Duclos* in *Oeuvres*, XIX, 95. See also *Première Lettre à Malesherbes* in XVII, 8; *Lettre à Moultou* in XVIII. 385; *Dial.* II in XVI, 202–3.
8. *Dial.* I in XVI, 10–11.
9. *Confessions* in *Oeuvres*, XIV, 202.

Chapter 7

1. *Écon. Pol.* in *Oeuvres*, I, 172, 175.
2. Ibid., 172.
3. Ibid., 177–221. Cf. also *Lettre à d'Alembert* in *Oeuvres*, IX, 146.
4. *Écon. Pol.* in *Oeuvres* I, 180 et seq.
5. Ibid., 176.
6. Ibid., 177.
7. *Contrat* in *Oeuvres*, II, 4.
8. Ibid., 5.
9. Ibid., 15.
10. Ibid., 16.
11. Ibid., chs. vi, vii, *etc.*
12. Ibid., 16.
13. Ibid., 17 *et seq.*; ch. viii, 21, 22, 26, 35 and 57; *Dial.* II in *Oeuvres*, XVI, 224 *et seq.*
14. *Émile* in *Oeuvres*, VII, 377–8.
15. *Fragments des institutions politiques: Des conditions du bonheur d'un peuple*, in Streckeisen-Moultou, p. 224.
16. *Contrat* in *Oeuvres*, II, 17.
17. Ibid., 17, 18.

Chapter 8

1. *Contrat* in *Oeuvres*, II, 30, 31 and 33.
2. *Écol. Pol.* in *Oeuvres*, I, 180.
3. Ibid. 184.
4. *Sur le luxe*, in Steckeisen-Moultou, p. 250.
5. *Écon. Pol.* in *Oeuvres*, I, 177.
6. Ibid., 178. The term 'good' here appears to bear a utilitarian significance.
7. Ibid.
8. Ibid., 178–9.
9. Ibid., 185.
10. Ibid., 196.
11. *Contrat* in *Oeuvres* II, 39.
12. Colm Kiernan, 'Science and the Enlightenment in eighteenth-century France.' *Studies on Voltaire and the Eighteenth Century*, Geneva, Institut et Musée Voltaire (1968), Vol. LIX, pp. 174–5.
13. *Écon. Pol.* in *Oeuvres* I, 186.
14. Ibid., 189.
15. J. S. Mill, *Representative Government*, ch. xvii.
16. *Econ. Pol.* in *Oeuvres*, I, 181, 185.
17. Ibid., 196.
18. *Contrat* in *Oeuvres*, II, 21.
19. Ibid.

Chapter 9

1. *Contrat* in *Oeuvres*, II, 117.
2. Godwin, *The Principles of Political Justice*, Vol. II, 140–1.
3. *Contrat* in *Oeuvres*, II, 117.
4. Ibid., 40.
5. Ibid., 30, 33–4; see also *Émile* in *Oeuvres*, VII, 377–8.
6. *Contrat* in *Oeuvres*, II, 33–4.
7. Ibid., 30.
8. *Écon. Pol.* in *Oeuvres*, I, 184–5.
9. *Contrat* in *Oeuvres*, II, 27.
10. Ibid., 30.
11. Ibid. 30–1.
12. Ibid., 31.
13. Ibid., 119–20.
14. Ibid., 121

References

15. Ibid., 121–2.
16. Ibid., 122.
17. Ibid., 122–3.
18. Ibid., 33, 34.
19. Ibid., 34; see also *Émile* in *Oeuvres*, VII, 378.
20. *Contrat* in *Oeuvres*, II, 40.
21. Ibid., 33.

Chapter 10

1. *Contrat* in *Oeuvres*, II, 32.
2. Ibid., 33.
3. Ibid., 20.
4. Ibid., 60.
5. Ibid., 20–1.
6. W. Belfort Bax, *The Last Episode of the French Revolution*, p. 215.
7. *Écon. Pol.* in *Oeuvres*, I, 210.
8. *Contrat* in *Oeuvres*, II, 22.
9. *Émile* in *Oeuvres*, VII, 378.
10. *Contrat* in *Oeuvres*, II, 22 and 23.
11. Ibid., 23.
12. Ibid.
13. Ibid., 24.
14. Ibid., 25.
15. Ibid., 25, 35, 58, 59, *etc.*
16. See p. 131 *et seq.*
17. *Contrat* in *Oeuvres*, II, 25; see also *Écon. Pol.* in *Oeuvres*, I, 195, 200, 220.
18. *Contrat* in *Oeuvres*, II, 25n.
19. Émile Faguet, *La Politique comparée de Montesquieu, de Rousseau et de Voltaire*, p. 100.
20. André Lichtenberger, *Le Socialisme et la Revolution Française*.
21. Thomas Paine, 'Agrarian justice' in *Miscellaneous Works*, p. 8 *et seq.*; see also 'A dissertation on the first principles of government, p. 18; *The Rights of Man*, Pt II, pp. 78 *et seq.*
22. Godwin, *The Principles of Political Justice*, Vol. I, Bk. III, chs. iv, v, vii; Vol. II, Bk. VII, chs. i, ii, iii, iv, v and vi.
23. *Contrat* in *Oeuvres*, II, 36, 37.
24. Ibid., 37.

Chapter 11

1. *Contrat* in *Oeuvres*, II, chs. i and ii.
2. Ibid., pp. 111–12.
3. Ibid., 112.
4. Ibid., 62, 101.
5. Ibid., 26, 108.
6. Ibid., 63.
7. Ibid.
8. Ibid., 113.
9. Ibid.

Chapter 12

1. *Contrat* in *Oeuvres*, II, 67.
2. Ibid., 66.
3. Ibid., 67–8.
4. Ibid., chs. ii–vi, viii, xii, xiii, *etc.* See also *Gouv. Pol.* in *Oeuvres*, II, chs. v and vii; *Jugement sur la paix perpetuelle* in *Oeuvres*, I, 262 *et seq.*; *Jugement sur la Polysynodie* in *Oeuvres*, I, 299 *et seq.*
5. *Contrat* in *Oeuvres*, II, 69–71.
6. Ibid., 72.
7. Ibid., 66.

References

Chapter 13

1. *Contrat* in *Oeuvres*, II, 86.
2. Ibid., 73–4; see also *Émile* in *Oeuvres*, VII, 384–6.
3. *Contrat* in *Oeuvres*, II, ch. iv.
4. Ibid., 74.
5. Cf. *Narcisse* in *Oeuvres*, IX, 220–5.
6. *Contrat* in *Oeuvres*, II, 75.
7. Ibid., 76.
8. *La Corse* in Streckeisen-Moultou, 67.
9. Ibid., 65.
10. Ibid., 71–2.
11. *Contrat* in *Oeuvres*, II, 77.
12. Ibid., 77–8.
13. John Locke, *Second Essay Concerning Civil Government*, ch. xiii.
14. *Contrat* in *Oeuvres*, II, 80.
15. Ibid., 83, *et seq*.
16. Ibid., 83–4. Topic discussed at length in *Gouv. Pol.*, *Oeuvres*, II, ch. viii.
17. *Contrat* in *Oeuvres*, II, 84–5.
18. *Gouv. Pol.* in *Oeuvres*, II, 196.
19. *Contrat* in *Oeuvres*, II, 108 *et seq*.
20. *La Corse* in Streckeisen-Moultou, 122.
21. *Contrat* in *Oeuvres*, II, 116.
22. *Inégalité* in *Oeuvres*, I, 98.
23. *Jugement sur la paix perpetuelle* in *Oeuvres*, I, 262–74.
24. *Narcisse* in *Oeuvres*, IX, 222–3; see also *Dial. III* in *Oeuvres*, XVI, 339.
25. *Gouv. Pol.* in *Oeuvres*, II, 187.
26. *Contrat* in *Oeuvres*, II, 104–5; see also *Nouv. Hel.* in Oeuvres, III, 23–4.
27. *La Corse* in Streckeisen-Moultou, 67.

Chapter 14

1. *Contrat* in *Oeuvres*, II, 50–2.
2. Alfred Cobban, *Rousseau and the Modern State*, p. 108.
3. *Contrat* in *Oeuvres*, II, 102, 103.
4. Godwin, *The Principles of Political Justice*, Vol. II, 100 *et seq*.
5. Ibid., 92–3.
6. Shelley, 'Prometheus Unbound', Act III, sc. iv, ll. 193–7 (Hutchinson, p. 253).
7. *Contrat* in *Oeuvres*, II: chapters on 'The death of the body politic', 'The means of preventing usurpations of governments', 'Of suffrages' and 'Of elections'.
8. Ibid., 116.
9. Ibid., chs. vi, vii, *etc*.
10. Ibid., 122–3.
11. Ibid., 104.
12. Ibid., 110.
13. *Political Justice*, Vol. II, 100 *et seq*.
14. *Econ. Pol.* in *Oeuvres*, I, 180–221.
15. *Contrat* in *Oeuvres*, II, 60; see also *La Corse* in Streckeisen-Moultou, 67, *etc*.
16. *Écon. Pol.* in *Oeuvres*, I, 195.
17. Ibid., 218.
18. Ibid., 210; cf. *Émile* in *Oeuvres*, VII, 378 *et seq*.

Chapter 15

1. *Gouv. Pol.*, *Oeuvres* III, 166.
2. Ibid., 172–3.
3. Ibid., chs. ii–iv.
4. Ibid., 172.
5. Ibid., 166.
6. Ibid., 172; see especially chs. ii–iv.
7. *Écon. Pol.* in *Oeuvres*, I, 196–200. Cf. *Gouv. Pol.* in *Oeuvres*, II, chs. ii–iv, *etc*.

References

8. *Écon. Pol.* in *Oeuvres*, I, 197.
9. Ibid., 198.
10. *Gouv. Pol.*, *Oeuvres*, II, 180.
11. *Contrat* in *Oeuvres*, II, 150.
12. Ibid., 151 *et seq.*
13. Ibid.
14. *Émile* in *Oeuvres*, VII, 100–1.
15. *Contrat* in *Oeuvres*, II, 153.
16. Ibid., 152–3.
17. Ibid., 153.
18. *Émile* in *Oeuvres*, VII, 68.
19. *Contrat* in *Oeuvres*, II, 154; cf. 'Profession de foi du vicaire savoyard' in *Émile*, *Oeuvres*, VII, 12–105.
20. *Contrat*, in *Oeuvres*, II, 154.
21. Ibid., 155.
22. Ibid., 157–8.
23. Ibid., 32.
24. Ibid., 158.
25. Ibid., 158–60.
26. Ibid., 33.

Chapter 16

1. *Ep.* 90, 6.
2. *Contrat* in *Oeuvres*, II, 42; cf. *Gouv. Pol.*, *Oeuvres*, II, ch. vii.
3. *Inégalité* in *Oeuvres*, I, 98; *Seconde lettre à Malesherbes* in *Oeuvres*, XVII, 8–13; 'See how I became an author almost in spite of myself'.
4. *Contrat* in *Oeuvres*, II, 43.
5. Ibid.
6. Ibid., 43–7.
7. Ibid., 43–4.
8. Ibid., 44.
9. Ibid., 46.
10. Ibid.
11. Ibid., 47.

Chapter 17

1. *Emile* in *Oeuvres*, VI, 141–2n.
2. *Confessions* in *Oeuvres*, XV, 488.
3. E. H. Carr, *Michael Bakunin*, p. 487.

Bibliography

Editions

Oeuvres complètes de Jean-Jacques Rousseau (20 vols.) Paris: Didot, 1801.
Oeuvres et correspondence inédités de Jean-Jacques Rousseau, ed. Georges Streckeisen-Moultou. Paris: Michel Lewers Frères, 1861.

Translations

Confessions, with an Introduction by R. Niklaus. London: Dent (*Everyman*, 859–60).
Confessions, trans. J. M. Cohen. Harmondsworth: Penguin, 1970.
Émile, with an Introduction by Peter D. Jimack. London: Dent (*Everyman*, 1518).
Eloisa (3 vols.) New York: Lennox Hill, 19—. (A reprint of the 1761 English edition of *Nouvelle Heloïse*).
Political Writings of Rousseau (2 vols.), ed. C. E. Vaughan. Cambridge University Press, 1915.
Political Writings, trans. and ed. F. Watkins. Edinburgh: Nelson, 1953.
Reveries of a Solitary, trans. J. G. Fletcher. London: Routledge (*Broadway Library of 18th-century French literature*), 1927.
The Social Contract, trans. M. Cranston. Harmondsworth: Penguin, 1969.
The Social Contract and Discourses, with an Introduction by G. D. H. Cole. London: Dent (*Everyman*, 660).

AQUINAS, ST THOMAS, *Opuscula Omnia necnon Minora*, ed. J. Perrier. Paris: Lethielleux, 1949.
—— *Summa Theologica*, Dominican translation, Vol. 7. London: Washbourne, 1913.
ARDREY, ROBERT, *The Social Contract*. London: Collins, 1970.
ARISTOTLE, *Basic Works*, ed. Richard McKeon. New York: Random House, 1941.

Bibliography

— *Metaphysics*, trans. H. Tredennick. London: Heinemann (*Loeb Classics*), 1961 (Bks. I–IX), 1962 (Bks. X–XIV).
— *Politics*, ed. Sir Ernest Barker. Oxford University Press, 1952.
— *Politics and Athenian Constitution*, ed. John Warrington, London: Dent, 1959.
 Politics (Bks. III and IV), trans. and ed. Richard Robinson, Oxford University Press, 1962.
 Physics, with an Introduction and Commentary by W. D. Ross. Oxford University Press, 1936.
 Physics (Bks. I and II), transl. with an Introduction and Notes by W. Charlton. Oxford University Press (Clarendon Aristotle Series), 1970.
BELFORT, BAX, W., *The Last Episode of the French Revolution*. London: Grant Richards, 1911.
BEVAN, EDWYN, *Stoics and Epicureans*. Oxford University Press, 1913.
BENTHAM, JEREMY, *Collected Works* (Vols. I and III), ed. John Bowing. Edinburgh: Tait, 1843.
BRINTON, CRANE, *Political Ideas of the English Romanticists*. Oxford University Press, 1926.
BROOME, J. H. *Rousseau: A Study of his Thought*. London: Edward Arnold, 1963.
BURKE, EDMUND, 'Reflections on the Revolution in France', in *Works*, Vol. II. London: Bell & Sons, 1882.
CARR, E. H., *Michael Bakunin*. London: Macmillan, 1937.
CARRIT, E. F., *Morals and Politics*. Oxford University Press, 1935.
CHAPMAN, J. W., *Rousseau, Totalitarian or Liberal?* New York: Columbia University Press, 1956.
CHARPENTIER, JOHN, *Rousseau, the Child of Nature*. London: Methuen, 1931.
CICERO, *De Re Publica, De Legibus*. London: Heinemann (Loeb Classical Library), 1952.
— *De Natura Deorum*. London: Heinemann (Loeb Classical Library), 1952.
COBBAN, ALFRED, *Rousseau and the Modern State*. London: Allen & Unwin, 1934.
——, *Dictatorship, Its History and Theory*. London: Cape, 1939.
——, 'New light on the political thought of Rousseau', *Science Quarterly* (1951), Vol. 66, pp. 272–84.
COHN, NORMAN, *The Pursuit of the Millennium*. London: Granada, Paladin, 1970.
COMPAYRE, GABRIEL, *J.-J. Rousseau and Education from Nature*, transl. R. P. Jago, London: Harrap, 1908.
COPLESTON, FREDERICK, *A History of Philosophy*, Vols. 1, 7 and 8. London: Burns, Oates, 1952–66.
COUNSON, ALBERT, 'L'influence de Sénèque le philosophe', *Musée Belge* (1903), Vol. 7, pp. 132–67.
DAVIDSON, W. L., *Political Thought in England: The Utilitarians from Bentham to J. S. Mill*. London: William & Norgate, 1919.
DIDEROT, DENIS, 'Essais sur les règnes de Claude et de Néron', in *Oeuvres Complètes*, Vol. 3. Paris: Garnier Frères, 1875.
ELIADE, MIRCEA, *Myths, Dreams and Mysteries*. London: Collins (Fontana Library), 1968.
ENGELS, F., *Socialism, Utopian and Scientific*, transl. E. Aveling. London: Swan, Sonnenscheim, 1892.

Bibliography

EPSTEIN, JOHN, *The Catholic Tradition of the Law of Nations.* London: Burns, Oates, 1935.

EYRE, EDWARD, *European Civilization, Its Origin and Development*, Vol. 3. Oxford University Press, 1935.

FAGUET, EMILE, *La Politique cimiarée de Montesquieu, de Rousseau et de Voltaire.* Paris: Société Française d'Imprimerie et de Librairie, 1900.

——, *Rousseau Penseur.* Paris: Société Française d'Imprimerie et de Librairie, 1900.

——, *Rousseau Penseur.* Paris: Société Française d'Imprimerie et de Librarie. n.d.

FRIEDRICH, HUGO, *Montaigne*, trad. de l'Allemand par Robert Rovini. Paris: Gallimard, 1968.

GIERKE, O., *Natural Law and the Theory of Society*, transl. Ernest Barker, Vol. I. Cambridge University Press, 1934 (reissued, 1950).

GODWIN, WILLIAM, *The Principles of Political Justice*, 2 vols. London: J. Watson, 1842.

GOSSMAN, LIONEL, 'Time and history in Rousseau.' *Studies on Voltaire and the Eighteenth Century* (1964), Vol. 30. Geneva: Institut et Musée Voltaire, 1964.

GOUGH, J. W., *The Social Contract: A Critical Study of its Origin and Development.* Oxford University Press, 1936 (reissued, 1957).

GREEN, F. C., *Jean-Jacques Rousseau.* Cambridge University Press, 1955.

GRIMSLEY, R., *Jean-Jacques Rousseau: A Study in Self-Awareness.* Cardiff: University of Wales Press, 1961.

GUEHENNO, JEAN, *Jean-Jacques Rousseau*, transl. John and Doreen Weightman, 2 vols. London: Routledge, 1966.

HEARNSHAW, F. J. C. (ed.), *Social and Political Ideas of Some Great Medieval Thinkers.* London: Dawson, Pall Mall, 1967.

HEARNSHAW, F. J. C. (ed.), *Social and Political Ideas of Some Representative Thinkers of the Renaissance and Reformation.* London: Dawson, Pall Mall, 1967.

——, *Social and Political Ideas of Some Representative Thinkers of the Sixteenth and Seventeenth Centuries.* London: Dawson, Pall Mall, 1967.

——, *Social and Political Ideas of Some Great English Thinkers of the Augustan Age.* London: Dawson, Pall Mall, 1967.

——, *Social and Political Ideas of Some Representative French Thinkers of the Age of Reason.* London: Dawson, Pall Mall, 1967.

——, *Social and Political Ideas of Some Representative Thinkers of the Revolutionary Age.* London: Dawson, Pall Mall, 1967.

HENDEL, CHARLES WILLIAM, *Jean-Jacques Rousseau, Moralist*, 2 vols. Oxford University Press, 1934.

HIGHET, GILBERT, *The Classical Tradition.* Oxford University Press, 1951.

HOBBES, THOMAS, *Leviathan.* London: Dent (Everyman, 392).

——, *Leviathan*, ed. Michael Oakeshott, with an Introduction by Richard Peters. New York: Collier Macmillan, 1967: London: Collier Macmillan, 1970.

——, *Leviathan*, ed. C. B. Macpherson. Harmondsworth: Penguin Books, 1968.

HOBHOUSE, L. T., *Liberalism.* London: William & Norgate, n.d.

JIMACK, PETER D. 'La Génèse et la rédaction de l'Émilé de Jean-Jacques Rousseau.' *Studies on Voltaire and the Eighteenth Century.* (1960), Vol. 13. Geneva: Institut et Musée Voltaire.

KIERNAN, COLM, 'Science and the Enlightenment in eighteenth-century France'.

Bibliography

Studies on Voltaire and the Eighteenth Century (1968), Vol. 59. Geneva: Institut et Musée Voltaire.

LEBLOND, M.-A., *L'Idéal du XIXe siècle*. Paris: Alcan, 1909.

LEMAITRE, JULES, *Jean-Jacques Rousseau*. Paris: Calmann-Levy, n.d.

LEVIN, H., *The Myth of the Golden Age in the Renaissance*. London: Faber, 1970.

LICHTENBERGER, ANDRÉ, *Le Socialisme et la Revolution Française*. Paris: Alcan, 1899.

LOCKE, JOHN, *Two Treatises concerning Civil Government*, ed. Peter Laslett. Cambridge University Press, 1967.

LOWENTHAL, MARVIN, *The Autobiography of Montaigne*. London: Routledge, 1935.

MACHIAVELLI, *The Prince*, trans. Marriott. London: Dent (*Everyman*, ——).

——, *The Prince*, trans. G. Bull. Harmondsworth: Penguin, 19—.

——, *The Discourses*, ed. Bernard Crick, trans. L. J. Walker. Harmondsworth: Penguin, 1970.

——, *The Prince and The Discourses*. New York: The Modern Library, 1940.

MADARIAGA, SALVADOR DE, *The Fall of the Spanish-American Empire*. London: Hollis & Carter, 1947.

MARITAIN, JACQUES, *Three Reformers*. London: Sheed & Ward, 1928.

MASSON, P. M., *Rousseau et la restauration religieuse*, 3 vols. Paris: Hachette, 1916.

MAY, G., *Rousseau par lui-même*. Paris: Editions de Seuil, 1961.

MAYOR, JOSEPH B., *M. Tullii Ciceronis: De Natura Deorum*. Cambridge University Press, 1880.

MILL, J. S., *Liberty and Representative Government*. Oxford University Press, 1946.

MOREAU-RENDU, S., *L'Idée de bonté naturelle chez Jean-Jacques Rousseau*. Paris: Marcel Rivière, 1929.

MORLEY, JOHN, *Diderot*, 2 vols. London: Macmillan, 1891.

——, *Rousseau*, 2 vols. London: Macmillan, 1910.

MORPHOS, PANOS, 'Renaissance tradition in Rousseau's second *Discourse*.' *Modern Language Quarterly* (1955), Vol. 13.

NICCOLINI, FAUSTO, 'Vico e Rousseau.' *Atti Aecademia Pontaniana*, nuova ser. (1950), Vol. 1, pp. 217–39. Naples.

PAINE, THOMAS, *The Age of Reason*. London: 1796.

——, *Miscellaneous Works*. London: W. T. Sherwin, 1817.

——, *The Rights of Man*, ed. H. Collins. Harmondsworth: Penguin, 1969.

PLUTARCH, *Lives*, transl. and ed. J. and W. Langhorne. London: Routledge, 1890.

——, *Select Essays*, 2 vols. transl. A. O. Prickard. Oxford, 1918.

POULENARD, ELIE, *Strindberg et Rousseau*. Paris: Presses Universitaires de France, 1959.

PROAL, LOUIS, *La Psychologie de Jean-Jacques Rousseau*. Paris: Alcan, 1928.

PROUDHON, P.-J., *What is property? First Memoir*, 2 vols., transl. B. R. Tucker. London: Reeves, 1969; New York: Dover, 1971.

REICHENBURG, MARGERITE, *Essai sur les lectures de Rousseau*. Philadelphia, Pa.: University of Pennsylvania, 1932. (Reprinted in part from *Annales de la Société Jean-Rousseau*, Vol. XXI).

RIST, J. M., *Stoic Philosophy*. Cambridge University Press, 1969.

ROMMEN, H. A., *The Natural Law*, transl. T. R. Hanley, St Louis & London: Herder, 1947.

SANTACRUZ, P., 'Ideas sociales de Seneca,' *Academia de Cordoba* (1933), Vol. 12, pp. 215–32.

Bibliography

SEILLIÈRE, ERNEST, *Les Origines romanesques de la morale et de la politique romantiques*. Paris: La Renaissance du Livre, 1920.

——, *Jean-Jacques Rousseau*. Paris: Garnier Frères, 1921.

SENECA, *Epistulae Morales*, Vols. 1, 2 and 3, London: Heinemann (Loeb Classical Library) 1917, 1920 and 1925.

——, *Epistulae Morales: Recognavit et Adnotatione Critica Instruxit*. (Vols. I and II). Revised and annotated by L. D. Reynolds. Oxford: Clarendon Press, 1965.

——, *Select Letters*, ed. W. C. Summers. London: Macmillan, 1932.

——, *Seneca: Moral Essays*, Vols. 1, 2 and 3, ed. J. W. Basore. London: Heinemann (Loeb Classical Library) and New York: Harvard University Press, 1963, 1964, 1965.

——, *Naturales Quaestiones*, Vols. 1 and 2, transl. P. Oltramare. Paris: Collection Budé, 1929.

——, *Thyestes-Phaedra*,ted. H. Moriocco. Turin, 1917.

SIMON, YVES, *The Nature and Function of Authority*. Milwaukee: Marquette University Press, 1941.

SOREL, GEORGES, *Reflections sur la violence*. Paris: Pages Libres, 1908.

TALMON, J. L., *The Origins of Totalitarian Democracy*. London: Secker & Warburg, 1952 (reissued, 1955).

——, *Political Messianism: The Romantic Phase*. London: Secker & Warburg, 1960.

——, *The Unique and the Universal*. London, Secker & Warburg, 1965.

THOMAS, P., 'Sénèque et Rousseau.' *Bulletin de l'Academie Royale de Belgique, Classe des Lettres, etc.* No. 5, p. 391 et seq. Brussels, 1900.

VAUGHAN, C. E., *Studies in the History of Political Philosophy before and after Rousseau*. Manchester University Press, 1939.

VILLEY, PIERRE, *Les Sources et l'évolution des essais de Montaigne*, 2 vols. Paris: Hachette, 1933.

WESTAWAY, K. M., *The Educational Theory of Plutarch*. London: 1922.

WICKWAR, W., *The Baron d'Holbach: A Prelude to the French Revolution*. London: Allen & Unwin, 1935.

WOODCOCK, GEORGE, *Anarchism*. Penguin: Harmondsworth, 1970.

ZELLER, E., *Stoics, Epicureans and Sceptics*, transl. O. J. Reichel. London: Longmans, Green, 1870.

Index

Age of Innocence, 16, 150, 158
Age of Reason, 34
'Agrarian Justice', 96, 167
agriculture, 123
American Colonies, 60
anarchism, 9, 132, 160, 161–2
anarchists, philosophical, 125
Archbishop of Paris, 158
Argenson, 147
aristocracy, 111, 115, 116
Aristotle, 3, 7; Aristotelian, 5
authority, 125, 135, 136, 140, 155, 161

Babeuf, 88, 94
Bakunin, 13, 41, 160, 169, 171
Bentham, Jeremy, 94, 95–6, 97, 125
Burke, Edmund, 65n

Cajot, Dom, ix
Calvin, 153
Catholic Church, 159
Church, xv, 135, 139, 142, 149, 160
Christianity, 14, 141, 142, 144, 146, 147; doctrines of, 13, 96
Chrysippus, 7, 15n
Cicero, 11, 13, 16n, 19
citizenship, 132
Civil Religion, 41, 141, 148, 149, 156
civilization, 5, 20, 138, 159
collectivity, xi, 160
community, xii, xiii, 127, 128, 134, 137, 147, 159
Confessions, 29, 32n, 55, 56n, 57, 58, 59

Condorcet, 17
constitutional machinery, 128
Contrat Social, xii, 41, 60, 64, 65n, 69, 79, 80, 83, 84n, 89, 90, 91n, 97, 113, 125, 128, 131, 147, 148, 152, 155, 160, 161
Corsica, 115, 122, 168
Corsicans, 110, 115, 123, 124, 132
cosmopolitanism, 2, 21, 137
Cynics, 5

De Beaumont, 15, 26, 42, 162
Deism, 51, 141, 144
Deity, 6, 15, 29, 31, 49
De Maïstre, 121
democracy, 102, 107, 108, 111, 112, 113, 114, 115, 117, 128
Dialogues, 24n, 51n, 58, 58n, 121
Diderot, 19
Dijon, Discourse to Academy of, x, 28
Discours sur l'Économie Politique, 41, 60, 68, 69, 79, 132, 134, 140, 163, 166, 167, 168, 169
Discours . . . les Sciences et les Arts, 2
Discours sur l'Origine de l'Inégalité des Conditions parmi les Hommes, 16, 28, 29, 30, 31, 32, 33n, 37n, 42, 61, 87, 88n, 114, 163, 165, 169
duty, xv, 159

Émile, x, xi, 8, 9, 15, 16n, 18, 22n, 23n, 33n, 39, 40, 42, 43, 45, 46, 47, 48, 49, 50, 51, 54n, 59, 62n, 67, 71,

175

Index

Émile–*cont.*
   72, 90, 160, 163, 164, 165, 166, 167, 168, 169
emotion, 5, 127
England, 109, 137, 143
Enlightened Despot, 118
Enlightenment, the, xii, xv, 1, 16, 17, 31
Epicureans, xv, xvi
evolution, 14
executive, 112, 120

Faguet, Émile, 20, 94
Fate, 9–10
federation, 120–2, 131
free will, 7, 9
freedom, 9, 162
French Revolution, 2

General Will, xi, xii, xiii, xiv, 2, 41, 63, 68, 69, 70, 71, 72, 73, 76, 78, 79, 80, 81, 82, 83, 84, 85, 87, 90, 95, 99, 101, 102, 103, 104, 106, 107, 108, 113, 120, 124, 125, 127, 129, 132, 133, 136, 140, 151, 155, 156, 157, 160–1
Geneva, 18, 21, 153, 154
Godwin, xv, xvi, 8, 17, 18, 44, 74, 77, 97, 125, 126, 127, 129, 131, 136
Golden Age, x, xi, xii, 10–14, 16, 18, 28, 43, 51
Gossman, Lionel, 43
Gouvernement de Pologne, 2, 41, 121, 131, 136, 140, 163, 165, 166, 167, 168, 169
government, 64, 100–4, 108–9, 111, 112, 112n, 113, 118, 128, 129, 131, 132, 137, 138, 139, 140, 141, 142, 143, 146
grace, 42, 159
Great King, the, 131, 138
Greece, 21, 75, 131

Hobbes, 30, 34, 36, 37, 143
House of Commons, 102

individual, 127, 153, 155, 160
inequality, 10, 13, 38, 133–4
instinct, xi, 5, 30, 127, 160
intolerance, 149
inventions, xi, xii, 5, 16

Jimack, Peter D., ix, xiv, 2n
Julie, 53, 146

laissez-faire, 96, 135
Lawgiver, the, 2, 109, 125, 150–7
legislature, 117, 129, 159
Lenin, 155
Lettre à d'Alembert, 52, 166
Lettre à Malesherbes, 24n, 166, 169
Lettre au Maréchal de Luxembourg, 58n
Lettre à Moultou, 166
Locke, 19, 34, 60, 81, 117, 135
Luther, 141
luxury, 13, 16, 134
Lycurgus, 121, 153

Machiavelli, xii, 75, 109, 110, 141, 145, 150, 151, 156, 157
Madariaga, 22
Mahomet, 153
Manichaean premises, 15, 158, 161
Marie Antoinette, 54
Maritain, Jacques, 56n
Marxism, xvi, 155
materialism, xv
Mill, John Stuart, 74, 96
monarchy, 111, 112n, 115, 117, 118, 120
Montaigne, 19, 20

Narcisse, 165
nationalism, 2, 136, 147
natural, xiv, 7, 127
Natural Law, 13, 95
Natural rights, 94–7
Nature, x, xi, xiv, 1, 3, 4, 8, 11, 12, 13, 14, 16, 18, 19, 20, 23, 24, 24n, 25, 28, 29, 34, 34n, 52, 55, 58, 59, 64, 73, 91, 127, 148, 152, 153, 154, 158, 160
necessity, 9, 45
'Noble Savage', 20
Nominalism, xv, xvi, 136
Nouvelle Héloïse, 32n, 54, 58, 165, 166, 170

Original Sin, 26, 158

Paine, Thomas, 49, 96–7, 112n, 119
palingenesis, 10n
panlogism, 7, 9
Paris, 52, 58
Parliament of England, 120
passion, 138, 152
patriotism, 115, 129, 138
Pire, Georges, ix, 2n, 3
Platonism, xv, 9

176

Index

Plutarch, ix, x, 19–21
Poles, 110, 122, 124, 131, 132, 139
Political Justice (Godwin), 8n, 9, 32, 77, 126, 131
Posidonius, xii, 8
positivism, 95
Prince, The, 50n, 151n
Projet de Constitution pour la Corse, 41, 69, 90, 168
Proménade, 32n
property, 10n, 13, 87, 88, 90, 92, 96, 165
prophet, 110, 150, 154
Protestant, 135, 144, 147
Proudhon, P.-J., 38n

radical tradition, 62, 135
ratio quidem, x, xii, 5, 10, 17, 39, 127, 158
reason, 126, 127, 158; Eternal, x, xii, xiv, 12; Supreme, 5
recta ratio, x, xi, xii, 5, 10, 12, 17, 39, 160
religion, xiv, 49, 141–9
responsibility: moral, 145, 161; personal, 19
Rêveries, 32n, 55, 58, 59
Rist, J. M., 8
Robinson Crusoe, 46
Rome, 13, 75, 142, 144, 154

San Marino, 125
Seillière, E., 164
Seneca, ix, xii, xiii, 2n, 3, 5, 8, 8n, 10, 11, 12, 13, 14, 15, 16, 16n, 21, 127, 136, 150, 163, 164; *Epistles*, x, xii, 2, 5, 8, 9, 15, 16, 18, 19, 20, 21, 30, 31, 34n, 37, 163, 164, 166
Shelley, 164, 168
Sidney, 19
Social Contract, xi, 17, 32, 37, 49, 55, 58, 60, 61, 62, 63, 64, 67, 69, 70, 73, 75, 76, 77, 78, 80, 81, 82, 83, 85, 86, 89, 90, 91, 92, 93, 98, 99, 117, 120, 122, 124, 129, 130, 142, 149, 150, 156, 157
Social Pact, 66, 81, 85, 86, 87, 88, 100, 106, 130, 147, 148, 149, 155

sociability, 127
socialism, 93, 94, 96, 134
Sophie, 15
Sorel, Georges, 56
Sovereign, 105, 106, 107, 120, 128, 129, 131, 133, 134, 140, 145, 147, 148
Sovereign People, xv, 17, 51, 58, 86, 97, 101, 102, 103, 104, 105, 129, 141, 147, 160, 161
Sovereignty of the People, 2, 49, 86, 116, 117, 131, 149, 155
Sparta, 121, 138, 154
St Germains, 28
State, xii, 13, 37, 49, 55, 58, 60, 61, 62, 63, 64, 67, 69, 70, 73, 75, 76, 77, 78, 80, 81, 82, 83, 85, 86, 89, 90, 92, 93, 94, 95, 96, 97, 98, 99, 100, 104, 105, 106, 107, 108, 109, 112, 113, 115, 117, 118, 119, 120, 121, 122, 124, 125, 126, 128, 130, 131, 132, 135, 136, 138, 139, 140, 142, 143, 144, 145, 146, 147, 150, 151, 154, 155, 156, 157, 159, 161
Stoicism, ix–xii, xv, 3, 5, 7, 9, 10, 11, 12, 13, 15, 19, 20, 21, 22, 31, 51, 161, 162
Stoics, xv, 2, 3, 5, 6, 7, 8, 9, 10, 13, 15, 15n, 17, 18, 19, 22, 23, 51, 55, 59, 69, 73, 121, 136
Streckeisen-Moultou, 51n, 164, 166, 168
suffrages, 80, 130
Supreme Being, xiv, 51, 160
Switzerland, 60, 115

taxation, 134
technology ('inventions'), xii
tyranny, 13, 111

unitary personality, xiii, 9, 31
universalism, 127, 142
Utilitarians, xvi, 79, 84, 94, 95, 96

Versailles, 54

will, xiii, xv, 7, 8n, 9, 10, 62, 63, 68, 70, 71, 76, 77, 78, 80, 83, 105, 107, 108, 109, 152, 155n

For Product Safety Concerns and Information please contact our EU
representative GPSR@taylorandfrancis.com
Taylor & Francis Verlag GmbH, Kaufingerstraße 24, 80331 München, Germany

www.ingramcontent.com/pod-product-compliance
Lightning Source LLC
Chambersburg PA
CBHW052121300426
44116CB00010B/1757